DATE DUE

Ronald C. Arnett

COMMUNICATION *and* COMMUNITY

Implications of
MARTIN BUBER'S DIALOGUE

Foreword by Maurice Friedman

SOUTHERN ILLINOIS UNIVERSITY PRESS
Carbondale and Edwardsville

89 88 87 86   4 3 2 1

Library of Congress Cataloging-in-Publication Data

Arnett, Ronald C., 1952–
  Communication and community.

  Bibliography: p.
  Includes index.
  1. Buber, Martin, 1878–1965. I. Title.
B3213.B84A87 1986   181'.06   85-30425
ISBN 0-8093-1283-2
ISBN 0-8093-1284-0 (pbk.)

CONTENTS

FOREWORD
MAURICE FRIEDMAN

THE implications of Martin Buber's philosophy of dialogue for the understanding of communication have been given much attention in recent years by scholars in the field of communication, including Ronald Arnett himself. What is not so well known or adequately understood is the indispensable context of that philosophy of dialogue—Buber's lifelong concern with community. Ronald Arnett's discussion of the implications of dialogic communication within the context of community is at the heart of Buber's life and work.

The Community Context of Buber's Dialogue

When he was twenty, Buber delivered a lecture to the Socialist Club of the University of Berlin on the thought of the nineteenth-century German socialist Ferdinard Lassalle, in whose life and work he had immersed himself. Shortly thereafter, Buber entered into an intense and lasting association with a leading communal socialist of early twentieth-century Germany, Gustav Landauer, a man whose life and death left a deep imprint on Buber's own life and thought. In 1905, Buber wrote an introduction to a collection of forty social-psychological monographs that he edited from 1906 to 1912 under the title *Die Gesellschaft*. In this introduction, Buber coined the term "das Zwischenmenschliche" (what is between person and person) and pointed beyond individual existence to the action or suffering of two or more persons together. In 1917, when he wrote an essay on "My Way to Hasidism," Buber characterized his childhood contact with this popular communal Jewish mysticism of Eastern Europe as one that showed him "debased, yet essentially intact, the living double kernel of humanity: genuine *community* and genuine *leadership.*"

In his first teaching in his own name, as opposed to the interpretation of Hasidism, his highly influential "Speeches on Judaism," Buber pointed to a community as lying at the center of the still uncompleted task of "Jewishness." In the common life of men, as nowhere else, he wrote, a formless mass is given us in which we can imprint the face of God. The human community is an important work that awaits us; a chaos that we must order, a diaspora that we must gather, a conflict that we must resolve.

Buber's summation of Landauer's socialism in 1927 also clearly expressed Buber's own view of socialism as community: "Gustav Landauer has recognized that the new community of mankind for which we hope cannot coalesce out of individuals, that it cannot arise out of the chaos in which we live, out of this atomizing of individuals . . . but that there must exist cells, small community cells out of which alone the great human community can be built." Buber modified sociologist Gustav Tönnies' simple contrast between organic community and atomized society in such a way as to bring the former nearer to a federalistic socialism such as Landauer's. Buber's "community" was not the natural community of the family or the village commune in which powerful instinctive traditions ruled, along with coercion, violence, exploitation of one's fellowmen, and disregard of their freedom and worth. Rather, Buber's community was a community of choice around a common center, the voluntary coming together of persons in direct relationship.

Buber's socialism was *social* and *decentralistic* in the strongest possible contrast to the political and highly centralized socialism that developed in the Soviet Union. Even in 1919, Buber saw the true nature of the socialist power state, which, in the name of compulsory justice and equality, makes impossible spontaneous community and genuine relationship between person and person. True to the "narrow ridge," Buber refused the clamoring "either/or" of the modern

world—the demand that one accept a centralized socialist state because of the defects of capitalism or a capitalist society because of the
defects of socialism. In the essays on community that he wrote just
after the First World War, Buber called on his fellows to break
through the shells of society, state, church, school, economy, and
public opinion to a direct contact with others, to practice directness
and betweeness, and to shape the shapeless into community. This
meant tearing away the veil born of the profit motive that leads
people to see each other not as persons but as members of a category
or a class. New laws are but empty shells when justice does not
manifest itself between persons. The true revolution demands a
powerful will toward community. The divine emerges in the possibility of genuine life between persons and wills to reveal itself only
through its realization in true community. This same teaching entered fully into Buber's Zionism and his support of the kibbutz, which
Buber saw then and later as a true embodiment of communal socialism. No socialist structure that leaves unchanged the life between
persons can bring about a true transformation of society, Buber
wrote. Many of the Jews who went to Palestine after the First World
War were motivated by Buber's call for the building of a new community.

These strands of the teaching of community come together in the
second part of I and Thou (1923), Buber' classical expression of the
life of dialogue. Politics, economics, and the state are not evil in
themselves, as they were for Gustav Landauer, except when they
become independent of the aim of building genuine community to
which they are legitimate means. Economics (the abode of the will to
profit) and the state (the abode of the will to be powerful) share in life
only as long as they share in the spirit—as long as the structures of our
communal life draw their living quality from the power to enter into
relationship. The statesman or economist who obeys the spirit
confirms the trust of the Thou in the world of It in accordance with
what is right and fitting each day and in each new situation. The
dualism that would keep "spirit" in one compartment and economics
and the state in the other would mean yielding up to tyranny once
and for all the provinces that are steeped in the world of It and
robbing the spirit completely of reality.

In the years following I and Thou, Buber continued to point to the
"between" as the true sphere of community. In the face of Fascism

not effacing the boundaries between the groups, circles, and parties, but communal recognition of the common reality and communal testing of the common responsibility." Vital dissociation—the sickness of the peoples of our age—is only seemingly healed by crowding individuals together. "Here, nothing can help other than persons from different circles of opinion honestly having to do with one another in a common opening out of a common ground."

In a 1935 letter to a disciple who founded and led a kibbutz in Palestine, Buber gave an essential hint about the relation of consciousness to a community. "Community has in common with sexual love the fact that too much consciousness is not conducive either to its growth or fruitfulness. By consciousness I mean, naturally, the discussing type—there is another, that of the whole being, but that lets growing take place, feels it, notices it and: is silent or sings." Three years later, when Buber himself immigrated to Palestine, he added an essential pillar to his teaching of community: the recognition that alongside the essential *Thou* there is also an essential *We* in which persons in a group have directly to do with one another. "Only persons who are capable of truly saying *Thou* to one another can truly say *We* with one another." In the same essay ("What Is Man?"), Buber asserted that the dominating significance of Freud's repression and sublimation for the whole structure of personal and communal life arises out of the crisis of confidence that undermines human communal existence today. Although the individual must often adapt his or her wishes to the command of the community in any society, only if the organic community disintegrates from within and mistrust becomes life's basic note does the repression acquire its dominating importance. "The unaffectedness of wishing is stifled by mistrust . . . agreement between one's own and the other's desire ceases, for there is no true coalescence or reconciliation with what is necessary to a sustaining community, and the dulled wishes creep hopelessly into the recesses of the soul. . . . The divorce between spirit and instincts is here, as often, the consequence of the divorce between man and man."

Buber's approach to community was not that of an idealist, but a meliorist. He did not call for absolute pacifism or total justice but for a redrawing of the demarcation line in every new situation. "It is true that we are not able to live in perfect justice, and in order to preserve the community of man, we are often compelled to accept wrongs in

and Nazism, this became more and more a critique of collectivism as
well as of individualism. In this context, Buber criticized "that
powerful modern point of view, according to which in the last resort
only . . . collectives are real, while significance is attached to persons
only as the workers or the tools of the collectives"—a precise definition of the totalitarian touchstone of reality. Such attempts give the
political province an exaggerated autonomy and remove it from the
responsibility of the real person who takes part in it. The totalitarian
states of left and right, bundled together without *Thou* and without *I*,
hostile and separated hosts, arch into the common abyss. True community emerges only out of the breakthrough from the repressed and
the pedestrian to the reality of the between. "No factory and no office
is so abandoned by creation that a creative glance could not fly up
from one working-place to another . . . an unsentimental and unre-
served exchange of glances between two men in an alien place." It is
with this truth of community that Buber confronted the dreadful
specter of Nazism in which the German Jews lived from 1933 on.

> "Israel" means to practice community for the sake of a common covenant
> in which our existence is founded; to practice in actual living and com-
> munity between being and being, person and person, toward which end
> creation was created. And today this means to preserve directness in a
> world which is becoming more and more indirect, in the face of the
> self-righteousness of collectivities to preserve the mystery of relationship,
> without which a people must perish an icy death.

The most remarkable aspect is that Buber, living in Nazi Germany,
could still affirm the body politic as the human world that seeks to
realize in its genuine formations our turning to one another in the
context of creation. "The person who has not ceased to love the
human world in all its degradation is able even today to envision
genuine social form."

The great community, Buber wrote in this same period, "is no
union of the like-minded, but a genuine living together of men of
similar or of complementary natures but of differing minds"—what I
have called "the community of otherness." "Community is the overcoming of *otherness* in living unity," Buber wrote. This is a question
of an awareness from the other side of the other's real relation to the
truth. "What is called for is . . . a living answering for one another . . .

decisions concerning the community. But what matters is that in every hour of decision we are aware of our responsibility and summon our conscience to weigh exactly how much is necessary to preserve the community, and accept just so much and no more." Buber saw this as a choice placed before Zionism, and he saw true Zionism as grounded in the biblical demand that Israel become a "kingship of God." Buber demanded of the Jews that they not use "the spirit of Israel" merely as a metaphorical mask for national egoism. "The true spirit of Israel is the divine demand implanted in our hearts," and this demand means building real community composed of real families, real neighborhoods, and real settlements, and a real nation that develops relationships of a fruitful and creative peace with its neighbors. Paraphrasing the prophet Jeremiah, Buber claimed that God demands from Israel and from all men not religion but community. "Here, where He blames a people for not having become a community, man's claim upon man takes precedence of God's claim." Similarly, Buber saw the uniqueness and greatness of Hasidism as lying not in its theoretical teaching but in its mode of life shaping a community.

To create new fellowship and social spontaneity in a world in which capitalism has left man lacking in organic social structure and in which communism has lost sight of social regeneration in favor of a rigid political centralism, Buber proposed a federalistic communal socialism. This social restructuring can find its progressively comprehensive embodiment in full cooperatives of ownership and work, village communes, and relations between communes, which lead to a community of communities, eventually broadening to a world confederation of commonwealths, a grouping of nations which, like the individual communes, will preserve the maximum social spontaneity compatible with the situation and the given time.

The most promising experiment in the village commune, in Buber's opinion, was that of the Jewish collective settlements in Palestine, the kibbutzim and kvuzot. These have been based on the needs of given local situations combined with socialistic and biblical teachings on social justice. These communes have worked together in close cooperation and at the same time have left complete freedom for the constant branching off of new forms and different types of social structure. What was essential to these communes was not intimacy, as it exists in the small one and is lost in the big, but openness. "A real community need not consist of people who are perpetually together; but it must consist of people who, precisely because they are comrades, have mutual access to one another and are ready for one another." In a meeting with the members of the largest kibbutz in Israel in 1963, Buber distinguished between *closeness* and *relation*, declaring any kibbutz of six or seven hundred members, let alone two thousand, to be a social monster that needed to be broken down into smaller, interlocking groups in which each person could feel a part of the group. He also emphasized the need for enough space for each individual to have some distance from his comrades, space through which alone he might enter into relation with them. During the last twenty years of his life, Buber repeatedly warned against that domination of the political principle that cleaved kibbutzim into party groups fighting one another and repeatedly led to the self-destruction of communities.[1]

Timely Relevance: Dialogue in Communication and Community

Martin Buber died in 1965. In the twenty years since then, the climate in America, as Ronald Arnett points out in this book, has changed from one of relative abundance to an economy of scarcity and limited resources. Not only have optimism and confidence in secure employment been undermined in this new period, but the whole ambience of the sixties and early seventies in which action for social welfare was combined with concern for the quality of human life has shifted. Now, not only the liberal arts and humanities, but precisely the values which Martin Buber espoused—dialogue, reciprocity, openness, experiencing the other side of the relationship, concern for relationship, and the "between"—seem to many a luxury that they can no longer afford. The great virtue of Ronald Arnett's book is that he continues to maintain the essential distinction between taking care of one's own needs and the reality of meeting:

[1]This presentation of Buber's teaching of community is based upon my three-volume biography *Martin Buber's Life and Work* (New York: E. P. Dutton, 1982, 1983, 1984). See in particular *The Early Years*, pp. 144 ff., 235, 238–45, 263 ff., 340 ff.; *The Middle Years*, pp. 115, 163, 190, 244, 268, 277, 279, 281; and *The Later Years*, pp. 6 ff., 34 ff., 43, 178 ff., 67–71, 389–92.

"'Real' life begins with two." Thus, Arnett's book is topical in exactly
the sense that Buber calls for, beginning with the actual situation in
which we find ourselves, rather than with abstract principles. Arnett
shows that the "between" is not a dispensable luxury, but on the
contrary is the very heart of what is essential and demanded in our
time.

In chapter 1, "The Communicative Crisis," Arnett speaks of the
polarized communication that arises from and exacerbates our current tendency to place people in one camp or another. This polarization also relates, as he shows, to that tendency of "seeming" to which
Buber points: desiring to be confirmed by others even inauthenti-
cally if necessary, people try to appear to be the way they imagine
others wish them to be. I have repeatedly pointed to this danger of
the polarization of communication in my book *The Hidden Human
Image* (1974).

> Polarization is necessary to destroy pseudoharmony, but it always goes
> beyond that to false dichotomies, pseudocategories. Finally we get the
> *politicization* of all social reality: The polarization already implicit in
> poverty and racism is converted into political slogans and catchwords. . . .
> This leads to *willful* misunderstanding in which people *refuse* to see the
> position of others from within. Finally, politicized persons become pro-
> grammed: Whatever they hear is fitted into the Either/Or of those who
> are *for* them or those who are *against* them. . . . Political slogans and
> catchwords obscure the concrete situation, and the hostilities grow on
> either side beyond the bounds of the actual conflict.
>
>   . . . No reconciliation was ever achieved through ignoring real differ-
> ences, or attempting to impose a sense of unity where there is none. But
> this is a very different thing from those who set out as a deliberate political
> tactic to sharpen and radicalize the polarities beyond the concrete reali-
> ties of the situation. . . . The notion of confrontation as being anything real
> when the other is a caricature and you are a caricature and there is mutual
> mistrust—this is the thing we have to fight. (333–38)
>
>   An . . . even more potent source of social and existential mistrust is the
> widespread tendency to polarize the concrete reality of our situation into a
> set of catchwords, a life-destroying, life-denying Either/Or that demands
> one be *for* the Establishment or *against*, *for* the Free World or *against*,
> *for* Black Power or *against*, *for* the state of Israel or *against*, *for* America
> or *against*. . . . Our life together has become so politicized that abstract

slogans are taken for concrete reality and qualifications of these slogans for equivocation. (382)

In entitling his second chapter "The Narrow Ridge," Arnett has placed in the forefront what is indeed Martin Buber's central metaphor. Originally, before it became three volumes, I was going to entitle my biography of Buber *Encounter on the Narrow Ridge*. A corollary of the concreteness and uniqueness of the narrow ridge, with its refusal of the timeless and situationless abstractions that tempt one on either side, is Arnett's emphasis upon an open mind, as opposed to a closed one. This is also a corollary of the central distinction that I make in my book *The Confirmation of Otherness: In Family, Community, and Society*[2] between the "community of otherness" and the "community of affinity" or like-mindedness. Community of like-mindedness is made up of people who huddle together for security—sons or daughters of the American Revolution, or Communists, or Jews, or Catholics, or Protestants, or born-again Christians. They imagine that they are safe and secure because they use the same slogans and the same language, even though they may not have much real relation with one another. Community of affinity is always ultimately false community; for it is concerned only with that coloration that makes its members feel secure because they are so afraid of conflict and opposition. The community of otherness, in contrast, begins with the recognition that even in a marriage or friendship or small family, there are still as many points of view as there are persons. The community of otherness is not one where people are alike but where they have a common concern, where they share in a common situation that they approach and respond to in different ways. The community of otherness is not an ideal but a direction of movement toward as much confirmation of otherness as the community has resources for at any given time. It avoids the blinders and hysteria that arise from the polarization of communication and the closing of mind and heart to the other for fear of conflict with it.

The close relationship to which Arnett points in chapter 3, "Existential Mistrust: The Failure to Listen," between inward focus and

[2]Maurice Friedman, *The Confirmation of Otherness: In Family, Community, and Society* (New York: Pilgrim Press, 1983).

the tendency to regard one's experience and thoughts as one's pos-
sessions is very much in tune with my own critique of "aiming at the
self" and with making the psyche *the* touchstone of reality, as Arnett
himself points out. The alternative to exploitative or possessive relation to experience and its corollary—the failure to listen—is taking
fully seriously the reality of the "between." Occasionally, one or
another of my students has chided me for encouraging discussion
instead of simply lecturing in my classes. What that student fails to
grasp is the full reality of what comes to pass *between* teacher and
student and among students, which is something quite other than the
"knowledge" that the teacher has in his or her mind. What Arnett has
to say on "Monologue: Centering on Self" in chapter 4 is a corollary of
this chapter on the failure to listen.

Sometimes history goes in a spiral. Arnett points that out neatly
when he unmasks the organizational involvement of the present as a
combination of the "organization man" of the fifties and the narcissism of the sixties and seventies—a social screen for collective privacy, as he puts it. In opposition to this topic of chapter 5, "Organizational Involvement: A Place of Hiding," is "The Search for the
Ethical Community" in chapter 6, the striving, as Arnett puts it, to
find "a commonality between dialogue and democracy" when democracy does not insist on conformity. Here again, Arnett and I share
a deeply felt common concern. *The Confirmation of Otherness*, as I
state in the conclusion of the book, "proposes nothing less than that
the old and tired polarities of individual versus society, individualism
versus collectivism, competition versus cooperation, free enterprise
versus socialism, capitalism versus communism, freedom versus social welfare be replaced by the confirmation of otherness as the *only*
meaningful direction of movement for friendship, marriage, family,
community, and society within a democracy." Chapter 7 of Arnett's
book, "Freedom: The Unity of Contraries," is precisely what the
confirming of otherness within dialogue makes possible: freedom to
be oneself, to address and respond from the ground of one's uniqueness within community rather than in isolation from it. In this same
chapter, Arnett emphasizes the importance of telling a story, thus
bringing out the central reality of dialogue with the event, not as a
mere retelling of the past but as a living happening of the present. If a
story is told as a present reliving of the event, as a new event in itself,
it is itself healing and helping.

In chapter 9, "Power and Responsibility," Arnett discusses a theme that was very close to Buber. Power is not evil, as the historian Jacob Burckhardt claimed; only power exercised without responsibility, power made an end in itself, is evil, as Nietzsche revealed in his doctrine of the "will to power." Commenting on Nietzsche's teaching, Buber wrote in "What Is Man?":

> Greatness by nature includes a power, but not a will to power. . . . The great man, whether we comprehend him in the most intense activity of his work or in the restful equipoise of his forces, is powerful, involuntarily and composedly powerful, but he is not avid for power. . . . This is the point from where we can understand the *responsibility* in which the powerful man is placed, namely whether, and how far, he is really serving his goal; and also the point from where we can understand the seduction by power, leading him to be unfaithful to the goal and yield to power along.[3]

Martin Buber's 1926 poem "Power and Love" gives incomparable expression to that necessary connection between power and responsibility to which Arnett points in this chapter. Arnett directly quotes that classic Buber poem and reveals its dialogic significance. The union of power and love embraces Buber's view of the dialogic narrow ridge being the "unity of contraries." Buber applied the dialogic union of power and love to society and politics in his 1942 essay "People and Leader" with its penetrating analysis of Mussolini and Hitler and its anticipation of a truly dialogic leadership. "Will to power as power leads from the self-aggrandizement of the individuals to the self-destruction of the people."[4]

In the final chapter, "The Community of Dialogue," Arnett appropriately calls attention to the need for "the courageous person who persists when others would have fled." Inviting dialogue within community is often dependent on one's ability to persevere when the common temptation may be to retreat from relational contact. Such a

[3]Martin Buber, *Between Man and Man*, trans. Ronald Gregor Smith with an introduction by Maurice Friedman (New York: Macmillan, 1965), pp. 150–52.

[4]Martin Buber, *Pointing the Way: Collected Essays*, ed. and trans. with an introduction by Maurice Friedman (New York: Harper & Row, 1957), pp. 148–60.

posture of determination is entirely consonant with Buber's insistence on meeting others *and* holding one's ground when one meets them.

Communication and Community is not only timely and situational. It is grounded in numerous concrete examples from everyday personal and professional life, making this scholarly work accessible on multiple levels of reading. Ronald Arnett has shown himself in *Dwell in Peace* and *Communication and Community* to be a true fellow of the "narrow ridge." One who walks the narrow ridge knows the joy of the community of dialogue but also the tragic limitations resulting from the drawing of the demarcation line each day anew, that continual rediscovery of the boundary between self and other in community through which we press forward and honor reality while we do so. The dialogic journey of the "narrow ridge" requires us to be together sometimes and at other times to walk alone; for, as Ronald Arnett quotes me, "the joy of finding unknown comrades walking beside one must also include the courage to walk alone again if it should prove necessary."

Walking the "narrow ridge" as Arnett does in *Communication and Community* encourages a distinction between effective social reality and surface political success, a discovery of the deeper currents in history and society, and alignment with them. For this reason, I cannot end this foreword any better than by quoting the final paragraphs of Buber's 1923 lecture to the Psychological Club of Zurich "On the Psychologizing of the World," because like Buber and myself, Ronald Arnett points to the limits of psychologism, while providing a liveable dialogic alternative.

> *Community* in a time like ours can only happen out of break-through, out of turning. Only the need aroused by the utmost sundering, the marginal phenomenon, provides the motive force for this. . . . Genuine community begins in a time like this with the discovery of the metapsychic character of reality and rests upon the belief in this reality.
>
> The *empirical community* is a dynamic fact. It does not take away from man his solitude but fills it, makes it positive. It thereby deepens the consciousness of responsibility of the individual—the place or responsibility is man's becoming solitary. The community does not have meaning in itself. It is the abode where the divine has not yet consumed itself, the abode of the coming theophany. If one knows this, then one also knows

that community in our time must ever again miscarry. The monstrous, the
dreadful phenomenon of psychologism so prevails that one cannot simply
bring about healing, rescue with a single blow. But the disappointments
belong to the way. There is no other way than that of this miscarrying.
That is the way of faithful faith.[5]

[5]*A Believing Humanism: Gleanings*, trans. with an introduction and ex-
planatory comments by Maurice Friedman (New York: Simon and Schuster,
1969), p. 151 ff.

ACKNOWLEDGMENTS

Communication and Community: Implications of Martin Buber's Dialogue is itself a community project. This work was given initial shape in conversations with my friend Dr. Paul Keller, shortly after the publication of my first book, *Dwell in Peace: Applying Nonviolence to Everyday Relationships*. Paul responded to some of the initial chapters and was always open to dialogue about the work.

I wish to extend thanks to my intellectual home, Marquette University, for encouraging an intellectual climate that seeks to examine issues such as human community. I am pleased to be associated with a university that takes both teaching and scholarship seriously, while providing a quality environment for discussion and the living of ethical and philosophical issues. In particular, I extend appreciation to my research assistant, Terry Griffin, whose patience was needed in long library searches.

The birth of this book was partially due to encouragement from my students at my former school, St. Cloud State University. My special thanks goes to my friend and colleague Dr. Don Sikkink, who is now the Dean of the College of Humanities and Fine Arts at St. Cloud, and to students associated with NOVA, Nonviolent Alternatives, for the "communication and community" they provided.

My colleagues Dr. Richard Johannesen and Dr. John Stewart continue to provide stimulation that assists my work. Dick read the completed manuscript; his helpful comments are reflected in this final product. Work with John on other "Buber-related" projects helped with the groundwork for this project.

Perhaps the most rewarding aspect of writing this book came from contact with Dr. Maurice Friedman, who provided a foreword. I have followed Dr. Friedman's work since my graduate-school days. My first book referenced much of his material, as does this one, with *Dwell in Peace: Applying Nonviolence to Everyday Relationships* using his concepts in a chapter title and two subheadings. In short, I appreciate Dr. Friedman's encouragement and willingness to be a significant part of this project.

Finally, I wish to thank my family, which continues to be my most significant sense of community. My wife and friend, Millie, put up with my workaholic tendencies and provided helpful suggestions throughout the project. She was the first to read every chapter and offered quality insights. In addition, she continues to provide our family with a sense of community, even in the midst of our busy schedules. My father-in-law, Dr. Emmert Bittinger, thoughtfully read and critiqued this book, as he did my first. And my father had the foresight to introduce this philosopher of communication to the benefits of some technological advances with the gift of a computer that significantly assisted this project.

I also appreciate the influence of my son, Adam Geoffrey, and my daughter, Aimee Gabrielle, who make being a parent the most rewarding role in my life. I dedicate this work to both of you. May you find community in the midst of a demanding world that now more than ever needs leaders willing to enter the uncertainty of dialogue in search of continuing visions of love, hope, and trust between people.

INTRODUCTION

Communication and Community: Implications of Martin Buber's Dialogue unfolds a vision of how communication can assist groups and organizations in becoming human communities, rather than just places of association. The impetus for this vision came from my work with the dialogic material of Martin Buber, a Jewish theologian and philosopher who has had a significant impact on human communication studies.[1] Each chapter is initiated with a quotation from Martin Buber, which sets the conceptual tone by commencing an interpretive study of the implications of Martin Buber's dialogue for inviting human community.

The goal of this book, however, is not just to retell Buber's orientation, but to use Buber's approach to investigate changes and demands placed upon today's communicator who seeks to invite community in interpersonal relationships, groups, and organizations. *Communication and Community* is not a "how-to" book detailing how to make groups and organizations into communities. Nor is *Communication and Community* a description of how we can "best" describe and adapt to what is today's communication fad or fashion in groups and organizations. More than a tale of what is, this book is a vision of what could be. This book unashamedly points toward communicative betterment, a utopia of sorts, from the roots of dialogic communication.[2]

1

Visions and utopias are generally suspect. Ever since Marx took Proudhon to task as a utopian visionary, the word "utopia" has gathered questionable responses.[3] Buber, in his classic piece on this subject, *Paths in Utopia*, attempted to offset the negative connotations of utopia and place the term in proper perspective. A utopia is a vision, a picture of a world that we can try to invite. It is not a reality, but a possibility that can draw a person toward the goal of a "better" situation for a human community.

> [What is common to] utopias that have passed into the spiritual history of mankind, is the fact that they are pictures, and pictures moreover of something not actually present but only represented. . . . The utopian picture is a picture of what "should be," and the visionary is one who wishes it to be. . . . What is at work here is the longing for the rightness which, in religious or philosophical vision, is experienced as revelation or idea, and which of its very nature cannot be realized in the individual, but only in human community. The vision of "what should be"—independent though it may sometimes appear of personal will—is yet inseparable from a critical and fundamental relationship to the existing condition of humanity. All suffering under a social order that is senseless prepares the soul for vision, and what the soul receives in this vision strengthens and deepens its insight into the perversity of what is perverted. The longing for the realization of "the seen" fashions the picture.[4]

The vision inherent in Buber's writings and reflected in *Communication and Community* is offered for dialogue. The reader is invited to encounter this book as a conversation between Buber and me that is open to a third partner. Some concerns within these pages may be identical to your own and others contrary to your vision. Use the former for confirmation and the latter for testing your own picture of communication and community. This book provides an opportunity to talk about what communication can and cannot do to generate human community. Perhaps this book can be viewed as a conversation of what might be or could be in the spirit of John F. Kennedy's and later Robert F. Kennedy's frequent quoting of George Bernard Shaw. "Some men [people] see things as they are and say why. I dream things that never were and say why not."[5] Hopefully, this book will encourage examination of how groups and organizations to which you belong are potential places to invite community, instead of just association.

Images—Past and Present

As a university professor, I am intrigued with the shift in emphasis that has taken place since my undergraduate years. My college experience was buffered by optimism, even in the midst of the Vietnam war. Kennedy's "New Frontier" and Johnson's "Great Society" provided a vision promising that no matter how big the problem, we could eventually solve it. I never worried about getting a job; instead, I asked what my role in this society should be. How could I best be of service to others? Since I took for granted the availability of jobs, I could turn my thoughts to more philosophical issues of role and contribution.

The image for many during the '60s and early '70s was one of optimism, abundance of resources, and enough jobs that one could be selective about the kind of position one took. In the 1980s, students seem to be articulating a much different image, one of pressure and concern, limited resources, and wondering if their college education will get them a job and keep them from being underemployed. As societal and cultural critic Christopher Lasch has stated, we have moved from a society of growth to one of people just wanting to survive.[6] Thus, the current images are centered around limited resources, not abundance. Such an image can generate a feeling that "if there is not enough to go around, how can I get mine first?" It seems to me that the dominant image[7] of today is how to get the "competitive edge."

This increased visibility of a Darwinian-type motif among young people[8] makes the discussion of community a countercultural activity. When so much time and energy are spent on surviving (at least attitudinally), little time is left for group-life concerns of human community, as indicated by Maslow's hierarchy of needs and Schutz's interpersonal need scales.[9]

There seems to be a return to a competitive and individualistic spirit. The perception of limited resources has encouraged the middle class to envision a lack of opportunity, necessitating a struggle for available resources. Whether perceived or real, the feeling of limited resources is affecting our communication strategies and questioning the importance of the notion of inviting community through our communication. Like a number of social critics from Christopher Lasch to Philip Slater, I see the time of "abundance" as over, not to return in the present or the forseeable future. As one historian wrote, "the age of abundance has ended. . . . The 'lessons' taught by the American past are today not merely irrelevant but dangerous."[10]

I acknowledge the image of limited resources, but I do not accept competitive struggle for survival of the fittest as described in social Darwinism[11] as the only possible interpretation of the changing environment. The implications of Martin Buber's work are that "real" life begins with two, not just taking care of one's own needs. Buber provided for us a vision that encourages giving up the "old" ways that may have been appropriate in times of abundance. But in times of scarcity and greater technological sophistication, a social Darwinian view becomes outmoded, even dangerous. The question before us is whether we can give up communicative strategies of the past and begin to discover ways to communicate and work together in the midst of limited resources and an uncertain future.

One of my colleagues, representing a contrary perspective, does not see us in a time of limited resources that would affect communication within community. Some polls are now reflecting an increased sense of optimism. Optimism for whom? My colleague's perspective and the interpretive position assumed in *Communication and Community* both reflect political overtones, a natural extension of any communication interpretation, as Carl Rogers learned of his own approach.[12] Buber's approach was keenly political with his commitment to religious socialism. Buber's view of the world, in contemporary social terms, might be reflected in such documents as the Catholic Bishop's Letter, calling for renewed sensitivity to the poor and commitment to their assistance.[13] Buber most probably would have affirmed the words of Ellen Goodman, who sees the current response to less or limited resources reflected in our not wanting to share with others. "If we are going to limit opportunities for those stuck in the Other America, it is much easier to think of these people as failures. If we are going to chip away at social programs for the have-nots, it is easier to name them losers. We used to call this blaming the victim. Now we call it winning."[14]

Daniel Yankelovich, well-known for his polling of American youth over the last three decades, stated the complexity of changes. But his general statements are consistent with the theme of this book.

> The 1980s—involves a very complex process of sorting things out as conditions change. . . . Affluence and limitlessness were the presuppositions of the 1960's and 1970's. . . . The feeling of limitlessness extended to the individual's feeling that self-fulfillment meant satisfying every need and desire. . . . One of the characteristics of the reigning social ethic of the 1980's is the shift from within the self to the world outside—the reality factor. . . . Selectivity and a sense of restraint have become part of this ethic along with a large dose of pragmatism. The emphasis is on winning rather than on principle. . . . Pragmatism has some unattractive features, especially when adopted by people who have no real training in self-restraint. If your objective is to win, you don't look so closely at the means, you cheat a little, cut some corners. That kind of behavior may not look too appealing to an older generation.[15]

The current mood seems to have swung from Buber's "narrow-ridge" concern for self and other to an increasing desire to protect what is one's own. As Ellen Goodman stated, it is no longer mandatory to help the "losers." The optimism some now sense may be largely a result of lowering expectations about who we will aid, thereby making more available to "our kind" of people. Such a perspective is affecting our communication in community. Increasing competition and struggle for resources is manifesting itself in a return to individualistic roots at odds with Buber's narrow-ridge view of community.

One of my favorite stories[16] describes the choice before us in a provocative metaphor. Once there was a meat-eating animal who was an excellent provider of plenty for himself and his family. This animal had a long pointed horn, of which he was very proud. The horn was used to capture and kill his prey. For centuries, this species of long-horned animal was successful at the task, which provided them with an abundance of fresh meat. But then came a severe winter, which drove all the game out of this animal's area. For the first time, the animal was without meat to feed his family.

In response to the changed environment, the long-horned animal began to work on strengthening and lengthening his powerful horn. His hope was that by enlarging his horn it would be only a matter of time before the game would "magically" return. This long-horned animal refused to alter his diet to take advantage of the plentiful vegetation around him. He clung to the hope that his tradition of the long horn was the only way to find a fulfilling life, so he persisted.

As time went by, the horn continued to grow until the animal could no longer raise his head. But he still refused to release his belief in the horn's magical qualities, even as his firm belief in the "old ways" was gradually killing him. Unable to lift his head and still refusing to change his diet, the long-horned animal began to die of starvation. Taken to his bed to die in the midst of family, the long-horned animal noticed that they looked somehow different. Then it became clear to him why the others were healthy and looked so strange. While he was working to enlarge his horn, the others had labored to rid themselves of what was no longer usable. The healthy animals had no horn at all!

The story of the long-horned species is a narration about change and adaptation. The hope is that our long horn of individualism and self-concern might be altered to include the pragmatic necessity of human community thinking. Both Buber's work and *Communication and Community* are grounded in this hope. But the values of dialogue and community are not offered as prescription. Rather, this perspective on communication and community is provided for conversation, debate, confirmation, and disagreement. Walking the narrow ridge between openness and advocacy[17] is the goal of *Communication and Community*; a clear opinion is provided, not to offer a final answer, but to initiate needed conversation about our collective future.

An Interpretive Inquiry

Both key terms of this interpretive inquiry, communication and community, have numerous definitions. Thus, following the advice of one of my graduate professors, I will not attempt to precisely define the obvious or the undefinable.[18] However, I do want to provide some guidelines for thinking about these terms within the confines of this book. Use of the term *communication* will adhere to Buber's definitions of monologue, technical dialogue, and dialogue.

> I know three kinds [of communication]. There is genuine dialogue—no matter whether spoken or silent—where each of the participants really has in mind the other or others in their present and particular being and

turns to them with the intention of establishing a living mutual relation between himself and them. There is technical dialogue, which is prompted solely by the need of objective understanding. And there is monologue disguised as dialogue, in which two or more men, meeting in space, speak each with himself in strangely tortuous and circuitous ways and yet imagine they have escaped the torment of being thrown back on their own resources. The first kind [dialogue], as I have said, has become rare; where it arises, in no matter how "unspiritual" a form, witness is borne on behalf of the continuance of the organic substance of the human spirit. The second [technical dialogue] belongs to the inalienable sterling quality of "modern existence." But real dialogue is here continually in all kinds of odd corners and, occasionally in an unseemly way, breaks surface surprisingly and inopportunely—certainly still oftener it is arrogantly tolerated than downright scandalizing—as in the tone of a railway guard's voice, in the glance of an old newspaper vendor, in the smile of the chimney-sweeper. And the third [monologue disguised as dialogue] . . . a *debate* in which the thoughts are not expressed in the way in which they existed in the mind but in the speaking are so pointed that they may strike home in the sharpest way, and moreover without the men that are spoken to being regarded in any way present as person, a *conversation* characterized by the need neither to communicate something, not to learn something, not to influence someone, not to come into connexion with someone, but solely by the desire to have one's own self-reliance confirmed.[19]

In short, self-centered conversation is monologue. Information-centered conversation that assumes neutrality is technical dialogue. Relationship-centered communication that is sensitive to what happens to both self and other approaches dialogic communication. All these forms of communication have an appropriate place in modern society. Buber did not want to make a technique out of dialogue. Dialogue can be invited, but not commanded. Buber further clarified his threefold understanding of communication in the first thirty-nine pages of *Between Man and Man*.

    Community can happen in groups and organizations when communication and living together go beyond association and begin to permit a sense of commitment to both the people and the ideals of the organization. To define the term community for this book, it is helpful to turn to the work of Maurice Friedman, a leading inter-

preter of Buber's material. Friedman discussed the notion of the
"community of otherness," which can be briefly summarized as
follows: Whenever one is concerned about the principles that ground
a group or organization or the persons within that group, in addition
to oneself, the beginning of a "community of otherness" surfaces. The
"community of otherness" permits a struggle over ideas and principles, while confirming one's adversary. In short, the "community of
otherness" holds in creative tension the importance of self, other,
and principles that ground a community, while encouraging confirmation of persons, even when their ideas clash with those of the
majority. Conflict is not feared in a "community of otherness"; it
provides the basis for growth of the person and community willing to
genuinely keep the triple focus of self, other, and community principle in creative tension.[20]

Organizations and groups can be helpful or detrimental, depend-
ing on how one is permitted and encouraged to relate with others and
whether or not the infusion of "new" ideas is tolerated. *Communication and Community* and Buber's dialogue are rooted in a concern for
self and other that sees the value of criticism and the danger of too
much self-protection. Much of this book discusses the dialogic community that Buber pointed to and the assistance that communication
can give to its development. Buber most clearly described his vision
of community in *Paths in Utopia*. The introduction to *Paths in Utopia*
provided a glimpse of how Buber came to root both communication
and community in a dialogic philosophy.

> Buber's researches into the lore and history of Hasidism had provided him
> with an ideal type of a truly humane community; and his immersion in
> biblical doctrine had given him unusual preparation for understanding
> the nature of messianism, as a permanent quest of man for a better order
> based on spiritual perspectives. It will be recalled that Buber started as an
> interpreter of the foundations of Hasidism, the seminal ideas of which—
> and in a larger sense of all authentic Judaism—he considered to be unity,
> conduct, and the future. His whole subsequent evolution as a religious
> existentialist philosopher, his system of "dialogical life," his interpreta-
> tion of social issues and his contributions to education, psychotherapy,
> and social philosophy, all flowed out of this primary orientation to the
> cardinal spiritual tenets of central prophetic Judaism as he interpreted it.[21]

One could say that for Buber the life worth living and struggling for required communication that embraced a vision that went beyond individual survival and invited community.

Buber worked as an interpretive researcher. He was not content to describe, but wanted to point to the significance of a particular happening. He did not search for a "covering law" model of communication and community. He brought his own uniqueness to bear on the subject matter, fully expecting another person to see different phenomena than he would conceptualize. Buber would have understood Gadamer's concern about the bad name that bias had received. One's historical bias is inevitable and impossible to prevent, according to many interpretive researchers.[22] The goal is not so much to prevent bias in interpretive research, but to acknowledge it as one view of an event or happening.

Interpretive research has become more common in human communication studies. The following examples are some of the recent contributions in interpretive research that are of importance to the study of communication in groups and organizations: groundbreaking work in organizational communication by Ian Mitroff and Karl Weick; critical theory approaches to management by Stanley Deetz; an entire volume of *Western Journal of Speech* (1982) devoted to interpretive inquiry in organizations; Putnam and Pacanowsky's well-received edited volume *Communication and Organizations: An Interpretive Approach*; and the fantasy-theme analysis of Ernest Bormann.

The uniqueness of *Communication and Community* as an interpretive study is that Buber's work is used as the guide for inviting human community through communication in groups and organizations. Examples, stories, and anecdotes about society, culture, and community are selectively used to support Buber's dialogical framework. This book is not a sociological analysis of communication in groups and organizations, but an interpretation of communication and community through Buber's dialogic vision.

Dialogic interpretation is an effort neither at objective, nor subjective exploration. Dialogic interpretation "walks the narrow ridge" between extremes, to use Buber's terms. Dialogic interpretation neither describes community as it "is," nor permits a subjective ignoring of the horizon of the text. Instead, dialogic interpretation

seeks to work within credible limits of the text with full knowledge
that the author will add to the text. In essence, dialogic interpretation
is the dialogue of two worlds: Buber's and mine. The result is not a
definitive statement that is irrefutable; rather, it is a perspective that
is open to conversation about communication and community.

As discussed later in the book, in times of rapid change and
uncertainty, a dialogic community may promote an atmosphere of
discussion and openness in the midst of multiple visions and numerous answers. In summary, the interpretive goal for this inquiry and
the theme of *Communication and Community* is to keep the discussion going in dialogic interpretation and on the issue of deliberate
building and invitation of human community.

Outline of a Dialogue

Communication and Community is divided into three sections. The
first, "Communication and Community in Crisis," sets the stage for
the rest of the book. Chapter 1, "The Communicative Crisis," describes the strain on communicators seeking community in a time of
limited resources. Acknowledging these limited resources, chapter
2, "The Narrow Ridge," lays out Buber's philosophy for inviting
community through communication in spite of our limitations. The
second part, "Communication Limiting Community," explores approaches to communication that might get in the way of our efforts at
inviting community. Chapter 3, "Existential Mistrust: The Failure to
Listen," points to the extent of mistrust in contemporary society and
its implications for dividing human community. Chapter 4, "Monologue: Centering on Self," explores our tendency to center communication not in relationship but around the self. Chapter 5, "Organizational Involvement: A Place of Hiding," continues the theme of
narcissism begun in chapter 4 and extends it to the renewed interest
in becoming "organization loyalists," while promoting self-interest.

The last part, "Inviting Dialogue in Community," examines basic
notions appropriate for discussion of communication and community
within a dialogical interpretation. Chapter 6, "The Search for the
Ethical Community," points to ethics as commitment to hearing
contrary perspectives. Chapter 7, "Freedom: The Unity of Contraries," describes the basic notion of dialogue as contradiction, not
logical syllogism. Chapter 8, "Meaning in Community: Is This All

There Is?" examines the notion of meaning for communication and community in a time of limited resources. Chapter 9, "Power and Responsibility," reveals the ontological nature of power and its implications for dialogue in community. Chapter 10, "The Community of Dialogue," summarizes the difficulty of inviting community in a time of limited resources and points to some reasons why we should maintain such a vision in the midst of a contrary social climate.

I hope this book initiates dialogue about communication and human community. I can personally acknowledge my own satisfaction, as well as frustration, with inviting community as implied by Buber. It is when I feel most protective of "my group" or "my view" that dialogue is violated. Perhaps the response to such a state of affairs is that dialogue is not for the faint-hearted, as my friend and colleague Paul Keller is fond of saying. Toward such a dialogue, I offer *Communication and Community: Implications of Martin Buber's Dialogue*.

PART ONE

COMMUNICATION and COMMUNITY in CRISIS

THE COMMUNICATIVE CRISIS

MARTIN Buber on communicative crisis:

> Man is more than ever inclined to see his own principle in its original
> purity and the opposing one in its present deterioration, especially if the
> forces of propaganda confirm his instincts in order to make better use of
> them. . . . He is convinced that his side is in order, the other side
> fundamentally out of order, that he is concerned with the recognition and
> realization of the right, his opponent with the masking of his selfish
> interest. Expressed in modern terminology, he believes that he has ideas,
> his opponent only ideologies. This obsession feeds the mistrust that
> incites the two camps.[1]

While delivering a lecture as a guest speaker on another college
campus, I was asked if I foresaw any one major communication
problem in the future. Ordinarily, such a question would seem
unanswerable because of the numerous problems we are facing and
will inevitably encounter. However, on this occasion I offered a
prediction with conviction. I answered that the major problem
within our human community for the remainder of this century and
into the next would be communication from polarized positions.
Polarized communication can be summarized as the inability to
believe or seriously consider one's own view as wrong and the other's
opinion as truth. Communication within human community becomes

typified by the rhetoric of "we" are right and "they" are misguided and wrong.

Before we can move on, the term *human community*, which is central to this work, should be clarified. In the introduction to this book, I relied upon Maurice Friedman's metaphor of a "community of otherness" to describe my understanding of community, involving a triple focus of self, other, and the principles of an organization, which must be held in creative dialogic tension. This book differentiates community from mere association with one another in groups and organizations. If the principles of a group are significant, but the relationships are minimized or viewed as irrelevant, then only association, not community is fostered. On the other hand, if association focuses on the self/other relationship, omitting the struggle over principle, relationships become narcissistic and self-serving, rather than the "community of otherness" that Friedman discussed.[2]

Perhaps another way to reveal my differentiation between association and community in groups and organizations is to examine Buber's discussion of this difference between the "interhuman" and the "social," respectively. In his classic essay "Elements of the Interhuman," Buber laid out four major differences between the "interhuman" and the "social." First, the "interhuman" realm is a personal relationship in which the individual is met as a noninterchangeable, nonobjectified contributor to the activity. On the other hand, the "social" realm has the person's function or role as the most significant concern. Second, the "interhuman" is the realm of the "between"; it is not a psychological construct. Meaning is found not in one partner, but "between" partners in interaction. In contrast, in the activity of the "social," meaning is possessed by one party or another. Third, the "interhuman" is grounded in the assumption that what one does is more vital than how one appears. (Buber called this *being*). The "social" life switches this emphasis. (Buber referred to this action as *seeming*.) Finally, the "interhuman" realm invites dialogue by permitting ideas to "unfold" in conversation, unlike the "social" realm, in which one pushes to "impose" a particular perspective prior to hearing the other's views. In short, the "interhuman" is based on relationship, nonpossession, the noninterchangeability of persons, and a reluctance to impose ideas on others.[3]

Buber's discussion of the "interhuman" and Friedman's description of the "community of otherness" provide the backdrop for my

distinction between association and community in groups and organizations. In addition, this work stresses the importance of principles
in groups, so that relationships are not permitted to govern what is
heard and permitted in community. Additionally, this book emphasizes the vitality of conflict within a community. If no conflict exists,
then, in all likelihood, someone is afraid to disagree.[4] In essence, the
usage of the word *community* in this book is not rooted in a precise
definition, but in an attitude sensitive to the dialogical tension between self, other, and the principles of a group or organization.

The view of community pointed to by Buber, Friedman, and
myself is violated as one embraces one's own position as solely right
and the other's view as inaccurate, misled, or even false, without
giving the other's view an honest hearing. Our "communicative
crisis" of polarized communication continues to pick up momentum.
It may become one of the major barriers to social progress and a
significant contributor to the deterioration and destruction of our
often fragile human community. Polarized communication appears to
be an epidemic infection in twentieth-century life, if the burgeoning
divorce rate, the problems in the Middle East, Asia, Africa, and
Central America, the increasing tension between the United States
and the Soviet Union, and assassination acts and attempts are taken
as indicators.

Within the boundaries of the United States, the struggles between
pro-abortion and anti-abortion forces, nuclear arms and energy advocates and protesters, and conservative and liberal political organizations lend further credence to the increasing reality of polarized
communication. In short, the ever-present character of polarized
communication with its devastating effects requires us to search for
ways to lessen its stronghold on our human community.

Looking Out for Number One

Polarized positions are fostered by groups and/or individuals looking
out for their own interests with little concern for others. In such a
communicative environment, the powerful party works to maintain
advantage and the underdog struggles to gain equal rights, or at least
to avoid losing further ground to those in control. Such behavior may
be the unfortunate consequence of hierarchial rankings that desig-
nate some positions as inferior to others, resulting in subordination of

the less powerful. For example, traditionally, management has controlled labor, administration has directed faculty, the teacher has
evaluated the student, and the male has dominated the female.
Although one may rightly argue that this is not and should not always
be the case, such relationships have occurred frequently enough that
subordinated groups have organized themselves for their own benefit. Labor unions, faculty organizations and unions, the student
protests and civil-rights actions of the 1960s and 1970s, and the
women's movement all sought or continue to seek to empower the
subordinate.

Such organization and unionization arise from a desire for power
parity or an equalization of power. There is an unwillingness to settle
for submissiveness. Such acts have led Rollo May to describe rebellion as a central element in one's humanness. "It is the capacity to
sense injustice and take a stand against it in the form of I will be
destroyed rather than submit. . . . [T]his elemental capacity to fight
against injustice remains the distinguishing characteristic of human
beings. It is, in short, the capacity to rebel."[5] Unhappily, as individuals rebel, they often discover that equalization of power does not
automatically solve the problem of polarized positions. A classic
example of this unfortunate reality is sometimes found in the parent/
child relationship during the "child's" adult years. Imagine a
hypothetical relationship between a woman, Tina, and her mother.
Tina felt distant from her mother as she grew up; she eagerly awaited
the day she would be a power equal with her mother. However, as
she accumulated the necessary power, the relationship remained
cold and detached. Being a power equal, it turned out, was not
enough. Tina's mother still withheld any obvious signs of love for her
daughter. Tina learned through painful experience that an increase
in power can begin to break the barriers of polarized positions only if
both people are able to prize the relationship above the desire to
dominate.

Consider another example, in which "looking out for number one"
only encouraged spending an inordinate amount of time probing
weaknesses in the other's defenses, in hopes of gaining power dominance or at least preventing the other from controlling the relationship. Tom and Mary had a traditional role relationship for a
number of years. Then Mary changed her career goals and began to
wield more equal power in the relationship, allowing a symmetrical

relationship to form. Yet Tom and Mary continued to have serious communication problems. Previously, silence meant resentment or indifference; later it implied calculation and a developing of strategies to maintain one's position and/or power.

In yet another familiar pattern involving a teenager and her parents, a fifteen-year-old girl with independent opinions and at odds with her parents felt too controlled and confined. To gain more influence, the youngster struggled for a more equal power relationship by running away from home and eventually returning only after being "guaranteed" treatment as an autonomous adult, capable of making her own decisions. Before running away, the parent/child relationship was composed of bitterness and mistrust. After the equalizing of power there was still no lessening of polarized communication. The relationship was then rooted in threats and fear of losing power parity.

It seems that neither a "complementary" relationship between persons of different status (superior to inferior, boss to employee, one-up to one-down) nor a "symmetrical" relationship (between equals) is enough to tame our communicative crisis.[6] Movement from a complementary relationship to a symmetrical communicative exchange between power equals is a first step, but alone it is often not sufficient to open up the channels of healthy communication within community. The chain that must be broken is that of calculation and strategy, which seeks to perpetuate only one's own position and advantage.

Six Ghostly Images

Gregory Bateson's discussion of runaway relationships, a phenomenon he referred to as schismogenesis, implicitly suggested a reason for the durability of polarized positions. Bateson's analysis pointed to the fact that equalizing power within a relationship may not lessen the extreme positions held by participants. Both symmetrical and complementary relationships can become dangerous or schismogenic. If a minority group is continually pushed into a complementary one-down position, a schismogenic process of continued oppression results. In a symmetrical relationship, such as the arms race between the United States and the Soviet Union, the constant competition between two approximately equal powers has led to schismogenesis. In both cases, the longer the progressive state of escalation persists, the more difficult it is to deter.[7]

In human community, complementary schismogenesis reflects the superior's desire to constantly have his or her position or viewpoint affirmed and the subordinate ignored or humiliated. However, if this situation changes to symmetrical schismogenesis, perhaps through unionization, superior and subordinate powers may become more equalized. But, unfortunately, both powers may continue to communicate from extreme positions. Take, for example, a situation in which a manager of a local company was asked if he would support a labor union in his plant. The answer was a forceful "no" to unionization. However, the employees in his plant felt exploited. They maintained that his dominant power position blinded him to their needs. The employees argued that unionization would help them equalize power, thereby developing a symmetrical relationship. However, if unionization had occurred and management and labor as parties of more equal power had continued to work only for their own benefits, a symmetrical schismogenic escalation could have replaced the old set of evils.

Gerald Nierenberg described such an instance in which the power relationship changed from a complementary relationship to symmetrical schismogenesis without ever altering the extreme positions. Bertram Powers, head of the printer's union in New York City, negotiated the contract he desired for his workers. But as a result, a number of newspapers folded. "The negotiation was successful, but the patient died."[8] Polarized positions of communication are typified by concern for one's own position and little regard for the other's viewpoint. Observation suggests that communication cognizant only of one's own viewpoint is destructive and counterproductive. Like the Powers example, a person can win a demand but destroy a part of, if not all of, the relationship.

In human community, the relationship styles of complementary schismogenesis and symmetrical schismogenesis appear rooted in opposing premises. Yet these apparently contrasting relationship styles have a common result—both promote polarized communicative positions. A superficial analysis of how both complementary schismogenesis and symmetrical schismogenesis can result in polarized communication often too quickly isolates the power component of each relationship style. One can too easily accept the cliché that "power corrupts" and fail to seek the fundamental roots of this communicative crisis. Numerous authors of human community reject this "power corruption" analysis in favor of the view that power is inevitable, as discussed by such authors as Rollo May, Martin Buber, Mahatma Gandhi, and Martin Luther King, Jr.[9] They prefer to view power as a neutral phenomenon that can be implemented for constructive or destructive ends.[10] In short, power in itself is insufficient to generate our communicative crisis. I am inclined to envision the overuse of comparative strategies as a more fundamental reason for the perpetuation of both symmetrical schismogenesis and complementary schismogenesis. Complementary schismogenesis involves a comparative strategy of keeping others in their places. Symmetrical schismogenesis requires a comparative strategy of making sure the opponent does not forge ahead in the struggle.

It is easy to visualize how perpetuation of a subordinate position results in polarized communication. But how does this same result occur from the symmetrical schismogenic impulse to keep up with one's opponent and then overtake him or her? In symmetrical schismogenesis, one develops a strategic concern about the other's image of oneself as a power-wielding agent, in hopes of outmaneuvering or outguessing one's opponent. Constantly measuring one's power against that of the other can result in the comparison getting out of hand. "Keeping up with the Jones" becomes a pathological preoccupation or fetish that can polarize the two parties.

Martin Buber spoke on the issue of strategic overconcern about perceptions as he discussed two people caught in a communicative exchange of image or appearance.

> Let us now imagine two men, whose life is dominated by appearance, sitting and talking together. Call them Peter and Paul. Let us list the different configurations which are involved. First, there is Peter, as he really appears to Paul, that is, Paul's image of Peter, which in general does not in the least coincide with what Peter wishes to see; and similarly there is the reverse situation. Further, there is Peter as he appears to himself, and Paul as he appears to himself. Lastly, there are the bodily Peter and bodily Paul. Two living beings and six ghostly appearances, which mingle in many ways in the conversation between the two. Where is there room for any genuine inter-human life?
>
> Whatever the meaning of the word "truth" may be in other realms, in

the interhuman realm it means that men communicate themselves to one another as what they are [not what they want to appear like or imagine themselves to be].[11]

Thus, Buber would say that the fundamental root of our communication crisis in human community is an overconcern for image and appearance. This critique strikes at the heart of the power parity problem. If relationships between power equals are based on outguessing one's opponent, then strategy, image, inauthenticity, and mistrust will widen the distance between polarized positions.

Our culture seems to encourage the strategy of images, with importance attached to high-level consciousness, which is directly related to Descartes' "I think, therefore I am." In an article on communication theory, Berger and Douglas took exception to the notion that all communication should be at a high level of strategic purpose, represented by the Peter and Paul example.[12] While strategic or purposeful communication sometimes has a necessary and helpful place in our culture, overuse of strategic communication can invite problems within human community.

At this point, I would like to add a cautionary note. A friend once asked, "Isn't it beneficial to strategize about ways to invite human community? Aren't you really just disagreeing with self-interest that ignores other's needs?" I agree that strategy only seeking self-interest goes against the human community theme of this book. However, we need to be cautious in strategizing about the construction of human community. I would be more eager to suggest encouraging an atmosphere that invites, but does not demand, human community. Strategic community formation can bring out the rebel in many of us. Buber invited community not by telling others what to do, but by looking for a common ground of shared interests that might encourage a triple focus of concern for self, other, and the principles of the group. He recognized that forcing community could result in the genuine independent character rebelling against the call to community.[13]

An invitation to human community needs to permit and encourage the emergence of human uniqueness. Comparative strategies that seek to keep someone down (complementary) or attempt to keep all the "same" (symmetrical) not only degrade human dignity, but limit the number of unique and new ideas available to a community. Since a complementary style of oppression can be easily visualized as detrimental to human uniqueness, we should concentrate on the symmetrical expression of the problem—the effort at sameness. For instance, at one educational institution, a professor became more "recognized" than the administrators of the institution. Since this institution took great pride in having no "heroes," the well-known faculty member was marginalized. Polarization emerged between her and those wanting to put her in a less significant position within the institution. If the communicative pressure were successful, this faculty person would have to lessen productivity in order to keep her professional visibility and success on the same level as her colleagues.

Unfortunately, there seems to be only a certain level of success that each group can tolerate from individual members. But if we simply excuse this behavior as normal and inevitable, we have sanctioned the pursuit of mediocrity. Healthy people need to admit that some are more gifted and talented in particular areas. In short, it is no more healthy for the less successful to *marginalize* a recognized leader than it is for those in power to continue to oppress the less advantaged.

The term *marginalization* refers to the action of a group or organization in which the power or influence of an individual is limited by placing that person on the outskirts of the group. A marginalized person is excluded from the decision-making center of the group. The organization permits and even encourages the marginalized person's continued involvement; however, the participation is controlled by the group, limited by the peripheral nature of the person's inclusion in the community. Such marginalization—whether of the less talented by the gifted, or vice versa—helps create an atmosphere of polarized communication. People can diminish the health of the human community by pursuing only their self-interests, whether it be through sameness and mediocrity disguised as equality, or through domination offered as legitimate authority.

Manipulating to Avoid Being Manipulated?

Further insight on the maintenance of polarized positions is provided by Anatol Rapoport's contrasting of strategic and conscience-oriented thinking. Rapoport contended that the strategist's concern for outguessing the other's next move relegates the opponent to an obstacle

that must be won or conquered. Rapoport's strategic thinker rejects
the role of emotion in decision making. A neutral stance is assumed
that permits doing a job without asking if that activity is worthy of
attention.

The neutrality of the strategist allows a feeling of detachment and
lack of responsibility that invites the completion of a job in an ethical
vacuum. Rapoport suggested that such a strategic viewpoint was part
of the foundation of Hitler's Germany. He recognized that many
Germans were coerced by the structures around them. It is not this
group he holds in disdain, but rather the strategist capable of doing a
job without affect or a willingness to ask, "Is it right?"

> The "detachment" of the strategist resembles not so much that of a
> surgeon as that of a butcher or still more that of the organizers of mass
> extermination. Those technicians too were for the most part "detached" in
> the sense that their work was not charged with affect. German chemists
> were detached when they built the gas chambers; German transportation
> experts were detached and efficient as they kept the trains moving,
> carrying people to the slaughter sites; German bookkeepers were de-
> tached while keeping tallies of the dispatched, etc. Doubtless many of
> those responsible for this activity took a certain pride in having overcome
> any inhibitions they might have had in this matter. They might have been
> sincerely convinced that the "Jewish question" was a problem to be solved
> in a detached and definitive manner, possibly for the good of humanity. In
> other words, the charge of depravity, sadism, etc., can not be made
> convincingly only against the entire corps of specialists who planned and
> carried out the extermination of the 1940's. These people did not go
> berserk. They were carrying out their duties methodically and systemati-
> cally. They were "normally functioning" human beings.[14]

Rapoport implicated the strategist as a person who does not question
the ethical consequences of an action. To be efficient is not enough;
one must carry an ethical conscience into one's vocation. Rapoport
posed the conscience-oriented thinker as an alternative to the
strategist, with the former asserting the importance of emotion,
values, and ethics in his or her decision making. The fundamental
distinction between these two orientations is that the conscience-
oriented thinker asks, "Is the projected outcome of this job an ethical
and helpful contribution to our human community?"[15]

In daily human communication, the strategist might be someone climbing the status ladder in an organization. When the climber talks to people, the human being is secondary and a "contact" or an "influential friend" is primary. The aim is to promote the right image and to maneuver for success. "The basic question in the strategist's mind is this: 'In a conflict how can I gain advantage over him?' The critic cannot disregard the question, 'If I gain advantage over him, what sort of person will I become?'"[16] If strategy and manipulation continually guide one's dealings with another, then polarized communication will continue and perhaps worsen the situation between strategic foes in an organization.

As problematic as strategic thinking may be, it is still the dominant mode of thought for many. Unfortunately, conscience thinking is usually viewed as an unrealistic and optimistic alternative. The strategist's claim to objectivity is a powerful persuasive tool that casts conscience thinking as naive and foolhardy; yet some consider the cloak of objectivity worn by the strategist to be equally biased.

Rapoport's attack on the objectivity of the strategic world view was not without considerable support, as well as controversy. The notion of inevitability of bias in human communication theory is still a point of contention, as suggested by Beltran.[17] However, philosophers such as Gadamer and Heidegger have supported Rapoport's assertion with their emphasis on historical situatedness—to be human is to be limited by one's context, which makes objectivity impossible.[18] The scientific basis for this statement has been established by Bohr's theory of complementarity, Einstein's theory of relativity, and Heisenberg's principle of uncertainty.[19] In addition, the philosophical and scientific basis for bias in communication has been described in a symposium on qualitative methodology[20] and by Martin Buber.[21]

It is Rapoport's contention that a person's values, not objective facts, develop a strategic perceptual outlook. Rapoport referred to human communication literature as uniformly describing the selective nature of perception. He suggested that the strategist's perceptual limits have imposed a vicious cycle, requiring one to look through "strategic glasses" only to constantly confirm the need for more and more strategy. Thus, it is a value, not a "fact," that links strategy and manipulation with "effective" human communication. Rapoport then concluded his critique of objectivity as the foundation for the strategic viewpoint with this poignant message. "On the basis of their 'objectivity' they accuse of muddleheadedness and naivete anyone who asks embarrassing questions about whether or not their games are worth playing, or whether one ought to identify with actors whose moral code resembles that of Louis XIV, Frederick the Great, and Catherine II at its best and that of Attila, Genghis Khan, and Hitler at its worst."[22]

Rapoport recognized little common ground between strategy-minded and conscience-minded persons. He was not optimistic about bridging the chasm between these opposing types of persons.[23] However, I view the relationship between these two types of thinking somewhat differently. Both strategic and conscience thinking are part of daily communication. It does not seem appropriate to try to become exclusively one type of thinker or another. The aim is to be aware that one is communicating from a value-laden perceptual viewpoint and not to attempt to hide behind a mask of "objectivity" and "factual analysis." At times, one may choose strategic thinking as the necessary communicative option, but one should make the choice with an awareness of this value-oriented decision and of its implications for one's interpersonal communication within a human community.[24]

Communication from Separate Camps

Strategic thought resulting in a polarized communication atmosphere of "us" versus "them" is increasingly reflected in daily interpersonal relationships. Toffler contended that "successful" people are able to terminate relationships in a skillful fashion. Some studies suggest that executives adept at climbing the status ladder are unusually smooth at dissolving friendships and relationships. Executives are sometimes even counseled on how to gracefully withdraw from lower-status associates detrimental to their movement into increasingly "higher" circles. Slater contended that some have refined the art of detachment to the extent that only those who can provide some obvious benefit or reward in terms of their careers or personal desires are termed important.[25]

Christopher Lasch, like Slater, warned of the increasing tendency to use another human being for benefit and success. Lasch has argued that "the narcissist has many traits that make for success in bureaucratic institutions which put a premium on the manipulation of interpersonal relations, and discourage the formation of deep personal attachments."[26] The strategy is to manipulate others for one's own benefit, which results in polarized communication of two groups—users and used. It is this form of polarization that tears at the heart of human community.

One may argue that Slater and Lasch are overstating the case. However, one may look at the great popularity of self-help books and conclude that such a pessimistic analysis is given some undeniable support.[27] Strategies to win and influence people and look out for one's own interests have signaled a switch from the Protestant work ethic to the quest for individual survival. The ethic is now increasingly becoming "us" versus "them." "'Growth' has become a euphemism for survival [and a justification of manipulative communication]."[28]

Although the reflective emphasis on "me," "my image," and "my success" is much more subtle and "civilized" than the overt manipulation of a totalitarian government, it is rooted in a similar strategy: How can I perpetuate my own regime or my own success? Unfortunately, our generation may be only beginning to see the damage and tension that polarized communication can inflict upon relationships. We are now aware of limitations of natural resources, social movements, and the buying power of incomes. As a result, some people are feeling a loss of control over their own ability to upgrade their position and status. It is likely that as resources become even more scarce and promotions more competitive, strategic interpersonal communication styles of how to outdo the other person will increase in popularity and use.

In essence, the communicative crisis within human community is twofold. First, we must recognize that power parity alone will not necessarily overcome polarized communicative positions. Second, we must understand that resorting to strategic interpersonal communication styles may allow some feeling of control, but further separates oneself from others. The continual use of strategic communication will widen the chasm between opposing people and their ideologies. Answers to problems within community that rely on quick or easily apparent solutions may actually contribute to the communicative crisis. Perhaps we need conscience-oriented thinkers, in Rapoport's terms, and attentive human beings in Buber's language.

> For the attentive man would no longer, as his custom is, "master" the situation the very moment after it stepped up to him: it would be laid upon him to go up to and into it. Moreover, nothing that he believed he possessed as always available would help him, no knowledge, no system and no programme; for now he would have to do with what cannot be classified, with concretion itself. . . . It will, then, be expected of the attentive man that he faces creation as it happens.[29]

Such a communication style within community necessitates that one work out problems in relationship with the other, not unilaterally or in solitude. The movement from strategic thinking to conscience thinking requires a shift from control to dialogue, from image to authenticity, from independence to interdependence, and finally from prescription to collaboration. Power holds only a partial answer to communication problems. To bridge the final span, one must risk developing solutions in dialogue with one's "opponent," while rejecting the temporary safety of technique and strategy.

Polarized positions of communication result in an either/or interpersonal communication style, demanding that the other accept one's proposed viewpoint or be regarded as an opponent and adversary. Martin Buber eloquently summarized the danger of polarized positions in an address entitled "Hope for This Hour." His comments are as appropriate today as they were in their original context.

> The human world is today, as never before, split into two camps, each of which understands the other as the embodiment of falsehood and itself as the embodiment of truth. Often in history, to be sure, national groups and religious associations have stood in so radical an opposition that the one side denied and condemned the other in its innermost existence. Now, however, it is the human population of our planet generally that is so divided, and with rare exceptions this division is everywhere seen as a necessity of existence in the world hour. He who makes himself an exception is suspected or ridiculed by both sides. Each side has assumed monopoly of the sunlight and has plunged its antagonist into night, and each side demands that you choose between day and night.[30]

Conscience-oriented thinkers must continue the search for alternatives to polarized communication by resisting overreliance on strategic-oriented thinking. The risk is real in such a search, but continuation of our present course may prove even riskier to our human community.

2

THE NARROW RIDGE

MARTIN Buber on the third alternative implied by the narrow ridge:

> In the most powerful moments of dialogic, where in truth "deep calls unto deep," it becomes unmistakably clear that it is not the wand of the individual or of the social, but of a third which draws the circle round the happening. On the far side of the subjective, on this side of the objective, on the narrow ridge, where I and Thou meet, there is the realm of "between."
>
> This reality, whose disclosure has begun in our time, shows the way, leading beyond individualism and collectivism, for the life decision of future generations. Here the genuine third alternative is indicated, the knowledge of which will help to bring about the genuine person again and to establish genuine community.[1]

Buber's "third alternative" requires walking the narrow ridge between extreme positions. Even when the selection of a polarized communicative position or "camp" is a temptation, it is not the only viable option. Some are able to embrace a conviction, while remaining open to the other's viewpoint. It is possible to remain sensitive to multiple facets of an issue, as one forms an opinion. Take the case of the conscientious objector whose friend was an Army chaplain for twenty years. These two men strongly disagreed on the appropriateness of the C.O. position. Fortunately, their relationship did not degenerate into polarized viewpoints. Even though neither was convinced by the other, each attempted to understand the other's viewpoint. Such a relationship is reminiscent of such historical figures as Samuel Johnson, who took delight in a Whig friend disagreeing with him, or Mahatma Gandhi, who willingly developed friendships with British opponents in the nonviolent campaign for Indian independence.[2]

Indeed, such examples shed a hopeful light on the long shadow of polarized communication. We can take heart that such a constructive communicative style need not be left to just extraordinary world citizens. Limiting polarized communication is at the very center of everyday communicative health. Martin Buber called this approach the "narrow ridge," bridging the chasm between opposing camps by opening up the possibilities of dialogue between persons. Buber spoke of the narrow ridge as an alternative to absolute positions that characterize communication in a polarized community. "I have occasionally described my standpoint to my friends as the 'narrow ridge.' I wanted by this to express that I did not rest on the broad upland of a system that includes a series of sure statements about the absolute, but on a narrow rocky ridge between the gulfs where there is no sureness of expressible knowledge but the certainty of meeting with the One who remains undisclosed."[3]

Before we proceed with a discussion of openness that is central to the narrow ridge, let us bear in mind that Buber did not advocate a relativistic nonjudgmental attitude. Sam Johnson, Mahatma Gandhi, Buber, and others of strong conviction stood their ground—what made them unique was their additional ability to learn from the opposition. They listened openly, yet if left unpersuaded by the other, they maintained their original conviction. On the other hand, if they were convinced by the power of another's argument, they changed positions.

Come On—Take a Side!

Attempting to understand an opposing opinion, yet not always being moved by it, may look suspiciously like a closed mind to the persuader. If we are arguing for a position and the other genuinely gives our side a legitimate hearing, we may expect him or her to change sides, or at least seek a compromise position between the opposing viewpoints. Milton Rokeach, known for his classic work *Open and Closed Mind*, pointed to the illegitimacy of such a viewpoint. He stated that a person can support a viewpoint in a closed fashion by refusing to listen to contrary information.[4] Rokeach cautioned against automatically equating the committed individual secure in his or her belief with someone who immediately rejects opposing viewpoints and persons.

> There are individual differences among us in the *absolute* extent to which we are willing to accept and reject others on this basis and there are relative degrees of preference for those with similar versus opposed beliefs. The reason Christ-like figures such as Gandhi and Schweitzer are idealized is that they have the capacity to love those who disagree with them no less than those who agree with them and to love all to a far greater extent than most men are capable of.[5]

A test of one's openness requires an honest answering of the following question: "Does the other have some chance of persuading me to his or her viewpoint?" If the answer is no, then polarized communication is inevitable. A resolution of this problem necessitates maintaining one's commitment as a tentative position, no matter how long that conviction has endured. Unfortunately, openness to contrary statements is not a common or popular stance. A more familiar attitude is expressed in an old *New Yorker* cartoon, in which two men are sitting at a bar. As one of the men is released from his inhibitions by his drunken state, he sticks his chin into the face of his timid companion and growls, "I know your cowardly type—always trying to see the other person's point of view." This cartoon, though exaggerated, represents an attitudinal reality typical of everyday thinking.

Polarized communication was initially at the heart of the 1979–1980 American hostage crisis in Iran. The Carter administration permitted the exiled Shah of Iran to come to the United States for medical treatment. Some Iranians saw the Shah as a despot not deserving special attention; rather, they wanted to place him on trial for crimes against the people. When he came to the United States, "radical" Iranian students occupied the American embassy in Iran, taking American personnel hostage. They demanded the Shah's return for the release of the hostages. At first, Carter's actions seemed to polarize the situation. He called for economic sanctions against Iran, and he referred to the demand for the return of the Shah as an irrelevant issue. The atrocities that the Shah was reported to have inflicted upon his people were not considered negotiable concerns. The problem was limited to resolving the "terrorist" act of kidnapping embassy personnel. Granted, all effort was and should have been put forward to aid the kidnapped individuals, who had been denied rights described by international law. But only recognition of both sides of the conflict, no matter how illegitimate we consider the demands, can temper the growing separation between opposing forces.

It was not until the Carter administration took a serious look at Iranian demands that polarized communication decreased. Such an effort at dialogue is necessary for healthy communication. The Carter administration finally began to walk the narrow ridge between opposing viewpoints. They recognized the limited usefulness of sanctions. "Inflicting pain upon an adversary government is, for a number of reasons, likely to be a poor way of getting them to change their mind. The government whose mind we want to change anticipated some costs when they decided to do what we do not like."[6]

Roger Fisher, well-known for his scholarship in international conflict, commented on the Iranian situation in an interview for "All Things Considered," a Public Broadcasting Service news and information radio program. He suggested that, historically, such actions have not worked in the long term. They tend to unite a country against a common foe. Fisher's view is in accordance with other conflict theorists, such as Lewis Coser, who have emphasized that internal group cohesion is heightened and maintained in the struggle against outside forces or opponents.[7]

Fisher offered similar advice during the Shiite Moslem hijacking of TWA Flight 847. As in the Iranian situation, Fisher in no way condoned the terrorists' actions. But he wanted to avoid a military confrontation by listening seriously to even the terrorists' position. Dialogically, Fisher in both instances called for the United States government to attend seriously to the opponents' view, even if it considered that view wrong or short-sighted, in order to facilitate a diffusion of the confrontation.[8]

Such a theory points to the need for interdependent action between opposing parties. No matter how illegitimate the other's claim, it cannot be ignored unless one is willing to constantly use power and force to diffuse the opponent's demands. Regrettably, the patience required for interdependent negotiation is rapidly becoming a political liability for decision makers. Meg Greenfield, in a *Newsweek* editorial, caught the mood of the nation with her opinion that interdependence has become a mere cliché of limited utility in today's world situations.[9] Polarized communication is often more politically marketable, because it appears "tough." Being open to opposing orientations may be seen as unpatriotic, perhaps even cowardly, by many voters.

Rejecting an interdependent view of human community invites a deceptive simplification of a conflict by splitting people into separate camps. This "us" versus "them" rhetoric is inherent in any revolutionary viewpoint that seeks to benefit from a class conflict or ideological confrontation.[10] Polarized communication neatly organizes events into contrasting categories, giving the illusion of sharpness of perception, when in reality there is a refusal to gain new insights by listening to the other's viewpoint. There is excessive polarized use of pressure techniques to force the opponent to capitulate, which ironically often leads to the strengthening of the opponent. Outside pressures generate internal cohesion in the opponent's ranks.

Another example of the breakdown of polarized communication was an integral part of the movie *Ordinary People*. A mother was unable to show love for her surviving son. Only with the help of a psychiatrist was the son able to "walk the narrow ridge" of understanding himself and his mother. He finally recognized what his mother had to feel with him surviving the boating accident, while her favorite son did not. The realization of his mother's unstated preference was painful to encounter, but it opened the boy's world. It was not just the knowledge that set the boy free. His ability to see the other side of the relationship ended his contribution to the polarized communication, even though his mother could not follow suit. The key to this story was rooted not only in self-knowledge, but in understanding the mother's position and not wanting to further her private agony.

In both of the above examples, one party was able to assume a position of conviction, while remaining open to "new" information. Buber recognized the necessity of both conviction and openness in order to open up dialogue. Ian Mitroff advocated a position that is somewhat akin to the conviction/openness orientation Buber stressed. Mitroff wanted to permit participants in managerial decision making to state consciously assumptions underlying a decision and also to listen to assumptions from a counterproposal. Recognizing the assumptions behind different decisions can sometimes generate a plan that incorporates quality components of each strategy.

There are several differences in the approaches of Mitroff and Buber. Mitroff was more committed to a Hegelian dialectic than to a dialogical stance. But both recognized the importance of bringing assumptions to the surface and permitting those assumptions to be challenged.[11] Conviction with openness was also the attitude embodied by Dag Hammarskjold, former secretary general of the United Nations. Hammarskjold appreciated Martin Buber's ability to combine conviction with openness. This trait was represented in Hammarskjold's writing as well. "We have to acquire a peace and balance of mind such that we can give every word of criticism its due weight, and humble ourselves before every word of praise."[12]

An Interpersonal Tightrope

Following Buber's "conviction in openness" theme may be as simple and as complex as the commandment "Love your neighbor as yourself." This theme is at the core of Frost and Wilmot's conviction that a mutually constructive communication and conflict style is "composed of two partially competing goals—*concern for self* and *concern for the other*, both of which must become part of one's decision-making process."[13] For relationships within human community, concern for both self and other requires acceptance of both leadership and subordinate positions at appropriate times. Usually both parties in a relationship have skills and insights that need to be affirmed and acknowledged, and at times followed.[14] Lederer and Jackson make a similar point in their book *Mirages of Marriage*. They discuss the concept of healthy "parallel" relationships in which both partners recognize the need for equality, shifting leadership, and a willingness to follow the other's advice when appropriate.[15] It is this style of sharing, listening, and sensitivity to others' needs as well as one's own that may interrupt the pattern of polarized communication.

As this chapter has revealed, the dual concern for oneself and the other person, not just redistribution of power, was the foundation of Martin Buber's notion of the "narrow ridge." Maurice Friedman considered Buber's narrow ridge a genuine third alternative to the common either/or thinking that gives rise to polarized communication.

> Buber's narrow ridge is no "happy middle" which ignores the reality of paradox and contradiction in order to escape from the suffering they produce. It is rather a paradoxical unity of what one usually understands only as alternatives—I and Thou, love and justice, dependence and freedom. . . . "According to the logical conception of trust only one of two contraries can be true, but in the reality as one lives it they are inseparable. . . . The unity of the contraries is the mystery at the innermost core of the dialogue."[16]

Aubrey Hodes, in *Martin Buber: An Intimate Portrait*, suggested that the narrow ridge is the meeting place of the human community, where an individual does not ask what can benefit himself or herself or his or her group; nor does he or she quietly acquiesce to another. The narrow ridge is a communication style that genuinely takes into account both self and other.[17] The notion of the narrow ridge does not rely on prescriptions such as a "suffering servant" or a selfish stereotype. Instead, the narrow ridge embodies a third alternative, assuming a genuine responsibility for both oneself and the other.

A metaphor for the "narrow ridge" might be a tightrope walker attempting to keep his or her balance; as he or she leans too far to one side, adjustment must be made and balance regained. The "narrow ridge" in human communication involves a balancing of one's concern for self and others. One must be open to the other's viewpoint and willing to alter one's position based upon appropriate and just cause, if necessary. However, as mentioned earlier, being concerned for oneself and the other does not necessarily mean a compromise or an acceptance of another's viewpoint. One *may* accept a compromise or even change to the other's viewpoint; such moves are done out of a commitment to finding the "best" principle or solution. As long as such shifts reflect a commitment to principle, rather than a "false peace," the narrow ridge has been followed. Of course, one can also remain unmoved by another's argument while displaying concern for self and other and giving the other's viewpoint an honest evaluation.

Buber called for a narrow-ridge attitude that embraces self and other not as a psychological construction, but as an ontological reality. Buber felt that it was impossible to live life without such an attitude, unless we excluded an *I–Thou* encounter in favor of the *I–It* at all times. "The *I–Thou* and *I–It* . . . are pointers to the human situation, in its intricate interweaving of the personal and the impersonal, of the world to be 'used' and the world to be 'met.'"[18] Although Buber considered both the *I–Thou* and the *I–It* necessary, he called the *I–Thou* the realm of relation and the *I–It*, or using of another, the realm of separation.[19] Walking the narrow ridge that seeks to be sensitive to the *I–Thou* relation of self and other is central to Buber's orientation.[20]

No formula or technique exists that can prescribe how to create an atmosphere of concern for both parties in a relationship. But if one is genuinely responsible and attentive, one can usually detect when too much concern for self and too little for the other, or vice versa, begins to interfere with interpersonal communication. In short, living the narrow-ridge philosophy requires a life of personal and interpersonal concern, which is likely to generate a more complicated existence than that of the egotist or the selfless martyr.

Tentative Commitment

Teaching the concept of the narrow ridge usually raises some common misperceptions. Various persons in the classroom or audience might say, "I know, it is a compromise." Another says, "It is a synthesis of viewpoints, like Hegel's dialectic." Someone else states, "The narrow ridge means maintaining your own view in the most adverse of circumstances." Yet another person describes the narrow ridge as "being open to an opponent's view." And finally, someone says, "The narrow ridge requires finding a solution that is novel to both parties in a confrontation." My response to these comments is that each individual is right, but also wrong. The narrow ridge can be any of the above interpersonal communication results. Yet any of the above could also occur without involving the narrow-ridge concept.

The narrow ridge is a philosophical stance that undergirds behavior. If two people manifest the same behavior, but one person's reason for the behavior does not embrace genuine dual concern for self and other, then the narrow ridge has not guided that person. Even if two people are engaging in the same behavior, the reasons for their actions may be quite different. The observable behavior can be called the carrier of communication. But the communicative event itself focuses on the behavior of the person and the reasons that underlie the behavior.

Take, for example, two hypothetical students who spend equal time studying and receive the same straight "A" grade report. We will call the first student, who is a strategic thinker, Anne. The second, Jane, is a conscience-oriented thinker, which is central to the narrow ridge. Anne does not care much for the knowledge she gains; status and recognition are her reasons for working long hours. Jane, on the other hand, loves to learn for the sake of learning; her success is a byproduct of her commitment. If one only looks at the carrier of communication, the behavior of studying, then two identical communication messages are witnessed. However, the reasons for studying and the final aim of each student are so different that the communicative happenings of these two individuals are worlds apart. Anne sees a means *to* an end and Jane sees the means *as* the end.[21] In narrow-ridge terminology of concern for self as well as others, the strategic student, Anne, would not share her notes with a competitor unless she could gain from such an act at a later time. But the conscience-oriented student would share such information without need of any reward other than encouraging herself and others to know the material. Her concern would be for both parties to learn; status recognition would not be the primary motivation.

Indeed compromise, synthesis, adherence to one's existing viewpoint, adoption of another's opinion, and finding a solution novel to both parties all can be rooted in strategic thinking for furthering one's own interests, *or* in a narrow-ridge viewpoint of concern for self and others. If the latter motivates one's interpersonal communication, there is an independent concern and openness that allows collaboration with one's opponent. The following classic scenes from "Fiddler on the Roof" are offered to reveal this orientation more fully.

The writer of "Fiddler on the Roof" caught the essence and struggle of the narrow ridge. In this drama, a universal message exists as

Tevye, the beleaguered father of a "traditional" family, is constantly torn between tradition and the modern ideas of his growing daughters.[22] First, Tevye's daughter Tzeitel refuses the man the traditional matchmaker has chosen for her and instead brings home a scrawny tailor, Motel. Motel asks Tevye's permission to marry his daughter. But Tevye is in pain because he knows that the Papa should, according to tradition, arrange the marriage. "Where do they think they are? . . . In Moscow? In Paris? In America? This isn't the way it's done. Not here, not now. Some things I will not, I cannot allow." There is in his voice the agony of a man who knows that he is vulnerable. And when Motel, pressing the request, says, "I promise you, Reb Tevye, your daughter will not starve," Tevye turns to the audience: "He's beginning to talk like a man. . . . On the other hand, what kind of match would that be, with a poor tailor? . . . On the other hand, he's an honest, hard worker. . . . On the other hand, he has absolutely nothing. . . . On the other hand, things cannot get worse for him, they can only get better." Ultimately, he says, "Well, children, when shall we make the wedding?" We are getting the image of a dedicated man struggling to balance his basic humanity with the demands of tradition. It is tearing him up; however, he recognizes the importance of walking the narrow ridge between his belief in strict adherence to tradition (self) and his daughter's wishes (other).

But his trials have just begun, for next comes his daughter Hodel, with her radical suitor Perchik, asking for her father's blessings on their plans to marry. He says "no," but Perchik shocks him into reality. "Reb Tevye," Perchik says, "You don't understand. We are not asking for your *permission*, only for your *blessing*." And when the father is able to pull himself together, he begins to reflect aloud. "He loves her. Love. It's a new style. On the other hand, our old ways were once new, weren't they? On the other hand, they decided without parents, without a matchmaker? After all, did Adam and Eve have a matchmaker? . . . Yes, they did. . . . Then it seems these two have the same matchmaker." And again he sings: "They're going over my head. Unthinkable. I'll lock her up in her room. I couldn't. . . . I should. But look at my daughter's eyes. She loves him." And he ends by saying, "Very well, children, you have my blessing and my permission."

That should be agony enough for one father. But it is not the end yet. Chava, sweet little Chava, the favorite child, is married without a matchmaker, without her father's permission, and outside the faith. Tevye cannot fathom it, cannot accept it, and turns his back on her. She begs him to accept them, but in a sorrowful soliloquy Tevye says: "Accept them? How can I accept them? Can I deny everything I believe in? On the other hand, can I deny my own child? . . . On the other hand, how can I turn my back on my faith, on my people? If I try to bend that far, I will break. . . . On the other hand . . . there is no other hand. No Chava. No . . . No . . . No . . ."

The thing that brings tears to our eyes in that play—the thing that makes Tevye believable—is that he walks the narrow ridge. If he were rigid, absolute, unfeeling, he would be nothing but a buffoon, a bearded Archie Bunker. In the narrow-ridge style, he walks between concern for his own tradition and his daughters' love for their men. His struggle allows us to see the difficulty of decision and the suffering that is sometimes present as one adopts such an interpersonal style. It is his suffering, the intense agony caused by the tension between love and responsibility, that makes us identify with him. We weep for him, but more than that, we weep for ourselves.

Standing Firm in Conviction

Buber's dialogue is too often misinterpreted by students and professional colleagues as a soft, expressionistic position. Richard Johannesen, in the second edition of *Ethics in Human Communication*, revealed how this perception is in error.[23] Buber was not fearful of tough stands. He did position himself on issues in an open fashion, but he made his point known when he was sure of his ground.

Martin Buber's own life also revealed that it is, indeed, possible to walk the narrow ridge regarding even the most sensitive of issues. From the very beginning of his life in Israel, he took the view that the Middle East should be a joint venture of Jews and Arabs. He refused to accept the idea that it was really Jewish land or Arab land. And so he offered concrete proposals for the joint development of the land— on several occasions risking his life in the face of bitter opposition from the patriots among his own people. We live today with the fear and terror produced by those on both sides who take the view that a joint development of land between Jews and Arabs is not at all feasible.

One of my favorite examples of Martin Buber walking the narrow ridge transpired in 1953, when he was awarded the peace prize of the German book trade in Frankfurt, Germany. Buber walked a narrow ridge in this speech; his caring was tough-minded, yet compassionate, and he listened to himself as well as to the others' viewpoint. Buber's acceptance speech, "Genuine Dialogue and the Possibilities of Peace," was given to the German audience less than a decade after the Jewish people had been so horribly massacred. In his acceptance speech, Martin Buber openly stated his heartfelt belief that no previous historical event had ever been so inhumane and cruel as the actions the German people had inflicted upon his people. "I, who am one of those who remained alive, have only in a formal sense a common humanity with those who took part in this action. They have so radically removed themselves from the human sphere, so transposed themselves into a sphere of monstrous inhumanity inaccessible to my conception, that not even hatred, much less an overcoming of hatred, was able to arise in me. And what am I that I could here presume to forgive."[24] Martin Buber shared his viewpoint, which revealed that he had neither forgotten nor forgiven the actions of the Nazis.

Buber could have concluded his address at this point. He could have revealed his self-talk and left without recognition of another viewpoint. Instead, he demonstrated that he cared enough to remain open to the opposing party, even regarding this emotionally significant part of his life and the lives of his people.

When I think of the German people of the days of Auschwitz and Treblinka, I behold, first of all, the great many who knew that the monstrous event was taking place and did not oppose it. But my heart, which is acquainted with the weakness of men, refuses to condemn my neighbor for not prevailing upon himself to become a martyr. Next there emerged before me the mass of those who remained ignorant of what was withheld from the German public, and who did not try to discover what reality lay behind the rumors which were circulating. When I have these men in mind, I am gripped by the thought of the anxiety, likewise well known to me, and of the human creature before a truth which he fears he cannot face. But finally there appears before me, from reliable reports, some who have become as familiar to me by sight, actions, and voice as if they were friends, those who refused to carry out the orders and suffered death, or put themselves to death and those who learned what was taking place and opposed it and were put to death, or those who learned what was taking place and because they could do nothing to stop it killed themselves. I see these men very near before me in that especial intimacy which binds us at times to the dead and them alone. Reverence and love for these Germans now fills my heart.[25]

The significance of Buber's speech is the living of a narrow-ridge philosophy under such adverse circumstances. He had the ability to walk the narrow ridge between commitment and openness to others' views. Surely, this was recognized by German youth in 1960 when they selected him as the third most influential spiritual leader of all time.[26]

During the trial of Adolph Eichmann, who supervised and ordered the execution of millions of Jewish people during the Nazi atrocities of World War II, Buber's living of the narrow ridge again stood a significant test. In the face of the tremendous pressures of that trial, Martin Buber openly stated his intense feeling toward Eichmann. Yet he did not want to treat Eichmann in the same violent and inhumane manner that had been applied to the Jews. Buber sought to follow a narrow ridge between hatred and revenge on the one hand and ignoring Eichmann's guilt on the other. Buber felt an imprisoned Eichmann would remain a symbol of guilt for the German people, which might result in a new wave of humanism. In the final verdict, however, the Buber initiative was overruled and Eichmann was executed.[27] Whether one agrees or disagrees with Buber's efforts, one must be impressed by his courage in pursuing the life of the narrow ridge—commitment with an openness to the other's experience.

Ivan Boszormenyi-Nagi, author of *Invisible Loyalties: Reciprocity in Intergene-Rational Family Therapy*, made it clear in an interview that Buber's narrow-ridge orientation was one of conviction and courage.

As I see it now, Buber is a man of *enormous* integrity and pure balancing and facing balances and drawing *hard* conclusions, at great cost. And balancing his survival on a razor's edge many times. That's the way I see him as a human being. . . . Here is this boy [Martin Buber], who is victimized by the tragedy of his mother, the shame of his mother running away. Somehow, I think to put all of this together, between these extremes of not talking probably about this and absorbing this as a child; on the other hand going back to the orthodoxy of his grandfather and the broken mind of his father . . . and broken heart. Making up for the missing mother, somehow exonerating her—doing the impossible . . . He's the only child, can't even turn to a sibling with whom to share this. . . .

[He] becomes eventually a self-styled, socialist Zionist, marrying a German girl; [he] becomes a great intellectual leader of Germany, leader of Zionist intellectualism, controversial Zionist political figure. Fair to the Arabs, defending what is a heroic legacy of Jews. [He] remains an intellectual figure, turning his energy toward the suffering of [the] psychologically ill . . . a *tremendous*, tremendous balancing of enormous human realms; at constant cost of misunderstanding and being victimized . . . all of this being done with great talent and tremendous intellectual power.[28]

Buber's balancing of human resources reflected his commitment to the narrow ridge. He was able to embrace contradictories as his very definition of dialogue. He saw life problems not in yes or no, but more often in yes *and* no simultaneously. In terms of the narrow ridge in community, Buber wanted communication to reflect both autonomy and loyalty.[29] He embraced life, not in spite of contradictions, but because of them.[30] As he stated himself, "every feeling has its place within a polar tension, obtaining its colour and significance not from itself alone, but also from the opposite pole: every feeling is conditioned by its opposite. . . . [C]omplete relation can be understood only in a bipolar way."[31] The richness of possibilities invigorates communication between persons and points to the importance of walking the narrow ridge between extremes. Buber wanted to search out a third alternative to an either/or position.[32]

When humans communicate from polar positions, they tend to forget the other's position and maximize their own. This form of communication will only augment our isolation from one another; it is the antithesis of interdependence. In its place, the practice of embracing one's own view while maintaining openness to that of the other is encouraged. A narrow-ridge view of communication can be central in the establishment of human community. This form of communication is not a formula or a technique that will guarantee the development of community; rather, it is a path, a guide, which emphasizes the need to search for genuine alternatives to extreme communicative positions.

PART TWO

COMMUNICATION LIMITING COMMUNITY

3

EXISTENTIAL MISTRUST:
THE FAILURE TO LISTEN

BUBER on the failure to listen:

> I had a friend whom I account one of the most considerable men of our age. He was a master of conversation, and he loved it: his genuineness as a speaker was evident. But once it happened that he was sitting with two friends and with the three wives, and a conversation arose in which by its nature the women were clearly not joining, although their presence in fact had a great influence. The conversation among the men soon developed into a duel between two of them (I was the third). The other "duelist," also a friend of mine, was of a noble nature; he too was a man of true conversation but given more to objective fairness than to the play of the intellect, and a stranger to any controversy. The friend whom I have called a master of conversation did not speak with his usual composure and strength, but he scintillated, he fought, he triumphed. The dialogue was destroyed.[1]

One contributor to polarized communication within community became clear to me in my first year of graduate school. As I pursued a counseling minor as a complement to an interpersonal communication doctorate, I found that many counseling students and faculty displayed a similar communicative pattern. People were slow to speak and when they did converse they often only paraphrased what had already been said. This reflective feedback assumed the judgmental tone of an "expert" advising a subordinate. I am convinced these people were attempting to provide a nonevaluative and supportive atmosphere. But, in reality, judgment was subtly handed by a superior to a subordinate in a one-up/one-down style.

The following exchange reveals the tense atmosphere created by this situation. A student requested a counseling professor to further explain a theoretical concept about counseling styles. Instead, the counselor paraphrased back to the student: "You are feeling some frustration with the lack of clarity in this material. You are puzzled about the material's helpfulness when it is so difficult to understand." The student then responded, "Why must you always look for a hidden motive? [In this case, frustration.] I would like some additional clarity; I am not in need of analysis." The professor's efforts to be supportive through the paraphrasing technique gave more of an impression of superiority than empathy. In effect, the professor was saying, "I heard what you said, but my training allows me to know what you really mean." At times, it may be necessary to look for a hidden reason in another's actions and words. But to do this continually can stir mistrust in place of understanding. Such action too often labels the "knower" as superior and the questioner as subordinate. Sometimes, as this example indicates, it is best to respond to the actual question asked.

At the time I became sensitive to this problem, I had great admiration for Carl Rogers, the founder of client-centered therapy. In reading Rogers' material and watching him on videotape, a nonevaluative and supportive relationship seemed a real possibility. My appreciation of Rogers made this question even more baffling: Why did relationships seem so tense and judgmental between graduate students and even some faculty members who purported to be Rogerians? Something is often lost in the translation from the founder of a theory to its followers. Carl Rogers, like other theoretical innovators, has no doubt occasionally shaken his head in disbelief and thought, "I'm glad I'm a Rogers and not a Rogerian!"[2]

Some distortion of a therapeutic system is inevitable as the system becomes part of common practice and language for a larger population of "experts." However, this diluting of the therapeutic system does not totally account for the source of judgment in a supposedly "nonjudgmental" system. I now suspect that the judgmental tone of the counselors was grounded in an impulse to look for a hidden motive behind what was actually said. What was said never carried as much weight as what the counselor felt the other really meant, but had not articulated. The constant hypothesizing about a latent or unconscious meaning is what Gordon Allport, a well-known psychologist, rebelled against. He even went so far as to suggest a "bold and new" technique for understanding people—ask them! He felt people should be trusted until proven otherwise, not the other way around.[3] In our court system, a person is considered innocent until proven guilty. It seems only plausible to give a person the same right in interpersonal communication. Should not a person be considered an honest speaker until proven unethical? Granted, sometimes people do mean what goes unsaid. But even with this realization, one must be careful not to overstress a hidden meaning—particularly when none may exist.

Buber did not suggest that one be naive and unquestioningly accept everything another person says. Suspended belief and suspicion are sometimes warranted. However, when suspicion about what the other really means is no longer an occasional response but has become commonplace, we have what Martin Buber termed existential mistrust.

> It is important to perceive clearly how the specifically modern mistrust differs from ancient mistrust, which is apparently inherent in the human being and which has left its mark in all cultures. There have always been countless situations in which a man in intercourse with a fellow-man is seized with the doubt whether he may trust him; that is, whether the other really means what he says and whether he will do what he says. There have always been countless situations in which a man believes his life-interest demands that he suspect the other of making it his object to appear otherwise than himself. . . . In our time something basically different has been added that is capable of undermining more powerfully the foundations of existence between men. One no longer merely fears that the other will voluntarily dissemble, but one simply takes it for granted that he cannot do otherwise.[4]

Buber's existential mistrust describes the uneasy feeling experienced with fellow counselors. The atmosphere of suspicion and judgment was the result of looking for a hidden meaning in what a person said or did. In short, polarized communication can be fueled in community when people lose the capacity to determine when it is appropriate and legitimate to look for a hidden motive.

Unmasking the Real

Certainly the previous discussion is not an indictment of the counseling profession. There are times when a counselor should look for a hidden motive. Danger arises, however, when the act of looking for a hidden motive becomes the everyday, not just the occasional action in interpersonal exchanges within a human community.

Viktor Frankl provided insight into the problem of existential mistrust as he explained the concept of "unmasking." He rightly suggested that Western civilization owes psychotherapy a great debt for its emphasis on unmasking, putting the finger on hidden motives. However, a good psychotherapist must know when to stop unmasking and when to believe what is being stated. To be listened to only at the level of the supposed rather than the stated is unproductive and debasing.[5] Frankl, like Buber, recognized that the danger of our communicative crisis is that some people seek to unmask the true and the authentic, and in the process they obscure our understanding of human life, rather than enrich it. Perhaps like the graduate students in counseling alluded to earlier, we become so suspicious that when the authentic does manifest itself we see only an actor playing a role in order to take advantage of us or the situation.

The following story displays some of the dangers of the unnecessary unmasking of existential mistrust. Some years ago, a group of Peace Corps volunteers were asked why they joined the Peace Corps. Many stated, "I want to share my skills with those in need of what I have to offer." The young people were then accused by their leader, a psychologist, of being seekers of superiority. It was suggested that they had come to the Peace Corps to service their own desires, not the needs of others. The volunteers believed in the psychologist and began to agree that he had to know their motives better than they did! The group's initial idealism was reduced to a hidden motive of superiority. As a result, the group members were left with suspicion of one another; each worked to unmask a hidden motive in the other's action, usually when none existed.[6] Had the psychologist accepted the initial enthusiasm and idealism of the young recruits, while silently knowing from past experience that some of the actions of Peace Corps individuals would be interpreted as self-serving by the communities they worked with, he might have dealt with the issue in a more constructive fashion.

Those advocating unmasking, like the psychologist in the above example, and individuals such as Buber, who question its use, are employing different interpretive frameworks. Examination of the clash of interpretive frameworks, known as "hermeneutics," aids in comprehending Buber's distrust of unmasking. Josef Bleicher, in a summary of hermeneutic or interpretive "schools," distinguished between constitutive or philosophical hermeneutics and deconstitutive or critical hermeneutics.[7] For our purposes, constitutive hermeneutics points to future possibilities; one attempts to see more by stretching or reaching out. On the other hand, deconstitutive hermeneutics unmasks the present; the goal is to find out more by reducing what was said or done to a more fundamental cause. Hermeneutic philosophy or constitutive hermeneutics can be historically traced to Dilthey and presently to Gadamer as a contemporary representative. Buber stated his indebtedness to Dilthey,[8] and, in an article on Buber, I described Gadamer as a contemporary extender of Buber's work.[9] Critical hermeneutics is more akin to the deconstitutive work of Freud and Marx, in which an underlying psyche or social oppression invalidates the manifest communicative meaning.

The clash between constitutive hermeneutics (Buber) and deconstitutive hermeneutics (unmasking) is represented today in the contrasting approaches of Gadamer (philosophical or constitutive hermeneutics) and Habermas (critical or deconstitutive hermeneutics). "Within hermeneutics there exists . . . debate which brings together Gadamer and Habermas. The latter, as a representative of *critical hermeneutics*, challenges the idealist assumptions underlying both hermeneutical theory and hermeneutic philosophy: the neglect to consider extra-linguistic factors which also help to constitute the context of thought and action, i.e. work and domination."[10] This quotation implies that those who assume a critical hermeneutic posture contend that external sources dominate us in such a way that even "normal" speech must be held suspect. Such an interpretive framework legitimizes unmasking, in order to offset forces of domination.

While Buber would not have disagreed with the need to be suspicious, he would have questioned overuse of the deconstitutive hermeneutic. Buber's dialogue opts for a constructive hermeneutic focused on future possibilities, not present shortcomings. Whereas the Peace Corps psychologist in the above example questioned present motives, I believe Buber would have suggested future possibilities in an exchange like the following: "I am pleased you really want to be of service to others. But I must be honest that not all who are so enthusiastic perform well in the field. We have found that the most successful are willing to learn from other cultures, as they give. Much of our work together will center on how we can learn from others, even more than give." Paulo Freire summarized this model of service in *Pedagogy of the Oppressed,* when he wrote that "education must begin the solution of the teacher-student contradiction by reconciling the poles of the contradiction so that both are simultaneously teachers *and* students."[11]

Perhaps the psychologist mentioned above could have built upon the idealism of those Peace Corps volunteers by attempting to ground it in a teacher/learning methodology sensitive to other cultures and the needs of others. The psychologist had an opportunity to leave those volunteers with more knowledge and skill, but he left them with less. Within that group of volunteers, human community was unnecessarily defiled by existential mistrust. In short, Buber's focus on constitutive hermeneutics and future possibilities brings people together. It builds human community, whereas unnecessary unmasking is a hermeneutic of suspicion and separation. Both are at times needed. But too much concentration on the latter will not permit our communication to invite community.

Even with an understanding of constitutive and deconstitutive hermeneutics, one wonders what has given rise to this modern mistrust of which Buber speaks. At one time, I suspected that anyone who saw meaning as internally grounded, that is, "the meaning is in the person," contributed to this problem.[12] However, my admiration for Carl Rogers' work required a reassessment of this position.[13]

Contrary to Rogers' inner focus, many of us in this culture too quickly equate an inner focus with control and ownership of experience. This is not the case with some Eastern philosophies that assume a more inner perspective. Abraham Maslow was aware of the philosophy of Tao, in which there is a simultaneous act of centering and letting go.[14] It is an oxymoron—a combination of opposing forces. However, with the exception of some very insightful and sensitive people like Rogers and Maslow, this dual act of centering and simultaneous letting go is difficult within our culture. We are more apt to center while keeping or possessing—at this point the problem of an inner focus emerges. Maslow and Rogers attempted to use language that centers—but on relationship, not just the self, and emphasizes letting go, rather than seeking to own an experience. When these cautions are not observed, the often close relationship between an internal view of meaning and ownership or possession of experience is appropriate.[15] Thus, locating where meaning arises in communication is crucial.[16]

One of the early descriptions of a meaning-centered approach to human communication was suggested by Dean Barnlund. He stated the importance of meaning, and he located it internally, inside the receiver and/or sender. "Communication, as I conceive it, is a word that describes the process of creating a meaning. . . . Messages may be generated from the outside—by a speaker, a television screen, a scolding parent—but meanings are generated from within."[17] Barnlund and others who advocated the internal view of meaning were not wrong to believe that the meaning of communication rests inside the person. They described one way to view communication as one participates with others. Meaning is made present where one looks. If one searches "inside" for "gut feelings," then meaning will arise there. However, if one is concerned that this introspective attitude may too quickly be perverted into a form of possessive individualism, then a different way of understanding meaning-centered communication is needed.

An experiment by William Pemberton illustrates how meaning can be uncovered in different places. Pemberton was convinced that people actually understand things differently because they start with contrasting assumptions. To test this hypothesis in his classroom, he gave a group of students pieces of paper dipped in phengl-thio-carbamide, a chemical that is tasteless to thirty percent of the people and considered bitter by seventy percent of the people. He then had everyone taste the paper and, of course, had varying responses ranging from "It's horrible!" to "I didn't taste a thing!" After this initial surprise and some arguing about who was right, the students discovered three distinct assumptions that guided their understanding of the question "Where did the taste originate?" The first student assumption was that the taste was in the paper; the second, that the taste was in the person. The final student assumption was that the taste was neither in the person nor the paper; it was a transaction between the two that allowed a taste or no taste to be made present. Without either the paper or person, the experiment was not even possible. Thus, both the person and the paper were interdependently involved.[18]

Pemberton's experiment suggests that the place in which meaning arises depends upon one's initial assumptions. This chapter is concerned with the distinction between a view of communication as occurring *inside* the person and a view of communication as arising *between* persons. The betweenness of meaning in interpersonal communication is central to the Buber's narrow ridge, which recognizes the essential nature of both persons in an exchange. Clearly, we cannot always walk the narrow ridge of concern for both self and others. However, the communicative crisis can be widened by thinking that oneself is the sole source of meaning; this seems only a short step from believing that one understands the other better than the self. Taken too far, the internal view of meaning can lead to an arrogance that is the antithesis of what Rogers and Maslow advocated.

An example of a changing relationship may reveal the distinctions inherent in an internal view of communication and a "between" or "narrow ridge" understanding of communication in human community. Both the man and woman in this troubled marriage felt that meaning emerged from inside each one of them. Their conviction was to follow gut impulses and individual needs. This action led to a suspicion of each other, as their pattern was, "If I am only concerned about myself, then the other person must only be concerned about himself/herself; I had better be on my guard with the other and question his/her motives!" In this case, an individual view of meaning was pushed to an extreme, eventuating in existential mistrust.

This couple was able to restore their marriage with outside help, by examining where meaning emerged in the relationship. As a couple, they decided to move from an individualized understanding to a relationship-based view of meaning. They made a pact to allow the narrow ridge of concern for both parties to guide their relationship. They found that it was difficult to define how to be sensitive to meaning emerging between them. But it was less difficult to tell when an internal, "me" view, or "outer," martyr view, just concern for the other, began to take over the relationship. When such signs

appeared, they talked with each other, seeking to restore the necessary balance. Of course, they continued to disagree at times on
issues. The narrow ridge does not always mean compromise or even
agreement; rather, it implies a genuine caring for the other. As they
began to move from an internalized view of meaning to a relationship-based conception, their mistrust of one another began to
lessen. It seems that when the meaning of communication emerges
with both parties' participation, there is less impulse to doubt. Each
party has some input into the communicative outcome.

The couple described here discovered, however, that what
worked for them did not automatically work elsewhere. Some of their
colleagues on the job were not willing to follow a narrow-ridge view
under any conditions. Eventually, they had to talk about the risks of
inviting a narrow-ridge view of meaning in communication with
those who refused to reciprocate. The lessening of existential mistrust is at times a real risk. Each one of us, it turns out, must decide
how much he or she will risk before retreating back into himself or
herself.

The Copernican Revolution

As stated previously, this internalized view of meaning in human
communication is not to be confused with helpful counseling and
therapy. Rather, it is an internal view of meaning that seeks ownership, not partnership of an experience that is of concern. One
begins to view meaning in human communication as control and
power over experience and others.

If one attempts to "own" an experience, questions emerge such as:
Will I profit from this encounter? What's in this for me? We begin to
apply capitalistic economic principles to interpersonal relationships.[19] Such an orientation may work as an economic guide, but
when applied to daily communication, it relegates people and experiences to objects and commodities to be possessed or ignored.

Maurice Friedman is a recurrent questioner of this possessive view
of communicative experience, which he and some others label "psychologism."

> To seek to "have" an experience is already to risk not having it; for the
> more we focus on it as a goal, the more we are in danger of removing it into

ourselves, or psychologizing it. The word *psychologism* is in no sense an attack either on psychology or psychotherapy when these observe their proper limits (refusal to unmask when the authentic is spoken or lived). It is an attack on the tendency to make the reality of our relationship to what is not ourselves—persons and cats, sunsets and trees—into what is essentially *within* ourselves.

The very notion of having experience, whether it be psychedelic, mystical, sexual, travel or adventure, robs us of what experience once meant—something which can catch us up, take us outside ourselves and bring us into relationship with the surprising, the unique, the other.[20]

Friedman's concern is the feeling of control and ownership associated with a possessive view of communication.

A true story about Martin Buber, told by Maurice Friedman, further reveals the difference between the impulse to own an experience and a willingness to respond to what emerges between oneself and another. As Buber worked with people in a lecture-discussion format, he mentioned to Maurice Friedman that he wished people would ask him more questions. A psychologistic and possessive interpretation of this would be that Buber felt he owned or possessed much knowledge and people would be foolish if they did not take advantage of this opportunity. However, Buber's meaning was far from this. "'If people would come to me with real questions, something would come into being between them and me that does not exist now!' The questioner is just as important as the answerer. A wise man is not a fountain of knowledge. On the contrary, he is helpless until someone brings to him a question great enough to evoke a profound response. He does not *have* the wisdom. It literally happens, comes to be, in the *between*."[21]

The essence of the above happening is translated into daily interpersonal terms by Sidney Jourard, who stated that a person never really gets to know himself or herself until disclosure to another occurs on a significant level. Jourard suggested that in relationships one may witness new revelations about oneself.[22] The speaker and the listener are equally important in the birth of these new insights.

The pervasiveness of psychologism is revealed by its connectedness to the possessive impulse of our culture. The taken-for-granted importance of "possessing" and "having" in Western culture discourages views of human communication that would reject possession of meaning. Martin Buber put this concern aptly: "The monstrous, the dreadful phenomenon of psychologism so prevails that one cannot simply bring about healing with a single blow."[23] To propose a shift from an internalized and possessive view of communication to a narrow ridge perspective is much like calling for a new Copernican revolution. Copernicus debunked Ptolemy's theory of the universe with the earth as the center, around which the moon, sun, and planets moved. Copernicus instead theorized that the earth was a participant in the universe, but not the primary point.

Like Copernicus, philosophers Buber, Friedman, Frankl, and others have an equally important perspective on the place of the person in communication within human community. Some viewpoints that recognize meaning as emerging from inside the person may be clinging to Ptolemy's hope of being the center of the universe. The Copernican revolution of communication suggests that one is a participant in life affecting others, while simultaneously being affected by them. In this style of communication, events happen between persons and one's feeling of ownership or total control over the situation is minimized.

We can call such listening within human communication the result of a Copernican revolution that walks the narrow ridge between too much and too little attention to the comments of both self and other in an exchange. For example, two students were in conflict with one another for a considerable period of time. As they disagreed, it was apparent that they saw each other as persons, not objects. They did not abuse each other, but neither did they withhold their variance in viewpoints. When the conflict ceased, they still did not agree, but because each felt confirmed as a person in the exchange, they were willing to talk again.

> Even in confrontation, the human who engages in dialogue confirms the other and . . . affirms the sanctity of the other's life. . . . [This orientation] can invite the other to meet in conversation and attend to the resolution answer that emerges "between" them. Perhaps no answer may be the temporary result that emerges, but confirmation of the other . . . may at least promote an atmosphere that invites and encourages the other to re-enter the negotiating arena.[24]

The other is needed to test one's viewpoints. As long as we are open to being persuaded and recognize that conviction would not be possible without challenge, meaning is not egocentric; it is relationship-based. Conviction with an openness to hear opposing viewpoints and a recognition of one's partner's noninterchangeable importance in the exchange are fundamental assumptions of this approach. Both parties are essential in such an exchange.

Exploitive and Dependent Listening

In concrete terms, communication within human community becomes a walking of the narrow ridge between so much concern for one's position that a dogma is displayed and so much openness to opposing viewpoints that "truth" becomes intolerably wishy-washy. Such listening is contrasted with two extreme forms of possessive listening. First is the arrogant listener who seeks to unmask internal feelings that may not even exist. Second is the dependent listener who constantly needs his or her internal messages reinforced by the reassuring comments of others.

Arrogant listening, in its most destructive form, is an effort to unmask the other's motives and use that information to one's advantage. An example of this listening style is revealed by the tragic events in November 1978 of Reverend Jim Jones' group, the Peoples Temple cultists, at Jonestown, Guyana. Jones' religious community was visited by Representative Leo J. Ryan, Democrat of California, and a group of American news correspondents investigating allegations that some members of the group were being held against their will, mentally and physically abused. Since many members of the temple were Americans and from California, including Reverend Jones, Representative Ryan felt impelled to investigate the situation. His visit apparently increased the fear and paranoia in the community to a frighteningly high level.

Some members of Jones' group shot and killed Representative Ryan and four members of his party as they were about to leave Guyana. Jones then commanded his followers to drink a poisonous mixture, while reluctant followers were shot. Jones apparently saw mass suicide and murder as the only way out of his self-imposed problem—a view that resulted in his own death and that of approximately nine hundred other human beings.[25] We might question how so many people could have consumed the poison and given their lives so willingly. Clearly, there is no simple answer to such tragedy, but a partial reason may be inherent in Jones' style of control gained by listening for the weakness of members and then skillfully exploiting that person's need for authority and direction.

Perhaps it is difficult to see how such exploitive listening, which led to existential mistrust in the form of great paranoia, could succeed. But we can all relate to occasions when somebody listens to us only to use that information to take advantage of our needs. If one experiences such situations too frequently, mistrust of others might become a significant problem. One is tempted to search for a hidden motive in a potential listener, in order to avoid the pain of being "used" and "taken for a fool" when sharing weakness.

For many human beings, the dating experience may reflect the negative characteristics of the exploitive listener. Such was the case with George, a bright, caring, and undemanding young man. He was attracted to a young woman who, because of his undemanding nature, used him as someone to eliminate the loneliness she felt when none of her better friends was around. This woman was important to George, and when he finally discovered her exploitive nature, the situation generated mistrust in his relationships with other women. When he finally did meet a genuine and loving person, he did not know how to respond. The relationship did not surpass a questioning of her motives, a technique George used to defend himself against further pain. Such mistrust caused George to lose that relationship and perhaps other relationships as well. Exploitive listening often generates more and more mistrust. Only the courage to risk encountering the authentic person without attempting to unmask what may not be there will break down the cycle of mistrust in human community.

A second consequence of a possessive view of meaning is the danger of excessive image consciousness. Chapter 1 showed that Buber believed that the roots of inauthenticity are in the fetish about one's image. He contended that excessive concern for image has the human always imagining events as happening through and in him. "Somewhat similar is the fact that many men are determined in their inner focus by how they appear to other men, that they all refer back to the image that they produce in others. They do not live from the core out, not to the other from their own center, but from the image that they produce in others."[26]

This concern for the perpetuation of one's image can eventuate in dependency on others to reinforce one's own image. Such a dependence on others is sometimes the downfall of entertainers, politicians, and others who thrive in the public eye. Brown and Keller suggested that Jimi Hendrix and Janis Joplin were too dependent on others for their own images.[27] They were compelled to listen constantly for reassuring support from others. Perhaps the tragedy of Freddie Prinze could be added to this list.

Carl Rogers warned of the danger of accepting the values of others without giving them proper thought. One accepts those values in order to gain a feeling of acceptance, not because one feels that those values are right.[28] People often seek acceptance at the price of their ability to evaluate their own actions. When a person becomes too other-directed, the comments of others play too significant a role in guiding his or her actions.[29]

Martin Buber wrote of the problem of listening to maximize one's acceptance by conforming to expectations. He contended that many people are content to seem like something they are not in order to please others, which they believe will please themselves.[30] But unlike some observers of this phenomenon, Buber attributed the fundamental reason for this problem to an internalized and possessive view of meaning, which ultimately results in existential mistrust. If people attempt to listen just for comments that reinforce their internal images, health within human community is unlikely. It is like an executive surrounding himself or herself with "yes" people in order to avoid any altering of his or her image as the decision maker. However, once this style is spotted, others may become wary and begin to feel used. Consequently, when an executive wants to honestly listen to employees, they may be too suspicious to share their real perceptions.

From Buber's perspective, exploitive listening and a dependent-conscious listening can actually have similar roots and consequences. Possession of meaning inside the self focuses attention on the self, not on what emerges from the relationship. Such possessive listening can encourage using the other, looking for a hidden motive by which to manipulate the other, and seeking comments to reinforce one's view of oneself. Possessive listening invites a ruggedly individualistic style of communication, rather than a community-based style. The possessive view of meaning is congruent with the world view of Ptolemy. The Copernican revolution, in contrast, is rooted in the importance of the relationship and the parties that compose it. Yet a Copernican revolution in our listening behavior does not guarantee success; expecting such a guarantee would assume total control over the situation, which is the problem inherent in a possessive and egocentric world view. But it does allow the opportunity to listen to and understand alternative viewpoints, an opportunity that is not present if one is locked into an image or a set of rigid assumptions.

The Copernican revolution offers a call to readjust assumptions and to begin altering our actions. The consequences of such a shift of focus are not completely visible. But the dangers of continuing a self-centered course are real, indeed. Martin Buber stated that "if psychologism becomes so intensified that the man can no longer bring his capacity for external relationship . . . to others, to the world, if his strength of relationship recoils backward into the I, if he has to encounter himself, if the doubt ever again appears to him, then that state exists that I call self-contradiction."[31] Buber suggested that the I is not fundamental enough. Each one of us is necessary, but not sufficient for quality life in human community to exist. We are participants, not the focal points. If we believe we are the pivotal foci and internally attempt to possess the world, we become self-contradictions, because we cannot exist alone. In human community as conceived by people like Buber, a possessive view of communicative meaning is a falsification of our original ground of being. We must begin with ourselves, but human community starts with us in relation with others.

4

MONOLOGUE:
CENTERING ON SELF

MARTIN Buber on self-centered monologue:

> Man can become whole not in virtue of a relation to himself but only in
> virtue of a relation to another self. This other may be just as limited and
> conditioned as he is; in being together the unlimited and the uncon-
> ditioned is experienced. . . . And monologue may certainly disguise itself
> ingeniously for a while as dialogue. . . . [But] when the man who has
> become solitary can no longer say "Thou" . . . then there certainly remains
> for him the sublime illusion of detached thought that he is a self-centered
> self; as man he is lost.[1]

Buber did not consider dialogue to be the communicative norm of
modern life. On the contrary, Buber saw monologue (self-centered
conversation) and technical dialogue (information-centered communication) as dominant in the majority of contemporary conversation.[2] Both monologue and technical dialogue are natural parts of
the world in which we live. Buber recognized that we live in a twofold
world of relation. The *I–It* (monologue and technical dialogue) is the
world of separation, and the *I–Thou* of dialogue invites the community of relation.[3]

However, as Buber acknowledged the appropriateness of monologue and technical dialogue, he also warned of the dangers of their

overuse. Maurice Friedman summarized Buber's position on too much reliance on the world of *I–It* that surrounds monologue and technical dialogue.

> Vital dissociation is the sickness of the peoples of our age. . . . "Direct, open dialogue is becoming ever more difficult and more rare; the abysses between man and man threaten ever more pitilessly to become unbridgeable." This difficulty of conversation is particularly discernible in the dominance of "false dialogue," or "monologue disguised as dialogue." In false dialogue the participants do not really have each other in mind, or they have each other in mind only as general and abstracted opponents and not as particular beings. There is no real turning to the other, no real desire to establish mutuality. "Technical dialogue" too is false dialogue because it "is prompted solely by the need of objective understanding and has no real concern with the other person as a person. It belongs, writes Buber in one of his rare notes of sarcasm, "to the inalienable sterling quality of 'modern existence.'" It is for monologue that disguises itself as dialogue, however, that Buber reserves his full scorn. Here men have the illusion of getting beyond themselves when actually each speaks only with himself. This type of "dialogue" is characteristic of our intensely social age, in which men are more alone than ever before.[1]

Buber's distaste for monologue is due to the separation that results from such a communicative style and its subsequent limitations on community. At times, monologue is encouraged as a "feeling-oriented" view of communication that can guide one's actions. When the primary feelings of concern are one's own, then the narrow ridge concern for both self and other in community is obscured. "Feeling-oriented" theories can be of value to the invitation of human community as long as the dual action of the narrow ridge is preserved.

Unfortunately, many feeling-oriented theories have come to be associated with popularized phrases such as "do your own thing," "follow your own impulses," "get in touch with your own feelings," and "trust the wisdom of your own body." The positive emphasis on affect, bodily impulses, or what has been termed "organismic impulses," was an effort to see the human in a more positive light than other theories provided. The most well known home of the affective or feeling-oriented school of thought has been in the field of psychology, in the branch called third-force or humanistic psychology. Psychologists Carl Rogers and Abraham Maslow (who is sometimes

referred to as the "father of humanistic psychology") were instrumental in its establishment.

I have much admiration for the work of Rogers and Maslow. I
believe that both Rogers and Maslow walked the narrow ridge.
However, the concern of this chapter is that their theories sometimes
lose the narrow-ridge quality when enacted by some practitioners.

The Humanistic Alternative

The origin of the term *third force* is significant because it ushered in a
third alternative to the then prevailing powers of Freudian and
behavioral psychology. Perhaps the major reason for the development of a humanistic alternative was that the image of the human
suggested by behavioral and psychoanalytic studies did not coincide
with the observations of many professional counselors like Rogers
and Maslow. The behavioral psychoanalytic schools of psychology
did not trust the individual decision-making ability of the human
organism.

Freud considered the human being impulsive and doomed forever
to do battle with irrational and unconscious desires. In fact, Sigmund
Freud contended that the only hope of civilization rested in an ability to keep the impulsive and irrational element of human nature
chained via conventions of social law and custom. He saw the fabric of
"modern civilization" as a delicate and frail covering over a pot of
hostility and inner rage.

The historical circumstances of Freud's writing surely influenced
his conception of human behavior. As a Jewish scholar in troubled
times prior to World War II, he must have sensed the rise of Hitler as
the emergence of the demonic. For in 1930 and 1931, while writing
Civilization and Its Discontents, he offered his pessimistic analysis of
the future of the human race in the curt phrase "I can offer them no
consolation."[5] Indeed, his fears of that historical era were more than
justified when over ten million captives met their deaths in the
concentration camps of Adolph Hitler.

One can also make a case for behaviorism as a manifestation of
historical circumstances. Behaviorism is based on the desire for
control, a characteristic perhaps inherent in the twentieth-century
pursuit of technology. B. F. Skinner, in his classic novel on a behavioral utopia, *Walden Two*, spoke of the importance of behavioral

engineering. He later detailed the theoretical implications of his theory in *Beyond Freedom and Dignity*. A "Skinnerian" quotation gleaned from a conference on "Methods in the Sciences and Social Sciences" details his pursuit.

> The point at which the scientific method will take superiority over the humanistic will be the point at which it gives man the techniques for the *manipulation* and *control* of human *behavior*. . . . We are on the verge of a great change in techniques of dealing with man in every sphere, which *will result in a great change in our concept of man*. Hence if we must make a choice, we will abandon the humanistic tradition for the greater advantage which will come through the plodding and careful methods of science. [italics added by Maurice Friedman][6]

Thus, early in Rogers' and Maslow's careers, two primary options were available—Freudian or behavioral approaches to psychology. The former required acceptance of the human being as destructive and the latter argued for control and manipulation of human behavior. Freud's perceived task was to keep the inner impulses in line, while Skinner required manipulation of the environment in order to produce a "properly" organized "civilization." From this context of uncomplimentary views of human nature emerged a genuine alternative, humanistic or third-force psychology. This approach has been called the most distinctively American contribution to the world of psychology and human communication.[7] It was rooted in an ethic of optimism and faith in the individual, in accordance with the mythology of Kennedy's slogan of the "New Frontier" and Johnson's "Great Society." The followers of third-force psychology rejected both Freudian and Skinnerian contentions with the assertion that each person strives for self-fulfillment and is innately constructive. The consensus of third-force psychologists was that the positive attributes of the human being had been overlooked for too long.

One can view the optimistic contribution of "humanistic psychology" as the forgotten element in the "dialectic of humanness" in psychology. The notion of dialectic involves the clashing of contrasting ideas. It requires a thesis or status quo position that collides with a novel approach or antithesis. One could liken the contribution of third-force psychology to the completing of Buber's notion of the unity of contraries—whenever there are female, there are male characteristics; wherever there is good, there is evil; and so forth. The thrust of this notion is that some concepts are most understandable when viewed in light of their opposites. In contrast to the images of human nature provided by behaviorism and Freudianism, humanistic psychology perceives the person in a positive light. In short a major contribution of "humanistic psychology" has been to emphasize positive psychological attributes. Viewed in this complementary fashion the work of humanistic psychology is of immense value.

Before going further, I want to affirm the value of all three approaches discussed above. Each orientation has significant value for understanding and helping humans. Within given contexts and problems, each image of the human being (psychoanalytic, behavioral and humanistic) is needed and beneficial. To an extent, Carl Rogers was open to other approaches throughout his career. He affirmed his own theory, while recognizing that his approach did not work at all times. On occasion, he even referred people to non-Rogerian counselors.[8] The flavor of Rogers' openness was announced early in his career following his discussion of the basic attitudes for successful client-centered therapy and interpersonal relationships.

> I would like to stress that these are hypotheses. . . . They are beginning hypotheses, not the final word. I regard it as entirely possible that there are other conditions which I have not described, which are also essential. Recently I had occasion to listen to some recorded interviews by a young counselor of elementary school children. She was very warm and positive in her attitude toward her clients, yet she was definitely ineffective. She seemed to be responding warmly only to the superficial aspects of each child and so the contacts were chatty, social, and friendly, but it was clear she was not reaching the real person of the child. Yet in a number of ways she rated reasonably high on each of the conditions I have described. So perhaps there are still elements missing which I have not captured in my formulation.[9]

Rogers retained a sense of commitment grounded in openness throughout his writing. In his latest book, he offered a plea for such commitment in openness that invites, rather than forces. "I go along with Martin Buber and the ancient Oriental Sages: 'He who imposes himself has the small, manifest might; he who does not impose himself has the great, secret might.'"[10]

In response to Rogers' remarks, one could conclude that the "dialectic of humanness" cannot be captured by any one approach, but must emerge at times in conflict between approaches. It seems to me that each of the three approaches offers some needed attribute—requiring knowledge of various theoretical premises in order to know which approach more appropriately fits a particular problem or situation.

Buber's narrow-ridge philosophy recognizes both the constructive and the destructive capabilities of the human character. The narrow ridge is akin to a child walking a balance beam. He or she must remain conscious of both sides of his or her body and not give one side undue attention. When the child momentarily becomes too concerned about keeping enough weight on the left foot while the right foot is temporarily ignored, he or she is in danger of falling. The same conclusion might be drawn about current humanistic theories. The optimistic component of the affective view was a necessary balancing of the pessimism of other theories. But perhaps the emphasis on feeling could now be complemented by a dialectic challenge that recognizes the inhumanity of human beings to others. We must search for a theory of human community that can address the increasing problem of polarized communication.

Self-Actualization or Relational Fulfillment?

The primacy of human feeling is advocated by some conflict resolution researchers such as Morton Deutsch. He described feeling as the major evaluator in judging whether a conflict has been successfully resolved. "A conflict clearly has destructive characteristics if the participants in it are dissatisfied with the outcomes and all feel they have lost as a result of the conflict. Similarly, a conflict has productive consequences if the participants all are satisfied with their outcomes and feel they have gained as a result of the conflict."[11] Granted, it is ideal if both parties in conflict "feel good" about the resolution of a conflict exchange. However, as some writers have detailed, not all appropriately resolved conflicts will produce good feelings.[12] Take for instance, the case of Henry, a college professor, who was known to be incompetent by many students and by his colleagues. However, it was difficult to discipline him because Henry and his family were appreciated as people. It was his professional competency that caused concern. Some people did make disciplinary contact informally with him, asking him to alter his unstructured and sloppily organized classroom teaching and extracurricular activities. He refused, stating that he did not concur with the negative judgment of his effectiveness. Eventually, Henry was fired with no one feeling good about the outcome. Henry felt used and manipulated and his colleagues felt bad about releasing someone they liked. No one felt victorious or good about the conclusion of Henry's unfortunate story. The most disturbing fact is that such cases are not uncommon in education or the business world, because some conflicts may not be resolvable to everyone's (or at times anyone's) "affective" satisfaction. In short, using feelings as the primary measure of the success of a conflict outcome is not always possible in our often imperfect world.

Another example further reveals the inability of an affective view to capture the total experience. A young man recalled the events of a trauma which had occurred five years earlier. He described vividly the suffering of his little daughter, who was dying of a blood disease. He was responsible for making the final decision concerning her life. As she was choking on her own blood, the nurses placed cotton balls in her throat to absorb the fluid. The little girl had no hope of living through the night. The father was given the choice of allowing her to die in the next five minutes. He chose to let her go. The father held her hand and watched her slip away. The agonized father felt far from good about the resolution of that conflict. Yet he knew it was the best decision possible. Feelings are very important, but cannot always be viewed as sufficient propellers of action. At times, we must say or do what does not, at least in the present, feel good.

Some would thus contend that feeling motivates much, but not all human action. The optimism of humanistic psychology has encouraged the following of inner feelings as innately good. These good feelings are then to propel one's self-actualization. Kurt Goldstein coined the phrase self-actualization, but it actually gained popularity under the influence of Abraham Maslow. Maslow did a study of private individuals and historic figures that were exceptionally emotionally healthy and successful. From that and subsequent studies, the term self-actualization has joined our common vocabulary. The following nutshell definition of self-actualization still motivates the actions of many people. "Self-actualization may be loosely described as the full use and exploitation of talents, capacities, potentialities, etc. Such people seem to be fulfilling themselves and to be doing the best that they are capable of doing, reminding us of Nietzsche's exhortation, 'Become what thou art!' They are people who have developed or are developing to the full stature of which they are capable."[13] Goldstein and Maslow were certainly not alone in their use and promotion of the self-actualization concept, as summarized and critiqued by Maurice Friedman.

> The concept of self-realization lies at the heart of Sartre's "project," of Heidegger's realization of one's ownmost, not to-be-outstripped, nonrelational possibility; of John Dewey's ethics of potentiality, and the thought of such varied psychologists and psychoanalysts as Rollo May, Carl Rogers, Medard Boss, Erich Fromm, Karen Horney, and Abraham Maslow. As a holistic approach to the person which sees his or her future actuality from the present possibility, it represents a decisive step forward toward the human image. Nevertheless this approach is not concrete or serious enough to grapple with the problem of finding authentic personal direction.[14]

Friedman acknowledged both the overemphasis on the affective approach to human communication, as well as its utility.

Perhaps an explanation of three major issues of the "affective" movement will make the implications of self-fulfillment for this discussion of human community more visible. The first contention of the "affective" movement is that the growth process is innate, which naturally results in the human striving for fulfillment. Second, this innate and natural movement to fulfillment is considered positive or at least neutral by its proponents. And third, it is the task of the communicator to further this constructive tendency in himself or herself and in others in daily conversation through two avenues: (1) seeking out communicators and activities that can aid in one's self-actualization, and (2) playing a nonjudgmental role with others in order to promote their self-actualization.

In order to examine in more depth the above three communication assumptions, we must observe them at work in the human community environment of teaching. Carl Rogers' Harvard address on education is an appropriate piece for study. The speech is persuasive because of the image Rogers presented of the student-teacher relationship.

So Rogers came before the Harvard group, explained that he wished to "present some very brief remarks, in the hope that if they bring forth any reaction from you, I may get some new light on my own ideas," and proceeded to give one of the shortest speeches he ever made, barely over a thousand words, taking about five minutes to deliver. Essentially, the points he made were: "My experience has been that I cannot teach another person how to teach. . . . It seems to me that anything that can be taught to another is inconsequential, and has little or no significant influence on behavior. . . . I realize increasingly that I am only interested in learnings which significantly influence behavior. . . . I have come to feel that only learning which significantly influences behavior is self-discovered, self-appropriated learning. . . . Such self-discovered learning, truth that has been personally appropriated and assimilated in experience, cannot be directly communicated to another. . . . As a consequence of the above, I realize that I have lost interest in being a teacher. . . . When I try to teach, as I sometimes do . . . it seems to cause the individual to distrust his own experience, and to stifle significant learning. Hence I have come to feel that the outcomes of teaching are either unimportant or hurtful."[15]

This speech and Rogers' classic work on education, *The Freedom to Learn*, reveal him as committed to the self-actualization of other human beings, which ultimately required a refusal to impose himself on another. This concern was shared by the father of third-force or humanistic psychology, Abraham Maslow, who often spoke of a Taoistic attitude as most beneficial to the growth of another person.[16] The Eastern religion of Tao is structured in a nonjudgmental framework and has been presented by Alan Watts for a Western audience.[17]

However, in order to affirm the notion of self-actualization, these theories require one to accept the asumption that the human being is innately good or at least neutral. As laudable as this image may be, it is not the only image of human nature held by well-known proponents of humanism.[18] Buber, Friedman, and Frankl are three outspoken voices of humanism who have rejected some of the optimistic tones of third-force advocates. Perhaps examination of a historic exchange between Buber and Rogers can shed some light on the variance in perspectives.

Judgment Reconsidered

Rogers and Buber met on April 18, 1957, as part of a Midwest conference on Martin Buber held by the University of Michigan. Maurice Friedman functioned as the moderator.[19] Interestingly, Friedman, known as a primary interpreter of Buber's work, saw the orientations of Rogers and Buber as very similar until that exchange. During the course of the Buber/Rogers dialogue, Friedman became aware of many conceptual differences between the philosophies of the two.[20]

Throughout the Buber/Rogers dialogue, Rogers spoke of trusting the other's self-actualizing movement and basing therapy in nonjudgmental acceptance. But Buber stated that he never lost track of the dual nature of every person—good and evil. He attempted to strengthen the positive side, but refused to recognize this as the only option. The events of the holocaust and his own study of human nature, which he called philosophical anthropology, led him to a much different conclusion than that held by Rogers.

If someone purports the notion of innate goodness,[21] another person can legitimately ask, "What then causes the events of our national and local news—war, greed, intervention in foreign countries, murder, rape, and social oppression?" From the Rogerian perspective, the answer would probably be that the human being, because of adverse environmental conditions, was not following his or her natural actualizing tendency. This implies that the person has lost a personal center and has become a follower. However, even though the notion of introjecting values has a clear connection to everyday living, it does not satisfactorily account for the magnitude of problems facing us today. The stress on following innate, inner impulses is not in line with some contending that the human being is a social creature needing guidance, implying that innately we have both good and bad potentials.[22] Maurice Friedman, in *Confirmation of Otherness*, took Rogers to task on this same issue.

> Equally serious is the tendency on Rogers' part to see what is happening in these communities in terms of an Either/Or—the individual versus the society or the organic whole, the inner versus the outer. Either "the welfare of the total organism, the state or nation is paramount . . . and each

person is helped to become conscious of being but one cell in a great organic structure" or there is "a stress on the importance of the individual." Rogers fails to see the third alternative that lies at the heart of the "community of otherness," namely the reality of the between that links the individual and the community. For this reason, he claims that "the locus of evaluation is in the person, not outside" and that "the good life is within, not dependent on outside sources." . . . [This approach] is inadequate to capture the reality of the community of otherness.[23]

For Friedman and Buber, the question of why goodness and destruction exist cannot be left to a conflict between self and society. Buber did not affirm an either/or interpretation of good and evil[24] or of the relation of self to society.[25] Both parts of the dialectic, in his opinion, are needed in the development of humanness. A narrow-ridge philosophy states that goodness must be nurtured by others. One should not necessarily fear adopting the values and hopes of others. However, one should continually examine such values as new information is made available. "As nowhere else in the early literature of the human race preserved to us, good and evil as principia are here brought together and put asunder. They come forth from a primary initial community as 'twins.' . . . Created man is ordained into the struggle for salvation as one who is himself called upon to choose between good and evil."[26]

To return to education, let us assume that a student is dissatisfied with the material assigned in the classroom. He does not want to learn this material; it does not seem accurate or applicable to his situation. One proposal might be to allow the student to study something else, centering on the student's self-actualization. However, a narrow-ridge response to this situation would require sensitivity to both self (teacher) and the other (student). In this dual sensitivity, the teacher may come to the conclusion that the material is important for the student to learn, even if the student does not want to read it. The teacher might say, "I appreciate your concern and your frankness, but in my judgment this material is needed in your study. However, if new information alters my opinion, I would be open to change."

A narrow-ridge response requires the teacher to be sensitive to the student, while still making a judgment. Such an orientation is similar to Paul Tillich's contention that people need to know that they are heard and accepted, even as their behavior is evaluated. "Without the experience of judgment, acceptance loses its depth."[27] Perhaps this is similar to the maxim that only a true friend chances telling you what he or she thinks, not just what you want to hear.

A narrow-ridge judgment is not a cause for fear as long as it is rooted in concern for both self and others. However, in the following example, this was not the case. Pete's actions were judged as inappropriate by college club members. Pete even viewed most of the criticisms as "on target." However, the manner in which the judging was initiated made agreement a humiliating experience. The club president delayed talking to Pete until a list of twelve items of dispute had been accumulated and then confronted him in front of peers. Caring for the other was absent in this typical example of "dumping" or "gunny sacking" another person. The narrow-ridge perspective advocates judgment as a natural and necessary part of human communication, but only with simultaneous accompaniment of caring.

Caring judgment has philosophical implications about the importance of human persons. It also has very pragmatic overtones as well. Suppose Sandra works on an assembly line and makes an error. The supervisor comes to her and, in full view of her peers, loudly announces how incompetent her action is. After the supervisor leaves, she may feel like taking this opportunity to get even and do a haphazard job. While the supervisor may discipline an employee in view of peers in order to avoid taking company time to find a private location (or worse, in order to make an "example" of him or her), the method may actually be quite inefficient. The employee may make a concerted effort to "get even" at a later date.

A narrow-ridge perspective in communication and community considers both persons' concerns in a situation and the special roles played by each. Our judgments are affected as much by our social roles as by our personalities. Different constraints are placed on a supervisor when he disagrees with Frank during the work day than when they disagree about where to eat after playing golf. A necessary component of an effective communicator is the ability to move in and out of role obligations smoothly. Parents often experience this difficulty as roles with their children shift throughout the years. A parent needs to be sensitive to his or her changing role, moving from protector to supervisor to co-adult. Sometimes, later problems with children are due to an inability on the parents' part to adjust roles as the children mature.

Consider another example, a counselor with a tendency to relate to family members as a counseling client. Imagine going home joyful over a well-done class assignment and your counselor-parent states, "You really feel good about this achievement; feel free to express your joy at this moment." The recognition of such role problems led Carl Rogers to reply emphatically, "Hell, no!" when asked if he functioned as a counselor with his children.[28] The seeming inability of some people to move out of their trained role indicates a learned incapacity. To deny changes in role is to deny changes in our judgment. Different roles frequently require a different set of judgment skills, in order to most fully participate in and benefit from human community.

The Search for Self or the Narrow Ridge

Both Rogers and Buber were sensitive to role requirements. However, Buber was more likely to see the viability of one-up expertise roles. Rogers, on the other hand, was more egalitarian. In a counseling setting, Rogers saw himself meeting another with an emphasis on equality and mutuality.[29] Buber encountered the other as more willing to acknowledge the limits of the helping role.[30] Buber did not see participation in hierarchial roles as inappropriate; he encouraged recognition of role differences and sensitivity to the demands of the situation.[31]

This divergent approach to roles and the limits of mutuality is partially due to the different starting points in communication implemented by the two men. Rogers began with self and worked to understand the other's self. Buber, on the other hand, recognized the narrow ridge as the primary goal. In order to understand how important the concept of self is to Rogers' theory, we must examine some of his writing on this subject.

Throughout numerous recorded interviews with clients, repeated references to self occur. It is unclear whether the self could develop without contact with others, or what actually forms the self.[32] However, one's view of the self changes and tends to be the integrating factor for behavior. Rogers defined self as follows:

. . . the organized, consistent conceptual gestalt composed of perceptions of the characteristics of the "I" or "me" and the perceptions of the relationships of the "I" or "me" to others and to various aspects of life, together with the values attached to these perceptions. It is a gestalt which is available to awareness though not necessarily in awareness. It is a fluid and changing gestalt, a process, but at any given moment it is a specific entity.[33]

Rogers contended that if one can accept oneself as one is, then change will automatically happen. Thus, therapy is an effort to get in touch with one's real self, which facilitates change as soon as one admits who one really is. This may require alteration of one's ideal goal of self and sometimes one must encounter painful realizations about who one actually is.

A good illustration of this is the classic tale of Ivan Ilych, lying on his death bed and finally coming to grips with his true self. He looks back upon his whole life as a facade without purpose.

It occurred to him that what had appeared perfectly impossible before, namely that he had not spent his life as he should have done, might after all be true. It occurred to him that his scarcely perceptible attempts to struggle against what was considered good by the highly placed people, those scarcely noticeable impulses which he had immediately suppressed, might have been the real thing, and all the rest false. And his professional duties and the whole arrangement of his life and of his family, and all his social and official interests, might all have been false. He tried to defend all those things to himself and suddenly felt the weakness of what he was defending. There was nothing to defend.[34]

The goal is for the human being to encounter himself or herself before meeting the unchangeable fate of Ivan Ilych. As previously stated, Rogers advocated the constructive possibilities of the person. If one can admit who one is, then change and movement in a constructive direction will naturally occur.

Unfortunately, some counselors do not emphasize Rogers' flowing, changing nature of the self. Rather, the major point of emphasis is getting in touch with one's "real" self. In communication, this generates a concern for finding a "noble self" or "real self" that Rogers never advocated. One can become too concerned about the search for who one actually is and fail to provide a constructive contribution to relationships with others. As Hart and Burks have described it, "rhetorical insensitivity" to others can result if the dominant thought is on self.[35]

We may look, for example, at the interpersonal events of a teacher we will call Tom. Tom wanted to get in touch with his "real self." In fact, this task became a manic goal for him. He tried to make a technique out of the flowing nature of the self by making a major life change every five years. In his career, he went from philosophy to pragmatism to administration, in pursuit of self. With each change, he sold his books and ridiculed his past activity. Each change was evaluated in a hierarchial rating with the newest being "the best." Whether or not Tom found himself is unknown. But it is known that he lost many friends in his rapid transitions. Tom failed to see that getting in touch with his self was not meant to become a goal in itself. Tom needed to view the development of self as a by-product of the numerous activities and persons with whom he shared. Who we are is a mystery that is never totally knowable. The situation calls out of us responses that may not be knowable before that moment.

Perhaps our infatuation with self-development is connected with our economic system: capitalism. The capitalistic myth assumes that accumulation of more will ensure happiness. Any time life becomes too focused on one activity, be it money, vocation, or self-development, life's possibilities are limited. Specifically, self-development as a sole focus becomes much like the accumulation of a great wealth. "If I can just have enough experiences, I will be happy." Take, for instance, the tourist who goes to Europe for the first time, running himself or herself ragged in order to build a reservoir of experiences. The assumption is that the more one sees, the better the trip, even if it means pushing to the point of exhaustion. This effort to develop self can encourage viewing others as commodities. One begins to use other people to further one's own self. "If I talk to that person, what is in it for me?" "Is this person able to provide me with new experiences and insights?" If one is not careful, the drive to develop self becomes an activity of looking out for number one to the detriment of others.

This chapter has discussed, in a number of different ways, views of the human being as the center of the universe, as the pivotal point. Polarized communication is quickly nourished by such self-centering. Gregory Bateson contended that we need an ethic of relating between persons and events that does not focus on the self, but recognizes our interdependence. The focus on the inner self as the decision-making center is not a new way of viewing the world, but old thinking that has led us into many errors.[36] Perhaps we should look toward a new Copernican revolution, as chapter 3 indicated, rejecting the ethnocentric person and responding to the demands of the situation, at least when the conflict requires one's commitment and attention.

Martin Buber called the overemphasis on self in communication monologue. He recognized that one must at times ask self-centered questions like "What is in this for me?" Such questions are not uncommon in Western culture, nor actually of great harm, unless such thinking becomes dominant in relationships. Buber's narrow-ridge philosophy requires concern for self and others. Life must start with one, but if "real living" is to be given birth, relationship must be established with others.

Buber spoke of the tendency to make monologue an everyday activity by masking the reason for engaging in a particular behavior. He considered monologue, the centering of the world around oneself, appropriate at times; but he contended that in recent times, it has become the frequent, the everyday, rather than the occasional. Buber revealed the style and danger of monologue that centers exclusively on self.

> There is monologue disguised as dialogue. . . . A *debate* in which the thoughts are not expressed in the way in which they existed in the mind but in the speaking are so pointed that they may strike home in the sharpest way, and moreover without the men that are spoken to being regarded in any present as persons; a *conversation* characterized by the need neither to communicate something, nor to learn something, nor to influence someone, nor to come into connexion with someone, but solely by the desire to have one's own self-reliance confirmed by marking the impression that is made, or if it has become unsteady to have it strengthened; a *friendly chat* in which each regards himself as absolute and legitimate and the other as relativized and questionable; a *lover's talk* in which both partners alike enjoy their own glorious soul and their precious experience—what an underworld of faceless spectres of dialogue![37]

In short, the "I" is fundamental, but not sufficient by itself to provide for a quality life of communication. We must begin with ourselves but we can never be content to end there—for real living occurs in relationship with others.

There is a positive benefit to the humanistic movement. However, some practitioners of this orientation have forgotten the narrow ridge needed for communicating in community. An intense focus on the "I" or self is at odds with Buber's dialogic invitation to community. "In typical Rogerian terminology of the organism: 'I felt, more fully than ever before, my strength and confidence in my organism.' The organic analogy which Rogers uses . . . is inadequate to capture the reality of the community of otherness."[38] Buber's sense of community does not result from following organismic impulses,[39] but from the complex workings of persons communicating with others and inviting human community.

5

ORGANIZATIONAL INVOLVEMENT:
A PLACE OF HIDING?

MARTIN Buber on the impersonal and mechanical relations in organizational life:

> [In the past] wherever historical destiny had brought a group of men together in a common fold, there was room for the growth of a genuine community. . . . A living togetherness, constantly renewing itself, was already there, and all that needed strengthtening was the immediacy of relationships. In the happiest instances common affairs were deliberated and decided not through representatives but in gatherings in the market-place; and the unity that was felt in public permeated all personal contacts. . . .
>
> All this, I may be told has gone irrevocably and for ever. . . . The pressure of numbers and the forms of organization have destroyed any real togetherness. Work forges other personal links than does leisure, sport again others than politics, the day is cleanly divided and the soul too. These links are material ones; though we follow our common interest and tendencies together, we have no use for "immediacy." The collectivity is not a warm, friendly gathering but a great link-up of economic and political forces inimical to the play of romantic fancies, only understandable in terms of quantity, expressing itself in actions and effects—a thing which the individual has to belong to with no intimacies of any kind but all the time conscious of his energetic contribution. Any "unions" that resist the inevitable trend of events must disappear.[1]

Martin Buber's warning words have a powerful ring of prediction. I used this quotation as the basis for a commencement speech I gave at my former "home" university. Tradition dictated that a resident faculty member share comments at the winter commencement. The audience was composed of close to two thousand students, parents, friends, faculty, and administrators. Being a Speech Communication professor, I knew that the audience's expectation level would be high in anticipation of a credible performance. This realization, in light of the diversity of the audience, brought a feeling of anxiety as the occasion drew closer. My dilemma was how to make contact with the life experiences of such a pluralistic group. In discussion with colleagues, the theme of organizational life emerged as a common and significant issue appropriate for all in attendance. As I accepted the theme of organizational life as my topic, I learned that the student speaker, an older nontraditional student, would be comparing his 1960s beginnings in higher education with his 1980s conclusion. Since I had also been a part of the turmoil of those years, a contrast of the 1960s and early 1970s with today in terms of organizational involvement seemed to fit together.

The theme of that commencement speech rings as clearly today as when it was first delivered—organizational life may become the home of narcissism in the 1980s and 1990s. The seventies were branded as the age of self-centering, psycho-babble, and "doing your own thing"—a time of narcissism.[2] Many assumed that as another decade emerged, we would leave behind the "me generation." But unfortunately, the changes that occurred in the new decade merely cloaked our narcissism in another garb.

The following story about a man I will call Ray is indicative of this position. Ray openly stated that his primary concern has always been himself first, and maybe others later, if some long-term benefit to himself could be foreseen. Changes in Ray's life from the turmoil of the 1960s to the present reflect the consistent theme of narcissism. It is now quite difficult to envision Ray as a "flower child" demanding a cultural revolution—yet two decades ago he was such a person. Currently, Ray is a successful businessman within a corporate structure that requires conformity to group expectations. Conformity is now an explicit rule, unlike his college years when it was more implicit. Ray has always been willing to conform as long as he was able to benefit from the organization that consumed his involvement at a particular time.

As one examines Ray's rise in the corporate business world and his previous leadership role in protest groups, a sequence of commonality emerges. Previously, he conformed to climb the ladder of success and influence in his countercultural group; now, he has done the same in a business organization. Ray's behavior has changed little— only now he supports the structure he once criticized. The 1960s and the 1980s are not the same, yet the motivation to climb within the organization is, at least in this case. The story of Ray is not unique. Ray may be a prototype of a new narcissism hidden within the walls of organizational security. The problems of self-centering may not be over, but continuing in a changed form.

A troubling consideration for the current competitive climate is the contrasting background for behavior. Even in the midst of Vietnam, the 1960s were rooted in the optimism of the "New Frontier" and "Great Society," while recent years have been grounded in limited resources, budget deficits, high unemployment, and retrenchment.[3] Such times bring forth increased membership in radical organizations, both left and right. Examples of this are the increased spectacle of the Ku Klux Klan, the re-emergence of the Weathermen, and the visibility of antinuclear groups. Something about the prospect of hardship brings people together. But the motivation of those gathered may not reflect a narrow-ridge concern for self, others, and principles of the group. Simply put, people sometimes use groups to promote their own welfare to the detriment of others. At times, just the desire for group protection from others can lead to problems. A person may give the group the mandate to be narcissistic by banding together against other groups in order to shelter himself or herself. Such was the tragic history of Adolph Hitler's constitutionally legitimate rise to power in a coalition government on January 30, 1933. Only later did Hitler seize power as a dictator.[4]

Philip Slater commented on this reshaping of narcissism. He suggested a cautionary look at changes that appear to be radical, but offer little difference. "An individual who 'converts' from one viewpoint to its exact opposite appears to himself and others to have made a gross change, but actually it involves only a very small shift in the balance of a persistent conflict. . . . Some of the most dedicated witch hunters of the 1950's were ex-communists."[5] Perhaps Ray's shift was not as unusual as it first appeared. It is possible to make a change that appears fundamental, when in actuality it may only be a change of allegiance.

Watzlawick, Weakland, and Fisch approach this issue in yet another way. They refer to the changes that do not make a real fundamental difference as first-order changes.[6] For example, let us suppose that Arthur is told to quit smoking or to die of a heart attack. He follows the instructions, only to eat too much and die of a heart attack. He experiences a first-order change. It would have been necessary to alter his stress level and basic life style, rather than to change only one aspect. The same can be said of Ray and the notion of narcissism within corporate life. In his rebellious years, Ray was out to gain status on the campus. Now, he is using the organization to gain money, status, and recognition from his business connection. He has only made a first-order change. The context is different, but the goal is the same—to further his own needs without following the narrow-ridge concern for both self and other.

In short, difficult times can generate a narcissism in which one uses an organization to obtain security, status, power, and so forth, to weather emotional or political adversity. On the surface level, it appears that the person is giving up all self-centering motivation in exchange for group involvement. However, on a deeper level of reflection, such behavior may be a transference of self-centering desires. Previously, the person was considered the center, but now the pivotal point is the organization. The phenomenon of "me-ism" or narcissism has shifted from the psychological to the sociological realm.

In Search of Courage

Classic experiments by Sherif have demonstrated the common-sense perception that social influence in groups is inevitable.[7] Buber was aware that group influence on the individual could be used for good or ill. He warned of the dangers of abandoning individual thought too quickly for the group perspective. Buber lamented the strength of the crowd mentality in which a person may submit without asking probing questions.[8] Marcuse warned that an individual may even follow the destructive path of the majority in order to remain loyal to the group or crowd.[9]

A system of checks and balances, such as in our governmental branches, may be devised to keep any group from moving in a direction detrimental to the larger community. However, when all is said and done, the final line of resistance to conformity in a group pursuing a dubious cause is the solitary individual—the one who can rise above the crowd and challenge its assumptions. As much as Buber supported community, he also saw the need for courage on the part of the solitary person. When such courage is absent, a totalitarian collective, not a community, is nourished. For this reason, Buber described the tendency to advance one's own cause through the collective as a major danger of his time. He spoke of this corporate narcissism as he addressed three German-Swiss universities in 1933.[10] Today, like then, there is a shift from a monological "me" to a monological "us." Responsible individual action is too often given up for individual advancement within an organization.

Buber pursued the question of the courage of the solitary person in an essay that examined Kierkegaard's "Question to the Single One." However, Buber saw Kierkegaard's call for the "single one" as unproductive, because it conceptualized association with other humans as a negative movement from direct contact with God. Rather, Buber saw the individual as requiring contact with others in order to be fully human. The depth of Buber's criticism of Kierkegaard's rejection of human association is revealed in the following quotation. "Kierkegaard behaves in our sight like a schizophrenist, who tries to win over the beloved individual into 'his' world as if it were the true one. But it is not the true one. We, ourselves wandering on the narrow ridge, must not shrink from the sight of the jutting rock on which he stands over the abyss; nor may we step on it. We have much to learn from him, but not the final lesson."[11]

Even though Buber rejected Kierkegaard's radical solution to the influences of the group, he did share much of Kierkegaard's critique of blind allegiance. Buber called for a thinking person who is willing to risk challenging the status quo. Collectives translate such willing submission into "true is what is ours."[12] Individual responsibility is given over to the group. As Philip Slater suggested, the one golden rule of a democracy is never to delegate upward. As soon as one makes such a tactical error, those willing to use power will establish the rules for all.[13]

In a collective, "truth" becomes politicized. Such "truth" is rooted in a tradition of consensus held together by domination, false consciousness, and propaganda emphasizing the insecurity of life without the corporate entity. Let us examine this phenomenon more deeply with an example from higher education. The faculty of an institution seemed to be frequently in conflict with one another. Whenever an issue of importance came before the faculty body, the struggle for positions commenced. The interesting part of this continuous struggle was that there was no clear pattern on how particular faculty members lined up on the issues. No voting blocs could be discerned. However, this style later began to shift as faculty members found themselves less mobile in job changes. The voting began to reflect the status quo or the "older" faculty versus the "newer" faculty who desired change. Truth then became politicized and groups polarized. It became difficult to cross over allegiances and vote with "them," even if "they" seemed to have the better proposal on a particular issue.

Before the perception of too few jobs for too many applicants emerged, the faculty were in healthy conflict pursuing the "best" solution. But later, polarized communication made party allegiance (monological "us") a higher criterion than the pursuit of truth. In a sense, the faculty were divided into two corporate entities with the younger faculty members claiming "foul" and the older faculty members demanding patience. The loser is the student who wants the institution to be a center for truth seeking, not a battleground for ideological struggle.

When interest groups emerge in any human community, their presence can be of significant benefit. But when "party" becomes more important than the pursuit of truth, we have walked into the problem of group narcissism. When groups become intolerant of independent judgment, trouble is brewing for a communicative crisis. In short, problems arise when one group does not permit another to dissent or protest. Appropriately, Martin Luther King, Jr., quoted John F. Kennedy: "Those that make peaceful revolution impossible will make violent revolution inevitable."[14] In order for an individual not to fall prey to collective totalitarian principles, the "single one," the person of conviction and courage, must be given a time and place to voice concerns and new perspectives on issues in question.

Both Buber and Kierkegaard saw the need for the single person to sometimes stand before a group or organization and refuse to submit, comply, or follow orders. "'What I speak of,' says Kierkegaard, 'is something simple and straightforward—that the truth for the Single One only exists in his producing it himself in action.' More precisely, man finds the truth to be true only when he stands its test. Human truth is here bound up with the responsibility of the person."[15] For Buber, it is the responsible individual, not someone hiding within organizational structures, that must bear the test of truth by sometimes taking a lonely stand that requires him or her to separate himself or herself from the crowd.

The Group for Me

It is unfortunate, but many fail the test of truth, as they attempt to fulfill themselves through group allegiance. As Bensman and Lilienfeld suggested, modern groups are providing "a social screen for a collective privacy."[16] Perhaps the critics of the conformity of the 1950s deserve another reading—David Riesman's "other-directed person," Erich Fromm's "market-place mentality," and William Whyte's *Organization Man*.[17] However, we must be wary of an individualism grounded in either the 1960s "do your own thing" or the 1980s climb in the organization for self gain.

One theme of the writers of the 1950s was that people can hide behind the value system of the group and fail to ask ethical questions about the taken-for-granted assumptions of the group.[18] The "me" becomes "we" in order to give "me" identity and security. When this happens, loyalty to the organization may be placed higher than the value of independent thinking. William Whyte, in *The Organization Man*, described the problem succinctly.

Another index of the difference between executive and trainee lies in the matter of conformity. In an inverse way, how much a man thinks himself a conformist tells a lot about how much spiritual fealty he feels for The Organization, and as subjective as this attitude may be, there is a discernible difference between older and younger men. The younger men are sanguine. They are well aware that organization work demands a measure of conformity—as a matter of fact, half their energies are devoted to finding out the right pattern to conform to. But the younger executive likes to explain that conforming is a kind of phase. . . .

Older executives learned better long ago. At a reunion dinner for business-school graduates a vice-president of a large steel company brought up the matter of conformity and, eyeing his table companions, asked if they felt as he did: he was, he said, becoming more of a conformist. There was almost an explosion of table thumping and head noddings. In the mass confessional that followed, everyone present tried to top the others in describing the extent of his conformity.[19]

"Me-ism" in this decade may once again fall prey to "introjection" of the values of others in order to fulfill one's narcissistic desires for status in a group and recognition in a community. Group life is vital and important, but such association should reflect alliance to the cause of the organization, not just acceptance of a value system in order to find status or safety.

Let us examine the life of yet another person who reflects this narcissistic desire to cling to a group. The man in this example, Jim, is in his early 50s; he is a low-level worker in his uncle's firm, where there is little respect for his skill. The uncle uses Jim's one-down position to make himself feel good. He abuses Jim with language that degrades him and makes him feel incompetent and inferior. The entire firm has caught on to this approach and follows suit by sharing negative comments about this person who, by now, you are probably calling "that poor man." However, additional information is needed to analyze this situation more clearly. Jim does not want to risk finding another means of livelihood. He is unwilling to leave a "safe" but "demasculated" situation. The result is that he associates with this group for the economic security provided by the uncle, even though the work is degrading. Indeed, Jim pays a tough price for his desire for economic security. He appears totally dependent, but he has accepted this dependence for his own individual reasons.

The above example reveals the close relationship between narcissism within the community structure and old-fashioned dependence. Jim's initial motivations may have been self-centered, but as he continued to give up individual responsibility to the group for safety and security, there emerged the ever-persistent danger of losing the courage to oppose the corporate view. A favorite quotation from Mahatma Gandhi describes this from the viewpoint of people in relationship to the large group called "the government." "No government can exist for a single moment without the cooperation of the people, willing or forced, and if people suddenly withdraw their cooperation in every detail, the Government will come to a standstill."[20]

Individual goals, whether economic security or hope of avoiding something worse, can propel people into a dependent alliance with a group. The irony is that many join a group to fulfill their own needs, but lose themselves in the process. As resources become more limited, the impulse to conform to fulfill one's individual goals of safety will become greater. One may fear that without the group, one cannot survive—yet, in some cases, group association is purchased at the price of one's own initiative and responsibility. Such a realization led Dietrich Bonhoeffer to encourage people to hold the values of the group at a higher level than the group itself. "Where . . . truth enjoins me to dissolve a fellowship for love's sake, there I will dissolve it, despite all the protests of my human love."[21]

A story about the fear of death provides a helpful look at the irony of losing oneself in the attempt to save oneself.

> Does this not bring to mind the story of Death in Teheran? A rich and mighty Persian once walked in his garden with one of his servants. The servant cried that he had just encountered Death, who had threatened him. He begged his master to give him his fastest horse so that he could make haste and flee to Teheran, which he could reach that same evening. The master consented and the servant galloped off on the horse. On returning to his house the master himself met Death, and questioned him, "Why did you terrify and threaten my servant?" "I did not threaten him; I only showed surprise in still finding him here when I planned to meet him tonight in Teheran," said Death.[22]

The analogous implication here is that searching for too much security may be the death of one's own integrity. Such an unfortunate state of affairs raises the question of how the individual can muster the courage to voice a view at odds with a group or organization.

Perhaps a glimpse of the answer to our question is reflected in still another story. Suzanne was a member of a political group that prided itself in raising questions about society, government, and culture. This group of "liberals," however, had fallen into a pattern of male leadership and domination, while the women remained quiet on issues. Suzanne wanted to challenge the power structure, but was told to remain silent for fear of destroying the only "liberal" group in the area. Suzanne did not remain quiet. Unlike the servant who attempted to flee from death, Suzanne was willing to confront the problem, risking the stability of the organization. She placed the ideals of the group higher than getting along with people in the group. The result of her courage strengthened the group and educated the males to the sexism inherent in their leadership styles. Clearly, we cannot always take such risks. But, like Suzanne, we must recognize that there are situations that call for actions that place one outside the crowd and into the cloak of the "single one"—announcing a new perspective, critiquing a questionable tradition.

Authentic Guilt

Like Suzanne, each of us at some time has sensed the need to hold a group accountable to the values it espouses. Unfortunately, however, if we failed to respond similarly, a feeling of authentic guilt might have been experienced. Martin Buber spoke of authentic guilt as different from neurotic guilt. Neurotic guilt is rootless and not tied to a specific action or inaction; it is a nagging feeling of discomfort that makes productive movement difficult as long as one's focus of attention is on the distress. This form of guilt often requires therapeutic attention.

Authentic guilt, on the other hand, may be put to rest by altering an action, repairing a relationship, or stating the unpopular when necessitated by conviction and circumstance.[23] The problem for the counselor, according to Buber, is to sort out the authentic guilt from the neurotic. Traditionally, psychotherapeutic techniques have been designed to assist with neurotic guilt, for which unmasking is of benefit. However, the counselor may sometimes label guilt as authentic—requiring a change in action.

> The psychotherapist into whose field of vision such manifestations of [true or authentic] guilt enter in all their forcefulness can no longer imagine that he is able to do justice to his task as doctor of guilt-ridden men merely

through the removal of guilt feelings. Here a limit is set to the tendency to derive guilt from the taboos of primeval society. The psychologist who sees what is here to be seen must be struck by the idea that guilt does not exist because a taboo exists to which one fails to give obedience, but rather that taboo and the placing of taboo have been made possible only through the fact that the leaders of early communities knew and made use of a primal fact of man as man—the fact that man can become guilty and know it. [24]

If the counselor works to relieve the pressure of the authentic guilt in the same manner he or she would relieve the neurotic form, then a communicative call for change has been dismissed.

Unlike some today, Buber did not feel that all guilt was destructive to the person. [25] He believed that some people should feel guilty, until they take the risk to say or act in a contrary fashion. A hint of the depth of this problem may be apparent when one examines a middle-age career crisis that brings up the question "Is this all there is?" The question may be examined as one of boredom or disappointment, or it can be looked at as a concern emerging out of a sense of guilt. What relationships have been torn asunder in order to gain one's present position? What products were not adequately tested in order to get them on the market more quickly? How many times did one disagree with the organization, yet fail to make one's voice heard?

Authentic guilt is a calling, a message that behavior needs concrete change. Apologies, resignations, changes in managerial style, reaffirmed concern for colleagues, employees, students, or family may be the required response. This authentic guilt can call one out of the security of a collective or group and call for action rooted in a personal responsibility. Groups are based on maxims and ideologies. The person who responds from a personal responsibility knows of the maxims and traditions, but is willing to challenge them to answer the needs of a concrete situation. Responsibility is not a blind call to carry out cultural and organizational dictates. Personal responsibility is a response grounded in training and tradition that bends, alters, or changes the acceptable laws that govern the general situation in order to meet the specific requirements of the moment. [26]

One may believe that such an attitude toward laws and maxims would instill chaos and lack of respect for authority. But there is already a historical precedent that flexible enactment of societal rules has been mandated by events and judgments of the twentieth century. One need only examine the records of the German war crime trials in Nuremburg[27] or the Vietnam War prosecution of Calley[28] to witness the message that "it is your personal responsibility to refuse corrupt orders." Not all orders can or should be followed. Certainly such refusal carries with it a risk of others not appreciating your personal responsibility. Yet without such a risk, our communication invites the mentality of the crowd, not human community.[29]

In the area of human communication, one can examine the career path of Carl Rogers as a case in point. He was trained in the scientific tradition of his time, but he felt his personal responsibility to clients required him to break new ground in therapeutic theory. He made a move toward the "less professional" and emphasized the importance of making contact with the client. He followed the path of non-convention pointed to by Otto Rank, emphasizing the importance of relationship.[30] Today, Carl Rogers is the well-known founder of client-centered therapy and many of his early detractors are long forgotten.[31] However, even in his success, Rogers has not followed an insensitive individualistic line of inquiry. He recognized the limits of his theory and, on occasion, recommended that a client work with a non-Rogerian therapist. His approach is more akin to that of the narrow ridge. He has broken from the mainstream, but is still sensitive to what the other can offer.

Rogers fits Buber's definition of a "great character," in that he is knowledgeable of his tradition, yet is able to stand above it and seek to answer tough ethical questions. The ability to rise above the crowd to state one's voice is summarized by Maurice Friedman. Notice that concern for both self and other is inherent in this action, even as they oppose one another. "Sometimes that dialogue can only mean standing one's ground in opposition to him, witnessing for what one believes in the face of his hostile reaction of it. Yet it can never mean being unconcerned for how he sees it or careless of the validity of his standing where he does. We must confirm him even as we oppose him, not in his 'error' but in his right to oppose us, in his existence as a human being whom we value even in opposing."[32] It is this concern for both self and other that encourages us to stand above the crowd and state our view without opting for an individualistic solution. Dialogically, we are called to contend with ideas and viewpoints without losing the ability to affirm simultaneously even our opponent. Such action may lessen polarized communication and enrich our human community with new insights. Buber's form of communicative courage can permit a life of integrity in organizations so that we do not have to hide our values in order to belong.

PART THREE

INVITING DIALOGUE in COMMUNITY

6

THE SEARCH FOR THE
ETHICAL COMMUNITY

MARTIN Buber on the maintenance of an ethical community:

> When Rabbi Yeheskel Landau came to Prague, he spoke to his congregation Sabbath after Sabbath of nothing else except the bitter need of the destitute in the city. . . . "Help! Go there even today in the evening and help. . . ."
>
> Then on a busy market day something wonderful took place. Right through the middle of the tumult came the rabbi and remained standing in the center of the thickest swarm as though he had wares to offer for sale. . . . Those that recognized him . . . stared at him, but not one dared to question him. Finally there broke from the lips of one who imagined himself intimate with him, "What is our rabbi doing here?"
>
> At once the Rabbi Yeheskel began:
>
> "If a table has three legs and a piece is broken off of one of the three legs, what does one do? One supports the leg as well as one can, and the table stands. But now if still another of the three legs breaks in two, there is no longer a support. What does one do then? One shortens the third leg too, and the table stands again.
>
> "Our sages say: 'The world stands on three things: on the teaching, on the service, and on the deeds of love.' When the holiness is destroyed, then the leg of the service breaks! Then our sages support it by saying: 'Service with the heart, that is what is meant by prayer.' But now when the acts of love disappear and the second leg suffers injury, how shall the

world still endure? Therefore, I have left the house of teaching and have come to the market place. We must shorten the leg of the teaching in order that the table of the world may again stand firm."[1]

Buber's story calls for balancing the various legs or aspects of human community in hopes of promoting an "ethical" community. There are multiple ethical perspectives that can guide our communication. Richard Johannesen described at least seven broad categories of ethics in human communication, with only one of them being dialogical.[2] Thus, Buber's dialogic perspective is clearly not universal as a communicative ethic, but rather it is a commitment to a particular ethical system.

Dialogic Ethic

Makay and Brown provided a list of characteristics considered essential to an ethical communication posture rooted in dialogue.

1. Human involvement from a felt need to communicate.
2. An atmosphere of openness, freedom, and responsibility.
3. Dealing with the real issues and ideas relevant to the communicator.
4. Appreciation of individual differences and uniqueness.
5. Acceptance of disagreement and conflict with the desire to resolve them.
6. Effective feedback and use of feedback.
7. Mutual respect and, hopefully, trust.
8. Sincerity and honesty in attitudes toward communication.
9. A positive attitude for understanding and learning.
10. A willingness to admit error and allow persuasion.[3]

Note that while Makay and Brown emphasize the importance of relationship, they simultaneously uplift the necessity of conflict, persuasion, and disagreement in a dialogical ethical perspective. The mix of conflict and caring is the earmark of a dialogic ethic of communication.[4] This unity of opposites or oxymoron is reflected in such titles as "Arguers as Lovers," by Wayne Brockriede,[5] *The Love-Fight*, by David Augsburger,[6] and "Interpersonal Dissent: The

Ethics of Dialogue," by Paul Keller, with each embracing the unity-of-opposites theme that is central to Buber's ethic of dialogue.

> But the chasm between those two ethics is wide and deep. It is the chasm of Ultimate Pride, the fearful insistence on what Ernest Becker calls the "heroic." It is made of the conviction that life requires a series of choices between the Self and Other, and that a life is served best by choosing the Self. The dialogic ethic tries to bridge the chasm. The fundamental tension, from which we can never escape, and in the midst of which we can grow, is the tension of living with the "between"—living, as Buber puts it, on the narrow ridge; foregoing a clear path either to Self or Other; looking always for the interlocking magic of the two. On such a fulcrum turns the dialogic ethic. Its central directive is: In any given situation, choose to do what is life-enhancing for both participants in the relationship. Avoid what is life-defeating for either.
>
> The movement of this ethic is constantly toward the ideal of human community, but it will continue to be challenged, as it has been in the past, by the voices that insist that "the law of the jungle" is ultimately more real.[7]

The key to the above authors' description of a dialogic or narrow-ridge ethic is that they acknowledge the difficulty, as well as the importance, of balancing relationship sensitivity and a willingness to encounter conflict in resolving a problem. Buber affirmed this dual focus in his short essay "Conversation with the Opponent" in *Between Man and Man*. Buber rejected the either/or of just being concerned about relationship or the opposite ploy of just struggling for the issue of contention.[8]

Buber's dual concern for relationship and principle is central to the introductory quotation on human community. Principle and relationship sensitivity are both crucial to a dialogic ethic, but the former seems to call for more immediate attention today, in order to invite a dialogic balance in communities. Clearly, there is a risk in such a proposal; human relationships are indeed very important. However, when loyalty to the group begins to service one's own needs to the exclusion of others (as discussed in chapter 5), a shift from relationship to principles in community maybe a necessary step.

Placing values and principles above relationships is a changed emphasis. Throughout most of human communication studies, relational sensitivity has been emphasized. However, my work as a consultant for church and business organizations and my career in academics have pointed to a need for a shift in emphasis. If too much concern is placed upon relationship in the short term, we may reap significant problems in the long-term health of the community. Let us examine, for instance, a business experiencing morale problems. For years, managers within this manufacturing firm were able to disagree with one another without any consistent voting patterns emerging. Friends were able to vote for or against each other when necessary, as revealed in the minutes of past meetings. However, this varied voting pattern drew to a close when managers ceased moving from one firm to another so readily. At that point, the managers began to take relationships more seriously than principles and ideas—voting blocs or cliques appeared for the first time. As the managers recognized the difficulty of moving from one firm to another, they began to think, "If I am to stay here for a career, I had better stick with my friends." As a result, voting patterns began to reflect friendship commitments, rather than the individuals' convictions about what was the "best" idea or proposal. The irony of this action was that as relationships became primary, morale and productivity declined. The focus on relationship divided the company into special-interest friendship cliques.

The work atmosphere became so unsatisfactory that the firm called me in as a conflict consultant. My primary job was to persuade the managers that a good work environment for them required quality relationships to be formed as by-products. Only when principles could motivate them in search of the "best" solution did their morale and productivity once again begin to rise.[9]

No community is ideal, but we can invite an ethical environment by balancing the legs of community as we limit relationship and uplift principles, or vice versa. There may be times, of course, when relationships must be given primary attention. Giving up the notion of an ideal community requires us to shift our emphasis from defense of the community to attempting to change the flaws present within community. Such action then points us toward an "ethical," not an ideal community. A favorite definition of community, shared by a Quaker (Society of Friends) who has committed his life to community living, seems appropriate here: "Community exists when the person you most dislike dies or moves away and someone worse comes and takes his or her place." Such a view of community, humorous as it may be, was shared in all seriousness. Similarly, Dietrich Bonhoeffer cautioned against joining human community to meet all one's personal needs.[10] Writers such as my Quaker colleague and Bonhoeffer want us to forego the illusion of ideal community life.

The essence of a lasting ethical community requires a conscious commitment to labeling and examining the shortcomings of the community. Shielding the community from scrutiny or criticism is not of long-term benefit to the organization.[11] A community can only strive to be ethical by listening closely to its critics.

When the flaws of community were discussed in a classroom setting one time, one student contended that a religious community could in no way be ethical by the above definition. He angrily stated that religious communities do not tolerate criticism. His passionate outburst was soon supported by many in the class. The anger of the group toward their experiences in religious organizations was overwhelming. Various students described how their home churches displayed little openness to new ideas. As one student said, "Only the move to the university allowed me to probe new ideas and to explore the world openly. I felt a great sense of fresh air by coming to a new environment."

Going with the students' interest, I began to discuss Rudy Wiebe's excellent book on intolerance to new ideas within a fictional Mennonite community. Wiebe referred to his novel *Peace Shall Destroy Many* as a war novel, not with arms, but with psychological oppression to innovation.[12] There are several situations within the book that reveal leaders' actions for another's "own good" as not turning out in that person's best interest, or in that of the community. As we discussed Wiebe's book, the students realized that leaders in the book did place principles above relationships, and they began to question the validity of doing so.

For example, one young man in Wiebe's community spoke the scriptures in English, rather than the required high-level German. His defense was that he was speaking to Indians who understood English, not German. He placed relationship or contact with these people at a high priority. However, the leaders insisted that German be used, in order to separate the community from the English-speaking culture. The principle of exclusive community was placed higher than open relationships with many. This young questioner was finally told that the community felt certain principles must be upheld, even to the extent of excluding certain relationships.[13]

As this example and many others in Wiebe's book reveal, this fictional community placed principle above relationship, sometimes to a destructive extent. What caused this community to be unethical, according to a narrow-ridge viewpoint, was the lack of openness to criticism. Adherence to principle must go hand in hand with the encouragement of critical scrutiny. Otherwise a totalitarian, not an ethical, environment is given reign.

Before going further, I would like to note that churches are not always unwilling to listen to minority viewpoints and frequently do respond to critics. An example of this is the Catholic church and its movement in Central America or its stand on nuclear weapons. Furthermore, the advances of the 1960s regarding civil rights were primarily put forth by the church leadership of people like Martin Luther King, Jr. But the students did have a legitimate point about the unethical nature of any community that does not permit criticism of its principles and attempts to stifle anyone seeking a measure of reform.

Good Old Boys

In a democratic culture, the marketplace of ideas requires us to be open to debate and discussion. Thomas Nilsen provided a summary of the marketplace ethic of debate. "We are touching here again, of course, on the marketplace of ideas principle. In a democratic society it is assumed that the best test (or at least the most workable test) of a social or political truth is its acceptance after public discussion."[14] In fact, bumper stickers from the Vietnam protest era that read "America: Love It or Leave It" were inherently undemocratic. Dissent is essential if we are to keep a democratic institution strong. Leaders need such reminders from their people, and churches could benefit from a theology of self-criticism. Every organization needs a questioner who does not permit the organization to run too smoothly.

In no way, however, is this to imply that leadership can be disbanded. The notion of leadership, like power, is not inevitably bad, if the health of the community is placed at a higher level than personal success. As Thomas Nilsen suggested, "hierarchical structures and authority appear to be essential to human organizations. But if human dignity is to be preserved, the structure must be flexible enough to adapt to the changing needs of people, and the authority limited, conditional, and exercised with prudence."[15] Nilsen's comments on flexible authority point to the difference between the Adams and Jefferson administrations. John Adams, as a Federalist president, did not want any questioning of his government. He implemented the Alien and Sedition Acts of 1798 to limit criticism. Jefferson then ran against this Federalist policy—he wanted the people to control the government, not vice versa. His victory as the third president of the United States was a triumph for the principles of debate and controversy within the political workings of a democracy.[16]

Today, we find many "Federalists" within organizations who would call Jefferson too radical in giving power to the people. Yet without questioning in an organization, we find a "good old boy" network. Most of us have experienced such a system at one time or another. If one is "in" with the "good old boys," there is little notice of this communication pattern. But if one is out of the relational and power network, control within such a system becomes obvious. For example, let us examine a high school setting with a well-established "good old boy" system. At this institution, decisions were often made in small groups by just a handful of people. One high school teacher, Tom, was seldom consulted on issues. In fact, the principal would talk to everyone but Tom. Then, in a faculty meeting, Tom would raise questions that made him appear foolish. Tom was without the necessary information to make a good decision or even to ask a sensible question, which caused him to look ill-prepared and further marginalized from the power center in the group. Tom was silenced by exclusion from the "good old boys" network, as he was kept from conversation with his colleagues.

This communicative game is played by a number of people with the goal of keeping themselves in power. It is an adult form of excluding some people from the popular "in" group at school. The game of community exclusion closely fits the definition of an interpersonal game system. "A game is defined as (1) a highly structured pattern (2) of complementary transactions, (3) with an ulterior motive, (4) leading to a well-defined, dramatic climax known as the payoff, (5) which serves as a substitute for intimacy in interpersonal relations."[17] This definition can be applied to analyze the case of Tom.

Clearly, the communicative game of keeping Tom out of the relational power structure was a highly developed pattern at the high school. Tom was excluded from knowledge, which put him in a complementary one-down position of having less information. The motive of this group was to keep itself in power and Tom on the fringes, which was a major part of their payoff, along with the intrigue and camaraderie generated among the "in" group, as they kept Tom out. The wholesome reward of intimacy of relationship in community was replaced by a narcissistic one of exclusion. The price paid for this intimacy was that someone was marginalized in order to give the others a feeling of power.

Indeed, not only religious organizations or high schools can act in an unethical fashion. Any group that denies the right of disagreement and the opportunity for an honest listening to opposing views must be held suspect. We should not be surprised to see a business, school, or social agency engaging in a lot of self-protective behavior that prohibits the articulation of dissent. But neither can we condone such self-serving oppression of dissent.

The Democratic Community

Numerous authors have examined the characteristics of an autocratic leader in contrast to a democratic one. Extrapolation of those findings to groups themselves is grounded in assumptions about "group-think," in which a group adopts a mind-set or a particular view.[18] In such a situation, not only might the leaders manifest autocratic dispositions toward new ideas, but if enough members of a community assume such a stance it can become the style of the community. This is in stark contrast to a democratic group process. The characteristics of autocratic and democratic groups[19] are illustrated in the following comparative overview:

Autocratic Community	Democratic Community
Group productivity is defined by those in power	Each group member is given opportunity for influence
Group goals are defined by power leaders	Alternative goals are discussed

Autocratic Community	Democratic Community
Discussion limited to the party line	Novel approaches to the status quo are explored
Effort to control the interaction	Effort to stimulate the initiation of new ideas
Inner circle controls knowledge and necessary decision-making information	Group maintenance is important; people are given available information
Attempts to move quickly	Waits for a group consensus to emerge
Group cohesion is measured by adherence to power elite's group values	Group cohesion involves affirmation of opposing viewpoints and relationships

The democratic group permits dissent without shunning the objector from relationship. The group goal is to learn, not blindly to preserve a tradition. As Maurice Friedman suggested, a group must hone out its common principles, while simultaneously permitting those ideals to be challenged. For unlike the autocratic community, there can be no "self-protection engaged in by the [democratic] community in casting out the person who raises anxieties or threatens its happy harmony."[20]

The prospering of a democratic community, according to Eric Hoffer, at least partially reflects the degree of support given to the fragile and difficult role of a dissenter in a community. In *Ordeal of Change*, Hoffer called attention to the fact that many people have been marginalized in our society. Hoffer made a salient point in maintaining that the very health of a community can be measured by the unrelenting courage of the "odd" person who will not necessarily give in and who is instrumental in changing the community.

The quality of a notion—its innermost worth—is made manifest by its dregs as they rise to the top: By how brave they are, how humane, how orderly, how skilled, how generous, how independent or servile; by the bounds they will not transgress in their dealings with a man's soul, with truth, and with honor. The average American of today bristles with indignation when he is told that this country was built, largely, by hordes of undesireables from Europe. Yet, far from being derogatory, this statement, if true, should be a cause for rejoicing, should fortify our pride in the stock from which we have sprung.[21]

From a narrow-ridge perspective, we cannot follow any single position in all instances; if we do, we cease to invite dialogue and begin to prescribe a technique. Such a critique applies to the notion of democracy, as well. We cannot at all times permit the majority viewpoint to control the arena of decision making. In some organizations, this would be the surest way to perpetuate mediocrity, with the "less able" or the "less caring" keeping themselves in power. Thus, in certain situations, the growth of a group is dependent not on democratic voting, but on the single-minded tenacity of the minority to challenge the status quo.

Em Griffin described the person unwilling to fit the group norm. He stated that if the "different" person can maintain his or her position long enough, others are often eventually persuaded to take the position seriously just out of the sheer power of the minority person's stance.[22] One of my former doctoral professors had a picture on his wall that typifies the power of this type of person. In the picture, a school of fish are all swimming in one direction, except one. As all the other fish pass this lone dissenter, they remark in classic form, "He must know something!"

We must ask ourselves if we have the insight to struggle against our own communities, if necessary, with the hope that someone will be convinced by our example and follow. Do we have the courage to swim upstream against custom, convention, and peer pressure? If your answer is yes, you are clearly a strong character. If your answer is no, at least you are honest! If your answer is maybe, you are in a hopeful position like many of us.

Any ethical movement in a community must recognize the difficulty inherent in confronting authority. Randy Hirokawa, in describing what we can learn from Japanese management, hit the issue of dissent and job security on the head with the following statement:

> The Japanese experience suggests that employee security can have a tremendous effect on organizational communication. It seems quite clear

that people are more likely to communicate openly and freely when they know that their jobs or long-awaited promotions or raises are not dependent on what they say. Unfortunately, this is not the case in many American organizations. A classic example is the case of the dismissal of William Niskanen, Jr., former chief economist for the Ford Motor Company. In late 1979, he advised his superiors that government-imposed quotas on Japanese cars would not solve Ford's problems. This view apparently was not popular among the company's top executives, because shortly thereafter he was dismissed. After learning of his dismissal, Niskanen told a reporter, "In the meeting in which I was informed that I was released, I was told, 'Bill, in general, people who do well in this company wait until they hear their superiors express their view, and then contribute something in support of that view.'"[23]

Fortunately, some American corporations, as well as universities, are now learning that they can benefit from the suggestions of employees. In fact, support staff at one university may receive financial rewards for helpful suggestions. Another university requires all its people to learn the procedure of debate and encourages it in the classroom. As stated earlier, Thomas Jefferson's non-Federalist statement that the best ideas must rise to the surface in the marketplace of debate is affirmed by some communities. Yet the fact remains that the rhetoric of debate is affirmed by many in principle, while in practice they adhere to the game of the "good old boys" to seek advancement.

The Price of Dissent

Many of us limit our own voices out of fear of reprisal. We may face very real consequences if we struggle for values and principles at odds with the power brokers. Some leaders become quite clever at short-cutting any process that might be critical of the community leadership. There are numerous ways to limit a voice in a community. Only three will be discussed here: ignoring, indiscrimination, and appeasement. Ignoring another human being within a community structure is a powerful way to limit his or her voice. Each of us at one time or another has angered someone who was unwilling to inform us of our infraction. Instead, they ignored us, leaving us in the dark about what we did to offend them and how we might best attempt reconciliation.

Shunning has been used for centuries as a paradoxical technique of collectively disciplining a person to bring him or her back into the group. This method may be the lesser of evils, however. As one of my friends keenly observed, shunning is better than death, which has been used in some groups to eliminate the deviant. Given these two bleak choices, most of us would probably choose being ignored. But we should not minimize the pain one can feel from such exclusion. As William James stated, there is no more fiendish behavior than to act as if another did not exist.[24]

To ignore another for whatever reason is to cease treating him or her as a human being and to begin responding to that individual as an object. Of course, we cannot affirm the behavior of everyone in community. But if we are to affirm an individual's humanness, we must continue to do so in the midst of our conflict or disagreement with him or her. Numerous philosophers reflecting on human care have stated that the human being is to be treated as an end, not a means. John Stewart stated that, in contemporary Western culture, some would ethically reject objectification of another out of an ethical ideal. "[John Stewart affirmed] the principle that an object could be treated as a means to an end, but that persons, because of their intrinsic value, should never be treated as the means to achieve some end, but should always be treated as an end in themselves. . . . You cannot value all human behavior positively, but you can value each human positively. That's another way we distinguish between things and people."[25]

A second major way of limiting another's voice in a community is through what we commonly call stereotyping. Frequently, we view discrimination as a problem, but in actuality we usually fail to discriminate properly. We tend to group all people into categories, such as feminist, radical, conservative, middle-of-the-road, and so forth. In short, the problem is indiscrimination. Instead of meeting each person as an individual with a unique opinion, we lump all such believers into a single category. The indiscriminate listener may say, "We have heard that before," when the speaker has not even begun yet! "There she goes telling her view again and we all know what that is going to be!" Indiscriminate listening does not give the other a chance to state a view in front of an impartial jury. At best, one is met with a judge waiting for an opportunity to marginalize the deviant.

Indiscriminate listening is akin to the abolition of a free press. It is a way of making sure that the other is not heard or taken seriously. As Camus wrote in *Resistance, Rebellion and Death*, "a free press can of course be good or bad, but, most certainly without freedom it will never be anything but bad. . . . With freedom of the press, nations are not sure of going toward justice and peace. But without it, they are sure of not going there."[26] However, indiscriminate listening is more subtle than forbidding a free press. It is easier to hide and cover up intolerant or totalitarian attitudes than printed ones. But in both cases, the goal is similar—to restrict the freedom of the person or community by eliminating the chance to influence others. Eliminating such closed-minded listening does not guarantee freedom within a community, nor will open listening solve all the problems within an organization. But at least if a forum for debate is present, some otherwise unexamined ideas will be probed.

In place of indiscriminate listening, Buber offered us a dialogic ethic.

> The one thing which has become clearer and clearer to me in the course of my life is that keeping an open mind is of utmost importance. The right kind of openness is the most precious human possession. I said, the right kind of openness. One can take a stand and hold to it passionately but one must remain open to the whole world, see what there is to see, experience what experience offers, and include all of experience in the effectuation of whatever cause one has decided for. Though constantly changing, our stand will yet remain true to itself, but deepened by an insight which grows more and more true to reality.[27]

It is this dual spirit of being willing to struggle for what one believes is true while remaining open to another's perspective that is crucial to a dialogic ethic.

Perhaps the most frustrating way of limiting a human voice is through the act of appeasement. This form of marginalization in a community is frequently also very subtle. Those in control go through the motions of helping or dealing with a request, but never intend to actually make any significant changes. It only appears that a request has been taken seriously. Unfortunately, appeasement at times can be a motivation behind the use of the encounter group. Some businesses and non-profit groups have used encounter groups in order to dissolve the problems within their organizations. Their primary motivation was not to solve problems or help people, but to let employees "air their views" without actually listening to their concerns. Through the encounter method, the workers got rid of their anger or at least diffused it, while the company made no changes. Voices were limited by creating the illusion that they had made a difference, when they had actually been marginalized through clever appeasement.

The communication and community model is ethical from a dialogical perspective if dissent from the party line is encouraged. An ethical community needs to affirm the voice of the person both in and outside the power elite. Granted, such a community may not always work smoothly, but even more troublesome are communities that seek to propagandize, rather than to sort out the best ideas available. The ethical stance of this chapter is best summarized by the following "rule": "A limitation has to be imposed on the majority itself; it must not stifle the opposition of any minority, however small its numbers or extreme its views, for unless dissenting voices can be heard today, tomorrow's decisions will not be democratic ones."[28]

Such a model of communication and community can be a radical call for dissent, as detailed by Thomas Emerson in his classic book on free speech. Emerson wrote that the impulse to limit both "rational" and "irrational" views contrary to one's own is a major problem in any culture.[29] Emerson was not naive about the problems of a democracy and insisted on making judgments about behavior, but he refused to limit speech no matter how controversial. While he saw it appropriate to punish *behavior* that goes against societal norms, he simultaneously advocated a system of free expression that permits and thrives on *verbal* dissent.[30]

Each of us has probably witnessed a "liberal" group that operates democratically in theory, but simultaneously does not permit dissent within its own community. Deviance from common views is difficult for even the best-intentioned community to encourage. Culturally, we try through our constitution, an independent judiciary, and an independent bar to assist in the maintenance of freedom of expression. We can legally only ensure a person's right to speak. But we cannot legislate the courage to do so. Frequently, it is left to the good will of those in power to encourage listening to opposing voices. Thus, an ethical community is left with developing ways of encouraging debate on issues, particularly when the opposition is contrary to the prevailing opinion.

There is a commonality between dialogue and democracy, but only if a democracy does not insist on conformity. Dissent must be permitted and recognized as vital for the community.[31] As Buber stated, "in a truly living community of opinion, the common opinion must ever again be tested and renewed in genuine meetings; the 'men who hold the same views' must ever again loosen up one another's views as they threaten to become encrusted, must ever again help one another to confront the changing reality in new, unprejudiced looking."[32] If one, for example, lives in a community committed to nonviolence, then one must go to considerable lengths to ensure that other opinions are not stifled. The protection of an idea or belief will only hurt a community in the long run. Opponents help us clarify our own opinions. If opposition is not permited, a totalitarian atmosphere will reign and the beliefs of the "in" group will atrophy without challenge.

The following are some guidelines for the establishment of an ethical community: One first needs to encourage debate on significant issues, no matter how central to the community. In the church, a theology of self-criticism is needed. In a community bound together for a basic purpose, whether it be to protect the environment or to advocate a nuclear freeze, a willingness to really listen to varying viewpoints must be encouraged. We must be open to our adversaries even as we oppose them. It is that openness that will keep life in community vibrant and alive, rather than oppressive. Second, an ethical community should consider rotating its leadership. The old adage that power corrupts does have some conventional wisdom. One can too quickly lose touch with the community and move too boldly ahead, or fail to change at all, while ignoring the voices of difference. Officers in a community structure might benefit from terms of not more than three to seven years. Also, the group might consider shifting a person completely out of leadership every few years. Many leaders simply go from one leadership position to another. An actual sabbatical leave from leadership may assist the person in power and the community itself. Finally, knowledge of and

movement from one community to another are helpful. It is important to have a home community, but also to venture out to investigate
other varieties of human gatherings. A former teacher was fond of
calling attention to the need for "translocals" in a community. These
individuals are able to evaluate the community realistically on the
basis of accurate comparative information. "Translocals" are knowledgeable about various other communities, as well as their own.[33]
Frequently, students coming home from a year abroad report that
their primary learning experience was a new perspective on the pros
and cons of living in the United States. In a world as diverse and as
troubled as ours, belonging to community because one believes in its
work and ideals is preferable to blind loyalty. Being born into a
community is not enough. The time of provincial communities is
over, if one wants to affirm the right of dissent and diversity of
opinion.

In short, the job of keeping a lively self-critical community is,
indeed, a demanding task. The thoughtful words of Sam Keen
summarize our responsibility. "No matter how hard our machines
labor, the creation of a loving community will always exercise the
human heart and hand to the fullest. Steel and computers wisely
managed may produce a sufficiency for survival; they cannot create
eros. So the best we can hope for is that every succeeding generation
will keep alive the high and fragile vocation of struggling to create a
more humane world."[34] The task of genuinely examining our community is not easy. The fear is that the community in which we
communicate may not be able to withstand the test of dissention and
die. But this may be a necessary risk, if we are to keep a dialogical
ethic for communication in community alive and nourished, rather
than self-protective and oppressive.

7

FREEDOM: THE UNITY
OF CONTRARIES

MARTIN Buber on the paradoxical nature of freedom in community:

> It is only when reality is turned into logic and A and non-A dare no longer
> dwell together, that we get determinism and indeterminism, a doctrine of
> predestination and a doctrine of freedom, each excluding the other.
> According to the logical conception of truth only one of two contraries can
> be true, but in truth reality of life as one lives life they are inseparable. . . .
> The unity of the contraries is the mystery at the innermost core of the
> dialogue.[1]

The question of freedom, as Martin Buber pointed out, cannot be
neatly or logically packaged. There is no set formula for or guarantee
of an individual's freedom within a community. Freedom is more
complex than just being able to do whatever one wants in community. A commitment to a narrow-ridge concern for self and other does
not permit such a simple definition. But the notion of freedom is
fundamental for communication within a human community seeking
to affirm both self and other.

For some of us, the notion of freedom is rarely discussed, because
we seldom experience its absence. Without an obvious threat, our
freedom is usually taken for granted. But for numerous people, the
full benefits of the civil rights and women's movement still need to be

realized. Perhaps what makes today unique is that high unemployment and widespread industrial retooling have also brought the cry for freedom to the lives of many middle-class persons.

For many college-educated people, the question of freedom is no longer an abstract issue. No longer do only certain unfortunate segments of our society see no visible means out of their predicaments. Now, some employed professionals are asking questions about freedom, as they find themselves unable to climb to "better" employment. Jobs are too few for too many, leaving some professionals unable to move in order to fulfill their dreams. The question "Where is my freedom?" has now become significant even for some of the privileged.

A Labor Department study says that 2.7 million of the estimated 10.4 million people receiving diplomas from the nation's universities in the decade ending in 1985 will work in jobs not traditionally filled by college students. . . . "It seems I never went to school," says Robinson [an interviewed graduate]. He had hoped for a $12,000–$15,000 job in consumer affairs or with the government but finds little call for his work at this stage of the economy. . . . Keating [another unhappy graduate] blames himself for picking the wrong career and blames the school for not informing the students that his field is overcrowded.[2]

Let us examine one result of this feeling of less freedom that has recently been experienced by the more privileged. During the 1970s, I noted that views of freedom and the underprivileged began to change. Because of an inability to control their future and little chance to become part of the American dream, there has historically been a tendency among the underprivileged not to delay gratification. Yet today it seems to be the middle-class student who does not want to delay gratification. Today's question, of course, is whether his or her degree will translate into a job as soon as possible. Now that the middle-class student does not feel the freedom to control his or her future as directly as before, the call to delay gratification goes almost unheeded. Even as studies emerge emphasizing the need for a strong liberal arts education,[3] students are still asking how that will help in vocational pursuits. The apparent lack of freedom has brought the middle class and the underprivileged closer together with a desire for immediate gratification.

Many readers may question whether freedom is an important issue in understanding communication within community. I admit that only recently have I come to this conclusion. When I completed my Ph.D. in the 1970s, the most significant communication concept was relationship. Now, relationship is taking a back seat to freedom. My observation is that there is movement back to a crowd mentality that encourages subordination to the will and whim of the group, as chapter 6 indicated. In short, our collective future may turn out to be more of a testing ground of freedom than in favor of its expansion.

Freedom, grounded in the narrow-ridge concern for both self and other, is both the attitudinal and practical web of community that prevents any group from becoming a tyrannically imposed gathering. The freedom of the narrow ridge works both to question community practices and to preserve the structure, if possible. It is the failure to have this dual interest of both critiquing and preserving that Buber questioned in the following statement: "Freedom—I love its flashing face: it flashes forth from the darkness and dies away, but it has made the heart invulnerable. I am devoted to it, I am always ready to join in the fight for it. . . . I give my left hand to the rebel and my right to the heretic; forward. But I do not trust them. They know how to die, but that is not enough. I love freedom, but I do not believe in it."[4] Buber considered freedom without limits irresponsible. He did not advocate anarchy. Like any motivating cry, "freedom" must be somewhat distrusted, even when it is rooted in the "best of causes."

Restraining Freedom

Freedom is generally restrained by the group. A community cannot permit total freedom for each individual member. Even so-called "countercultural" groups must confront individual actions that violate the intent of the group. For example, I was informed that, at a local draft registration protest rally some years ago, one individual arrived with a sign reading "Rednecks Suck." To say the least, many in the group were upset by this crude statement so unrelated to the group's purpose. The protest group attempted to put pressure on this young man to put down his obnoxious message. At first, the group members sat down and waited for this fellow to lay down his sign. When he did not, the group of protesters went to the other side of the street to protest without him. That evening the local paper's headline read, "Protesters Protest Protester," generating humor for the whole community! However, a crucial point was frequently missed in conversations about the headline. Any group, even one protesting the status quo, will encounter the reality that not all behavior is acceptable within guidelines of the group norms.

The above example also reveals that not all efforts at nonviolent protest can be equated. Gandhi distinguished between *satyagraha* and *duragraha*, with the former affirming the importance of the person and the latter ignoring the opponent's humanness and being rooted in stubborn persistence.[5] The lone protester was involved in *duragraha*, which violated the intent of the group. In short, even in civil disobedience and protest, one does not have total freedom. In exercising freedom against the tradition, we are limited even within a dissenting group.

Every group generates rules that curtail action—and to a degree this is necessary and beneficial. While chapter 6 discussed the need for rule violation within community, this chapter is suggesting that rule violation is significantly different than rule error (in which there is only a tacit sense of the rule) or rule ignorance. Both rule error and rule ignorance limit freedom. Not to know the rules of a game makes it difficult to play, let alone win. Maximizing freedom within a community necessitates a knowledge of the rules.[6] Every group must restrain freedom to an extent; however, we cannot permit simple ignorance of community rules to limit our freedom. Knowledge of rules is necessary to get along with others and in order to communicate our vision for change within the community.

One of the implicit and sometimes explicit rules that affects our human community and that has been an underlying theme of this book is the reality of limited resources. While this is not an overt concern to all, there is a major constraint on natural and human resources for many. Michael Parenti stated that for tens of millions of middle-income Americans, from middle-level managers to clerical workers, life is less than ideal.

> A goodly number of persons in the white-collar and service sectors, like most blue-collar workers, live under the chronic threat of economic insecurity, forced early retirement, unemployment, inflation, high taxes, and heavy debts, and are employed at some of the most underpaid, menial, and mindless jobs any modern civilization could produce. Occupational disability, job insecurity, job dissatisfaction, constant financial

anxieties, mental stress and depression, alcoholism, and conflictful domestic relations are common woes among the mass of middle Americans who compose the aching "backbone" of America. Even if not suffering from acute want, few if any exercise much control over the conditions of their lives. If not as severely buffeted and exploited as the very poor, they still number among the powerless in regard to most of the crucial decisions affecting their livelihoods, their communities, and their nation.[7]

This book does not address the economic issues pointed to by Parenti. The point is, however, that the middle-class worker is facing some of the problems that poor people have endured for centuries. Buber did not avoid the political and may have called for direct political action to change such wrongs. But, in addition, he would have tried to locate a freedom of attitude that could assist in enduring the reality of today until a "better" tomorrow could materialize.

Attitudinal Freedom

Buber encouraged uncovering attitudinal freedom in situations where others saw none. Generally, we look for freedom in novel places, new environments, or utopias claiming to permit us to do whatever we choose. But Buber indicated that freedom is as much an attitude as a place. For this reason, it is possible for one person to find freedom within the routine of life, while another fails to discover it even in change. The following material, from Buber's *Between Man and Man*, provides us with some of the flavor of this attitude of freedom.

> Those who stake themselves, as individuals or as a community, may leap and crash out into the swaying void where senses and sense fail, or through it and beyond into some kind of existence. But they must not make freedom into a theorem or a programme. . . . Let us realize the true meaning of being free of a bond: it means that a quite personal responsibility takes the place of one shared with many generations. Life lived in freedom is personal responsibility or it is a pathetic farce. . . . As we "become free" this leaning on something is more and more denied to us, and our responsibility must become personal and solitary.[8]

Attitudinal freedom is a central theme in the novel *Siddhartha* by Herman Hesse. Siddhartha searches for meaning in life through philosophies as diverse as Buddhism and hedonism. Yet his struggle to find adventure and wisdom leaves his life unfulfilled. Finally, Siddhartha returns to the river he crossed years earlier. He watches in awe as the old ferryman again crosses the great river as if for the first time. Siddhartha now listens intently to the ferryman's philosophy of the river, which is actually a statement on attitudinal freedom.

> "Love this river, stay by it, learn from it." Yes, he [Siddhartha] wanted to learn from it, he wanted to listen to it. It seemed to him that whoever understood this river and its secrets, would understand much more, many secrets, all secrets.
>
> But today he only saw one of the river's secrets, one that gripped his soul. He saw that the water continually flowed and flowed and yet it was always there; it was always the same and yet every moment it was new.[9]

Hesse's story brings to awareness an image of someone consistently dissatisfied with routine and forever seeking new horizons. Many of us may be sympathetic to such a search, but it entails some danger. What happens to this person when he or she can no longer be promoted and has reached a plateau of competence? Perhaps, like Siddhartha, this person will have to realize that freedom can be discovered in everyday activity. Like Siddhartha, one may begin to recognize that each crossing, each routine, is unique. To a considerable degree, freedom is contingent upon our attitudinal approach to the world.

Viktor Frankl called our final freedom that attitude with which we approach the unchangeable. If a person is dying of cancer, freedom can be found not in the hope of continued life but in the attitude with which he or she approaches death. As Frankl recorded, even in the agony of the concentration camps of World War II, some were able to find freedom through their attitude toward seemingly unchangeable circumstances. Some acted like swine, but others behaved like saints, caring for the sick and those less able to deal with the danger of the time.[10] Frankl's story is one of assurance of the real possibility of discovering freedom. Even in the midst of such daily danger, people can transcend a feeling of entrapment.

On an everyday level, we may examine a task as mundane as doing dishes for the family. Such a routine can generate a feeling of boredom and imprisonment. However, if another dries the dishes, the possibility of quality conversation can be pursued. Such activities as washing dishes, taking care of a house, grading papers, and so forth, leave us with the option of boredom or with the possibility of discovering freedom in the midst of routine. The attitude of freedom finding can make one a hero in a time of limited resources and community building. Unlike most of us who desire each action to be "worthy of our time," the hero of limited resources can lead others to unlock significance and freedom in the midst of routine. The question is: What permits a communicator to assume the attitude of the hero of limited resources?

It seems that attitudinal freedom requires the development of a philosophical system that can guide one's communicative vision. Gordon Allport, in the preface to *Man's Search for Meaning*, stated that those who best survived the dangers and torture of the concentration camps had a philosophical system that ordered their understanding of events. "Frankl is fond of quoting Nietzsche, 'He who has a why to live can bear with almost any *how.*' In the concentration camp every circumstance conspires to make the prisoner lose his hold. All the familiar goals in life are snatched away. What alone remains is 'the last of human freedom'—the ability to 'choose one's attitude in a given set of circumstances.' This ultimate freedom . . . takes on significance in Frankl's story."[11]

For Buber, Frankl, and Allport, a philosophical system can provide a structure that results in attitudinal freedom. Philosophy, in this case, is meant as a way to self-understanding. This view of philosophy is fundamental to Martin Buber's work, which he referred to as philosophical anthropology.[12] Buber's orientation was significantly influenced by Ludwig Feuerbach.

Feuerbach's forceful characterization of philosophy as "nothing but" the process of human self-understanding, as the attempt at human self-knowledge, carries him beyond either the transcendental precincts of speculative idealism, whether of Kant or of Hegel, or the reductive precincts of traditional empiricism, whether British or French. The process of human self-consciousness he describes is one that is directly expressive of human feelings, human needs, human actions. Once philosophy is understood in this way, says Feuerbach . . . philosophy . . . is recognized, in its "positive" content, for what it is—namely, anthropology.[13]

For Feuerbach and Buber, philosophy was not something abstract and distant; it was a vital part of everyday communication. It is this understanding of a philosophy of communication that makes it possible to find meaning in the midst of routine, or what Buber called "hallowing of the everyday."[14] This hallowing requires courage to walk with uncertainty into human meetings without technique, formula, or prediction.

Buber's emphasis on rejecting technique did not in any way ignore the value of tradition, preparation, or invitation. What is pointed to by Buber's insistence on meeting the moment is a recognition that life can not be lived a priori to the event. Yes, we know our tradition, but the "dialogical communicator" adapts his or her training to the needs of the historical moment. Without this flexibility, we begin to exhibit a "trained incapacity"; we become locked into the formula or method in which we were trained.[15] For instance, as an undergraduate psychology major, my first efforts at paraphrasing with my wife were less than helpful. I had learned a technique that I failed to use in a relationship-sensitive manner. Instead, I crudely paraphrased and repeated back whatever my wife said. My technique was brought to an abrupt halt when she said, "Enough! Add something to the conversation, but please stop retelling what I have just told you!"

Emphasis on a priori technique fails to take into account the full "hermeneutic circle," interpretive meaning emerging between interpreter and the event. With too much concentration on an imposed method, the significance of the interpreter and event is forgotten. Steven Strasser laid out the philosophical danger of not recognizing the "hermeneutic horizon" or the limits of one's method.[16] Thus, no method is right for every situation, as can be seen from the example of my clumsy use of paraphrasing years ago. Emphasis on the "hermeneutic circle" opens up a call for a sensitive inquirer who knows the limits of method and the need for dialogue between person and event.[17] Emphasis on an a priori method or technique does not permit that dialogue to take place.

John Stewart brought the "hermeneutic circle" (rather than rigid technique) to the study of listening. He focused on trained flexibility in his discussion of hermeneutic listening, utilizing Gadamer's and Ricoeur's emphasis on play. "Interpretive listening follows the dynamic of play. . . . [e]ach participant must, to some extent, give herself up to the game in order to play . . . because of the open-endedness of the enterpise, each genuinely 'playful' conversation is creative, productive of insight not simply reproductive of individual psychological states [or limited within one method of technique]."[18] This emphasis on "hermeneutic circle," "play," and dialogue between person and event reveals the importance of a training and preparation modified to meet the moment given birth in relation, not simply played out in accordance with a predetermined strategy. One must be open to the unexpected even in the midst of the everyday routine.

Finding freedom in the midst of routine is what Kant was able to do through his regimen of a daily walk. It is told that some people actually set their clocks by Kant's routine. Kant's action was not generated from uncontrollable compulsion; rather, he freely chose to structure his life around his desire for *faire une promenade* on a regular basis.[19] Kant's freely chosen discipline of walking seemed to put his life in order. Some sense of order in life seems necessary for the emergence of freedom. Yet it is clear that order itself is not sufficient for freedom to be felt; alone, it leaves us merely with routine.

Perhaps for the contemporary communicator, the hidden ingredient for the discovery of freedom out of an ordered response is what William James called old-fashioned "will." While the term may conjure up many questionable images, I no longer hesitate to use it. I see so many students who, because of a lack of "will," are in need of remedial skills training. For example, given a writing assignment, some students simply lack the "will" to glue themselves to a chair long enough to get something on paper.

In terms of recent communication theory, there seems to be no constitutive rule that provides a "will" to get things done. A constitutive rule is defined as a rule that gives stability, provides a way of understanding the world, and is rooted in a high awareness about the pattern of our behavior in community with one another.[20] In other words, such a rule would allow us to be aware of our ordering principle and how it shapes our life. A constitutive rule encompassing the notion of "will" seems to be the ordering process that pulls life together and pushes forward. As Rollo May stated, "will is the capacity to organize one's self so that movement in a certain direction or towards a certain goal may take place."[21]

The discussion of will in the work of Leslie Farber, whose understanding of this notion was significantly influenced by Buber,[22] is consistent with my use of the term. Farber described two realms of will: the first grounded in relation (and similar to my use of the term) and the second given birth by an isolated imposition of oneself on another person or event. Farber's distinction between the two realms of will centers on the importance of relation and the ability to hear a call and answer it with a unique response.

> The problem of will lies in our recurring temptation to apply the will of the second realm to those portions of life that not only will not comply, but that will become distorted under such coercion. Let me give a few examples: I can will knowledge, but not wisdom; going to bed, but not sleeping; eating, but not hunger; meekness, but not humility; scrupulosity, but not virtue; self-assertion or bravado, but not courage; lust, but not love; commiseration, but not sympathy; congratulations, but not admiration; religiosity, but not faith; reading, but not understanding. . . . I can will speech or silence, but not conversation.[23]

Farber's relational realm of will includes person and event in the midst of rules or tradition that can be adjusted as needed by the historical moment. This dialogical approach to the notion of will is at the heart of Friedman's "courage to address and respond," which implies a courage to be open to hearing an address and a need to respond out of one's own uniqueness.[24]

Even more fundamental than types of will, for some, is the question of whether or not a free will exists that can organize life toward a goal. The question of free will versus determinism is an old-standing issue. Perhaps the most sensible suggestion to resolve this question comes from William James. James felt that he could not logically prove the existence of a free will, but he contended that life would be unbearable without such a notion. Thus, he chose to accept the power of free will as his first act of exercising it.[25] In communication terms, "will" then becomes a constitutive rule that governed his behavior.

This motivator of the human being which James called free will is similar to Buber's notion of "direction."[26] But Buber did not see direction emerging in a vacuum; rather, it was central to his understanding of communication constituting community. "Direction" or "will" is not an egocentric construct within the person. A Buberian view of will or direction, which Farber extrapolated upon, is seen as a transaction between person and event. A narrow-ridge philosophy of communication recognizes the person as a necessary part, but as not alone sufficient for will to be a force in life. The person must be called out by the moment and then provide his or her own unique response.[27]

Perhaps this form of will is best illustrated in an anecdote told by Carl Rogers. A "schizophrenic" patient was in counseling, but seldom even talked to the counselor. Then, in the middle of a session, the patient mentioned others who had recently been released from the hospital. He said little more, except, "If some of them can do it, maybe I can too." And within a short period of time, the former "schizophrenic" patient was released to return home.[28] A Buberian understanding of will or direction for the former schizophrenic was that the situation seemed to call forth a response to life and the person responded. Will, then, is the transaction of the call of the situation and our response to it. Dialogically, we do not muster the will or courage to act without a call, and the call is nothing if not responded to by the individual.

Friedman, in a discussion of Buber's manner of interaction, pointed to the need for the situation to draw from us a response that we are capable of in transaction, but not by ourselves. He suggested that the presence of other events and people allows "new" insights to emerge.[29] Similarly, Sidney Jourard emphasized that by talking about ourselves to others, we learn about ourselves.[30] Something happens in the exchange that permits us to discover new possibilities.

Philosophically, this means that we need to be open to events and people in order for new combinations of ideas and actions to emerge. Otherwise, our philosophical system becomes a law, rather than a flowing set of possibilities. It seems that our behavior tends to become more standardized as additional transactions become part of our person. It is the call of the situation giving birth to will or the desire to get something done that can shake us up and open our possibilities.

Communicative Call—"Signs"

Buber would contend that "signs" call us into freedom and out of the comfort of the past. Buber spoke of signs addressing us or of the situation speaking to us. For instance, the young psychiatric patient heard the sign and responded. This sensitivity is needed for an active will.

> Each of us is encased in an armor whose task is to ward off signs. Signs happen to us without respite; living means being addressed, we would need only to present ourselves and to perceive. But the risk is too dangerous for us, the soundless thunderings seem to threaten us with annihilation, and from generation to generation we perfect the defense apparatus. All our knowledge assures us, "Be calm, everything happens as it must happen, but nothing is directed at you, you are not meant; it is just 'the world,' you can experience it as you like, but whatever you make of it in yourself proceeds from you alone, nothing is required of you, you are not addressed, all is quiet."[31]

Buber's reference to signs that can claim our attention in no way forgets the person. Each person's uniqueness permits a response to a sign or call of an event that is unique. The transaction of this sign or call of the event in combination with the uniqueness of the person is what we could call will. Maurice Friedman told the following Hasidic tale that reveals the importance of both the call, in this case to be a Hasidic rabbi, and one's uniqueness. "When Rabbi Noah, Rabbi Mordecai's son, assumed the succession after his father's death, his disciples noticed that there were a number of ways in which he conducted himself differently from his father, and asked him about this. 'I do just as my father did,' he replied. 'He did not imitate, and I do not imitate.' The paradox of the image of man is that it is at once unique and universal, but universal only through the unique."[32] Within human community, a narrow-ridge understanding of freedom requires us to organize our lives through a transactional definition of will that involves bringing together a listening to the situation (what Buber referred to as call) and one's own personal response.[33]

Freedom grounded in the driving force of our transactional view of will opens up possibilities within an organizational structure. This sense of freedom permits us to learn from others. This understanding of freedom is akin to that of Martin Heidegger and allows the event to reveal itself as it is,[34] while permitting our own presuppositions to influence our hearing.[35] Freedom then becomes an act of the person changing events, while simultaneously being willing to be changed by them.

A common problem within an organization may serve as an example. A secretary and one of her employers do not get along well. They both find petty grievances about each other. Finally, both agree to discuss the problem. Ideally, both need to recognize a call to address the issue openly and to bring their own uniqueness to the interpretation of the event. An act of will begins the possibility of freedom, if both listen openly. If one comes with a closed mind, no new possibilities or freedom will be discovered—for freedom involves the discovery of new possibilities whether they be practical or attitudinal. Unfortunately, the boss has determined the outcome of the communication before sitting down. Freedom of new possibilities is crushed by the boss's approach and both parties are left dissatisfied with the outcome.

Such a view of freedom can build community, while simultaneously challenging it. A narrow-ridge view of freedom cannot be given birth without placing a high value on being responsive to both self and other. Freedom, then, is intricately bound to others and the world around us. It was a view of freedom without this boundedness that Buber feared and distrusted. It was freedom among and with others that sparked Buber's hope. Thomas Merton, in his classic work *No Man Is an Island*, pointed to a view of freedom similar to that of Buber.

> Only when we see ourselves in our true human context, as members of a race which is intended to be one organism and "one body," will we begin to understand the positive importance not only of the successes but of the failures and accidents in our lives. My successes are not my own. The way to them was prepared by others. The fruit of my labors is not my own: for I am preparing the way for the achievements of another. Nor are my failures my own. They may spring from the failure of another, but they are also compensated for by another's achievement. Therefore the meaning of my life is not to be looked for merely in the sum total of my own achievements. It is seen only in the complete integration of my achievements and failures with the achievements and failures of my own generation, and society, and time. . . .
>
> Every other man is a piece of myself, for I am a part and a member of mankind.[36]

For Buber and Merton, the essence of human life is one's connection to others. Friedman summarized Buber's viewpoint by saying that real life began in meeting another person in relationship.[37] Perhaps we could expand on this and suggest that real freedom occurs only in community, where one's responsibility is propelled by a "will" or "direction" that turns toward another's needs, as well as one's own. Freedom begins not apart from, but in the heart of, relationship.

Telling the Story

Buber and Merton believed that, through our togetherness, freedom is made possible. They believed in nourishing the connectedness through "telling the story" of the people. Freedom in a community is deeply tied to the narration of its own history. Both Buber and Merton experienced freedom in religious groups that paid particular attention to telling their own story of why and how the community was formed and nourished.

The myth of Prometheus, the God who brought mortals fire, and Io, Zeus' lover, illustrates how freedom can be found by telling a story to others. One day Prometheus meets a creature that looks like a heifer, but speaks like a woman. The two begin to talk, to tell each other their stories about how Zeus mistreated Prometheus and how Hera inflicted pain on Io, because Hera's husband, Zeus, was in love with Io.

Later, Io has to contend not only with being a beast, but with captivity as well. With the help of Zeus' son, Hermes, Io almost escapes her misery. But Hera, seeing this, has a gadfly sting her to madness. In the midst of this immense pain, Prometheus tries to comfort Io with a narrative that extends her community into the future.

> Prometheus tried to comfort her, but he could point her only to the distant future. What lay immediately before her was still more wandering and in fearsome lands. To be sure, the part of the sea she first ran along in her frenzy would be called Ionian after her, and the Bosphorus, which means the Ford of the Cow would preserve the memory of when she went through it, but her real consolation must be that at long last she would reach the Nile, where Zeus would restore her to her human form. She would bear him a son Epaphus, and live forever after happy and honored. And Io's descendant would be Hercules, greatest of heroes, than whom

hardly the gods were greater, and to whom Prometheus would owe his freedom.[38]

The above "freedom" narrative provided by Prometheus brings optimism for Io's future. It details the importance of a future event that provides a vision of freedom for Io's descendents. Many parents continue to hope that their children will be able to have better lives than they did. Telling the story about how a group or family will be able to look to the future, as did Martin Luther King, Jr., and say "We Shall Overcome Some Day" seems necessary for the health of community.

Narration not only gives us hope of a better future, it enables us to critique the ongoing community. Stories about community give us a vision of a "just" and "right" community. Such an understanding of narration was present in the Kennedy brothers' frequent paraphrasing of George Bernard Shaw: "Some men see things as they are and say why. I dream things that never were and say why not."[39] Freedom in community can only be found when what we take for granted is critiqued against a narrated vision of how things "should" be. Stanley Hauerwas analyzed the importance of narration, which can later become a lasting story within a culture. "Good and just societies require a narrative, therefore, which helps them know the truth about existence and fight the constant temptation to self-deception."[40]

In everyday association, this means that our freedom is bound to knowing our tradition. To know a history is to follow it, fight it, change it, or develop a stance toward it that permits us to view things in a new perspective. Thus, listening to the old stories told by earlier generations can be of benefit, as we understand who we were collectively and what we may become. In short, telling a story helps us make sense out of our past. It binds us together, and it can provide us with a vision for the future toward which to strive or change.

For Buber, the most sacred things were told in stories and analogies,[41] not in the clear-cut statements that some of our "how-to" books offer today. To be told precisely how to do something limits freedom. But to be pointed in a direction through analogy and story permits the person to encounter freedom through his or her own uniqueness. Freedom through narration invites a dialectic between the tradition and the uniqueness of a person. Perhaps this view of freedom is best described by Buber's narration about the educated person, one who knows the rules, regulations, and traditions, but can violate them when necessary.[42] Ultimately, Buber's narrow-ridge view of freedom is a story in itself that communicates to the person to be wary of breaking with the past, while simultaneously not letting himself or herself be chained to it. Similarly, one of my associates, who has lived in a close working relationship with a religious community, stated that we have freedom in community as long as we can keep the conversation going. When we cease to talk, we rupture our collective web and make it virtually impossible to learn from one another.[43] In short, being able to tell our story and to listen to somebody else's narration does not guarantee freedom within community, but without it both a sense of tradition and the need for change may go unnoticed. Freedom within community is intricately tied to our telling of the story.

8

MEANING IN COMMUNITY:
IS THIS ALL THERE IS?

MARTIN Buber on the complexity of "meaning" in community life:

> The hasidic movement . . . teaches that the true meaning of love of one's neighbor is not that it is a command from God which we are to fulfill, but that through it and in it we meet God. This is shown by the interpretation of this command. It is not just written, "Love thy neighbor as thyself," as though the sentence ended there, but it goes on. "Love thy neighbor as thyself, I am the Lord" (Leviticus 19:18). The grammatical construction of the original text shows quite clearly that the meaning is: You shall deal lovingly with your "neighbor," that is, with everyone you meet along life's road, and you shall deal with him as with one equal to yourself. The second part, however, adds, "I am the Lord"—and here the hasidic interpretation comes in: "You think I am far away from you, but in your love for your neighbor you will find Me; not in his love for you but in yours for him." He who loves brings God and the world together.
>
> The hasidic teaching is the consummation of Judaism. And this is its message to all: You yourself must begin. Existence will remain meaningless for you if you yourself do not penetrate into it with active love and if you do not in this way discover its meaning for yourself. Everything is waiting to be hallowed by you; it is waiting to be disclosed in its meaning and to be realized in it by you.[1]

Martin Buber viewed the world as ordained with meaning in the meeting of others and events in community. For Buber, participation

with others is the key to a meaningful existence. Buber recognized
the world as sometimes chaotic, confused, and veiled from understanding, but he did not conceptualize the world as forever absurd.[2]
Ultimately, for Buber, life worth living together would be meaningful. Buber believed that meaning was discovered by actively meeting
others, not by waiting for others to meet us. He would have responded well to President Kennedy's famous line in his 1960 presidential inaugural address: "And so, my fellow Americans, ask not
what your country can do for you: Ask what you can do for your
country. My fellow citizens of the world: Ask not what America will
do for you, but what together we can do for the freedom of man."[3]
Buber would most probably have substituted community, world, or
life, for Kennedy's "country," but he was in agreement with the
message that we are to reach out for meaning by doing, rather than by
waiting to be served.

It seems that we could benefit from Buber's sense of meaning
today. Unfortunately, the third leading cause of death among individuals younger than twenty-five is suicide. The problem is so significant that some high-school curricula are being revised to include
suicide prevention.[4] Statistics also reveal that job satisfaction of
American workers is on a steady decline. "Unhappy American workers are a growing breed, according to an ongoing U.S. Department of
Labor study. The study has been monitoring attitudes of 5,000
workers since 1966 and has found job satisfaction declining over the
past several years."[5] In short, the question "Is this all there is?" did
not vanish with the supposed conclusion of the "me" decade.

Perhaps our age is in such transition and trouble that this historical
period is qualitatively different from others. One of my respected
professors was fond of saying that no historical period is any less
demanding than another; each time has its own set of difficulties.
However, no one can deny the severity of our problems. Our children are now dealing with nuclear anxiety. Millions of viewers hov-
ered in front of the television to watch the movie "The Day After," a
drama about a nuclear war. In recent years, we have witnessed the
assassinations of John F. Kennedy, Robert F. Kennedy, Martin
Luther King, Jr., Anwar Sadat, and Indira Gandhi, as well as
attempts on the lives of many others, from presidents to the Pope. In
my lifetime, American troops have died in Korea, Vietnam, Cambo-
dia, Laos, Lebanon, El Salvador, Grenada, and Iran. This short

historical period has indeed been consumed with complex and, at times, world-threatening problems.

As a university professor, I have heard students lament, "If I died, it would make no difference. I feel so powerless and insignificant!" These words seem to reinforce the results of an informal poll taken in two of my interpersonal communication classes, according to which one-third of the business majors said they were majoring in something they did not like. The students felt so powerless that they were compelled to study subject matter that was of no interest to them. Philip Slater described this dilemma. "Working at a job you don't like, making something you don't want, for people who will have to be persuaded to buy it, is a sign that something is amiss, something that can't be justified in terms of the economy."[6] Seemingly, the intensity of our time is exaggerating a feeling of meaninglessness. Stability in life is no longer as prevalent. Traditions that previously provided a consistent meaningful understanding of the world are now questioned, making us less sure of values and philosophies. The question of meaning is even more troublesome as the pluralistic set of possibilities and choices before us both confuse and, hopefully, enrich our lives.[7]

For many, the ability to control their immediate world appears increasingly limited; futures seem determined without one's influence. For students in the 1980s, the predominant concern is jobs; and too few jobs for too many qualified workers in a variety of areas is the predicted future. "The surplus of college-trained workers, and some further slowing of job growth in traditional sectors of demand, add up to a keenly competitive situation."[8] The 1984 survey of job prospects for college graduates concluded that experienced but unemployed workers would make it tough for current graduates as they seek entry-level positions. Those with experience will have an edge.[9] Russell W. Rumberger, a senior research associate on educational finance and governance at Stanford described the future in even more bleak terms for the emerging college graduate. Rumberger maintained that there will be three phenomena that many graduates will experience: overeducation, underutilization, and underemployment.[10] Similar findings can be gleaned from a wide array of periodicals on higher education. But the common theme is that students can no longer count on the job of their choice at an entry level, or even later in some cases.[11]

Problems today seem to present few simple answers; we have inherited a seven-headed beast. We need nuclear power, or so we are told, but where do we put the waste? We need to collect garbage, but who wants to live next to a landfill? Within communities we need a clear vision, but who wants to risk articulating a potential inaccuracy? Robert Jay Lifton stated that we can almost stereotype the twentieth century as the age of meaninglessness. No single meaning or form can capture the imagination. Instead, we are faced with choices, few of which compel commitment and enthusiasm.[12] The current confusion of our plight seems analogous to the chaos represented in the following story of a nineteenth-century feud.

> From 1868 to 1873, DeWitt County, Texas, was the setting for a savage feud between the Taylor and Sutton families. Bloody gun battles between them included cousins and friends. Taverns, general stores, jailhouses, and streets regularly became scenes of ambushes, knife fights, and shootouts. Late in 1873, a weeklong battle took place between the warring factions ending with the deaths of the heads of family members and allies.
> Strangely, no one could say for sure what had caused the conflict.[13]

The senselessness of the above feud reflects the confusion of our time. People were dead; yet no one knew the origin of the conflict. The events of this nineteenth-century tragedy seem no more explainable than John Hinckley's attempt to kill President Reagan, because Hinckley was in love with movie star Jodi Foster, whom he had never met. Is this any less logical than the previous example of students majoring in subjects they dislike, preparing for careers they do not want, in hopes that a job will be open for them after they finish their "time" at the university? I do not believe it is. It seems that many of us live in an era of confusion and lack of meaning, ranging from dissatisfied workers and self-destructive students to irrational assassins.

The existential movement of the sixties termed this confusion and meaninglessness *absurdity*.[14] Although absurdity is no longer discussed as much as it was in the 1960s, it makes more sense to me than ever before. The sixties were a time of pseudo-absurdity and pseudo-depression. Optimism seemed to prevail, even in the midst of our supposed disenchantment with society. Ronald Glasser, well known for his "reality therapy," visited my undergraduate college almost two decades ago and stated that the "average" student was most concerned about his or her role in society; participation and influence in society were taken for granted. Of course, Glasser was speaking to a predominantly white middle-class audience. But even with that qualification, such a speech would probably go unheeded today. As indicated above, many of my current students are not asking, "What is my role?" Today, the question is "Will I get a job?"

The optimism of Kennedy's New Frontier and Johnson's Great Society served as a backdrop for discussions about meaninglessness in the sixties. While one might have faced depression and temporarily lost a sense of meaning, in the back of one's mind was the assumption that meaning would be discovered again, that the rights of minorities would eventually be protected, and that the error of Vietnam would soon be rectified. The question of today is whether or not such optimism any longer serves as a backdrop for the feeling that life is absurd. If the answer is no, as I contend, then our communication is grounded in assumptions of fear and survival, not optimism and growth.

Blind Faith

The optimism of the 1960s then gave way to the so-called age of narcissism. The 1970s were known as the "me generation." As chapter 5 emphasized, this age of narcissism did not vanish with the end of the decade; rather, it went underground in the guise of organizational loyalty. [15] A danger of looking for meaning in powerful groups is revealed by a brief examination of Albert Camus' writing for a French resistance paper during World War II. In answering the German charge that the French were not loyal to their country, he made it clear that love and meaning must not be blind, but thoughtful, reflective, and even critical.

This is what I wanted to answer to your remark, "You don't love your country," which is still haunting me. But I want to be clear with you. I believe that France lost her power and her sway for a long time to come and that for a long time she will need a desperate patience, a vigilant revolt to recover the element of prestige necessary for any culture. But I believe she has lost all that for reasons that are pure. And this is why I have not lost hope. . . . I belong to an admirable and persevering nation which, admitting her errors and weaknesses, has not lost the idea that constitutes her whole greatness. . . . This country is worthy of the difficult and demanding love that is mine. And I believe she is decidedly worth fighting for since she is worthy of a higher love. And I say that your nation, on the other hand, has received from its sons only the love it deserved, which was blind. A nation is not justified by such love. That will be your undoing. And you who were already conquered in your greatest victories, what will you be in the approaching defeat?[16]

Camus' comments are even more foreboding when compared with those of a German news commentator on PBS radio during one of our presidential political conventions. When asked his evaluation of the convention, he stated that not since the rise of Hitler's Germany had he witnessed such unthinking patriotism!

Recently, the following example of absurdity masking itself as a legitimate task occurred in a business context. A corporate document on strategic planning required each departmental unit to speculate about its future anticipated success in various markets. Such an exercise is common and can assist with the strengthening of a business. However, this event reflected more of the theatre of the absurd than the pursuit of truth. First, the document asked for "projected sales" to be submitted by December 20. However, the main corporate office refused to release the needed information until January 20. Second, the document requested empirical support of assertions. Yet one of the corporate vice-presidents had stated that only subjective impressions were necessary. While the document was to be submitted by December 20, this same vice-president said that it was not expected that many would complete the report by that time. How absurd that what was asked for was not available and what was requested was not what was expected! Such requests are an insult to a place in which creative thinking is supposed to assist productivity.

Many of us do not see the absurdity of what we take for granted as normality. When we begin to take the absurd seriously, as the backdrop for our communication within an organization, we may fear isolation and rejection without relational bonds, perhaps without a job. Much of the 1960s literature on absurdity concluded on the desperate note of the individual in isolation.

This theme of isolation is endlessly repeated in modern literature: Hardy's Jude the Obscure, dying, deserted by everyone, with Job's curse on his lips; Camus' "Stranger," aware of that slow wind blowing from the future that destroys all the false ideas of human brotherhood and solidarity that men put forward in the "unreal years" before death; Kafka's K., attaining a freedom greater than anyone has ever had—and equally meaningless; Sartre's Matthieu, unable to belong to any person or group because he cannot commit himself or cherish any value beyond his own freedom.[17]

One may surmise that the origin of today's fear of isolation is in our psychological roots. However, today it seems that our social environment, not just our psychological make-up, is generating fear in our lives. We live in a time that places us under pressure because we fear isolation through loss of job, difficulty in promotion, or simply social estrangement in an organization. Acceptance of the absurd as normal may be grounded in our perception of limited resources. If a communicator views the world as limited and not full of endless possibilities, then a struggle for those resources is more likely to commence. Unless one works alone, that struggle will have to take place within an organization with the standards for success being set by others, not ourselves.[18]

Again, there are many similarities between this decade and the earlier era of the 1950s. The "other-oriented" person and "the market-place personality" are returning to us in the guise of the new narcissism. The 1950s witnessed a group-think mentality that brought us Joseph McCarthy and the "Red scare." Matthew Rothschild has stated his belief that this need to belong now permits the Central Intelligence Agency to recruit from the "best" of our academic "think tanks." Rothschild contended that the chance to belong, to have a job, and to find a career propels people into choices they would have not even considered in an earlier decade.[19] It seems that only the totally successful and the unsuccessful are free of the race for success defined by organizational conformity.[20] The perception of limited resources has made the stakes high enough that some prefer to be absorbed by group expectations rather than to risk exclusion with an original proposal.

In higher education today, there is a significant trend toward making particular departments "marketable." I have seen faculty ignore their own principles and those of an institution in order to bend to the consumer interests of students. Job security has become such a high priority that some faculty members have adapted to values at odds with beliefs they held earlier in a time of abundance. Christopher Jencks stated the dilemma well. "If selfish individuals can set educational policy, schools will probably ignore moral issues. I will leave to you to draw your own conclusions about what is actually happening today."[21] Jencks' concern is that catering to the "market" cannot be the primary goal of educators. Such a goal is important, but must be relegated to secondary status behind the fundamental issue of educating people to live for others, as well as themselves. In Buber's terms, the education must call the student to the narrow-ridge concern for both self and other, not just market what is fashionable.

Let us examine two communicators who were able to identify and reject the absurdity of a situation, rather than adapt to it for their own survival. James was a faculty member in his mid-forties. He was considered an excellent teacher, perhaps one of the best. But he was repeatedly denied promotion because of a lack of publications. James felt a calling to be a teacher, read the current ideas in his field, and was conversant with them. But he did not believe that he had anything new to add to the literature through publication. After one of his promotion rejections, James became angry and despondent. He no longer felt appreciation from his colleagues. However, he did not reside in self-pity and resentment for too long. When asked to be a guest lecturer in a class, James used the opportunity to discuss how he had liberated himself from his own pain. His lecture consisted of reading an obituary about himself!

James wanted to illustrate the death of a man who lived by others' rules. James saw publications as essential for a university, but he felt it absurd to require all to contribute the same talents to a university. He did not reject the importance of publication; he rejected the mandate that all must conform to the same criteria for evaluation. In James' words, "This is not a death, but a birth. Today, I take the responsibility to find my own meaning for life and as a professional educator. No longer will I just look to others for statements about my significance." In short, James found meaning by no longer playing the game. He gave up the pursuit of the absurd by not following their rules and contented himself with his own integrity.[22]

The second example is somewhat different in that Rob was in his mid-fifties, had been a departmental chair, a dean, and a published full professor. Rob had "made it" and used his expertise and power to fight for younger faculty, argue for free speech, and call university operations absurd when others were too timid. Rob's older friends were often surprised at the younger faculty members Rob chose to affirm. Rob appreciated "young blood" that questioned the system. Unlike many of his older counterparts, Rob wanted to improve educational institutions, not just conform to standards that kept the status quo in power. Rob found the fear of new ideas absurd at a university, a place in which innovation is supposed to be welcomed and then critically examined.

As stated earlier, frequently only the most successful or those that drop out can violate the norms of an organization. But I would prefer to think that the motivation of the two people in the previous examples was more in keeping with their own integrity. Both were unwilling to call absurdity truth. Both believed that it was absurd to alienate themselves from what they felt they had to do just in order to belong.[23]

Meaning does not always come from refusing to conform, of course. However, conformity should be done with integrity and one should not comply when absurdity masquerades as normality. Through their communicative stances, both Rob and James wanted to invite a human community that affirmed integrity, encouraged identification of the absurd, and promoted constructive social criticism. Sam Keen commented about Carlos Castaneda and Don Juan that "things are seldom what they seem. In sharing the sources of his sorcery, Don Juan sought to develop in Carlos the ability to see the everyday world with wondering eyes. Don Juan knows the world of commonsense is a product of social reality."[24] In short, we can and we do as groups of people construct a social world through the community of conversation, and if we adapt to absurdity instead of challenging it, we reinforce relations that limit the possibilities of human community.[25]

Meaning: Propaganda or Social Reality?

When we begin to see meaning as a socially accepted reality, we become more cautious about dictating truth.[26] We cannot allow just one person or group (even if that person or group shares our vision) to dictate what all people should believe. Meaning should be discovered only after careful evaluation, not handed down unthinkingly from a group or person, as propaganda is.

Martin Buber warned of the problem of propaganda in modern

culture. Buber stated that the propagandist communicates control of the social reality so that there are no apparent alternative proposals.[27] We have all seen this type of person in action. The propagandized reality is discussed as knowledge that can be possessed and known—to disagree with a particular assumption is simply to be wrong. Take, for example, the message of Isaac Bashevis Singer's "Yentl, the Yeshiva Boy," from which the movie *Yentl* was made. Yentl was a woman with a love of learning, but in a time and culture where women were not permitted to study—particularly not the *Talmud*. Yentl proceeded through the learning process with determination, but disguised as a man! She had to deny her own gender to study. Such sexist propaganda is still with us, but in more subtle forms. Any time we are given a social reality and are not permitted to violate it, we should question the nature of the demand.[28] Jacques Ellul, in his classic work on propaganda, stated the issue as follows:

> The only true serious attitude—serious because the danger of man's destruction by propaganda . . . is to show people the extreme effective-ness of the weapon used against them, to rouse them to defend them-selves by making them aware of their frailty and their vulnerability, instead of soothing them with the worst illusion, that of a security that neither man's nature nor the techniques of propaganda permit him to possess. It is merely convenient to realize that the side of freedom and truth for man has not yet lost, but that it may well lose—and that in this game, propaganda is undoubtedly the most formidable power, acting in only one direction (toward the destruction of truth and freedom), no matter what the good intentions or the good will may be of those who manipulate it.[29]

Once a communicator questions the "given" social reality as com-municating potential propaganda, the inevitable question arises. Are not some things sacred? Are there not some absolute truths that we can pass on? The answer is, of course, that some traditions should be perpetuated. But people need to choose to affirm a tradition only after recognizing its faults and limits. The narrow ridge requires us to walk between pushing a particular construction of reality on people and leaving them with no foundation at all. Whatever tradition is communicated in community, it should be challenged, perhaps mod-ified, before being accepted. If truth is to be pursued, we must challenge and permit our own information to be tested or we run the risk of protecting ideas as antiquated as those of Yentl's historical contemporaries.

When people struggle to communicate a particular social reality in a time of pluralistic alternatives, the chances of human community dividing into camps is great. When a uniform description of the world is accepted, less polarized communication occurs. And when resources seem plentiful, there is often more tolerance of multiple perspectives. However, today we are left with multiple meanings in a time of limited resources. The result is a struggle for dominance of a social reality in order to ensure distribution to the benefit of oneself or one's own group.[30]

In recent communication theory, Barnett Pearce and associates have attempted to limit polarized exchanges in an era of multiple social realities by approaching communication through "the coordinated management of meaning." Pearce captured the communicative art in human community with the assertion that it is most important to coordinate diversity, not impose a single reality. "Anthropologists also report that some rituals work precisely because leaders and celebrants do not attach the same meanings to conjoint actions. We thus come to focus on coordination per se rather than upon one's specific means to it."[31]

Pearce spoke of a communicative casualty as someone who cannot deal with multiple meanings in our pluralistic modern society.[32] Although their theory is in the initial stages, Pearce and his colleagues pointed to the notion that multiple meanings require us to negotiate together, in order to ensure that all persons can find trust and affirmation within community. The rules that govern a community must reflect not only one person, but variable views within the community.

> It is our suspicion that modern America's emphasis on assigning . . .
> authority (self) to rules produces serious social problems. As individuals
> change via participation in multiple systems, it is most difficult to maintain stable relationships with others if rules for meaning and action are
> regarded as flowing from an inviolate self. Modern society requires that its
> members have the ability to trust in negotiated rules, or they are condemned to a string of very short run relationships.[33]

This conception of human community governed more by communicative negotiation of rules and standards than by ideology points to one way of limiting polarization in human community. Of course, there would need to be an effort to negotiate certain standards in order to find a common ground on which we could function together. We must seek a narrow ridge between expecting all to accept a social reality and permitting each to do his or her own thing. Pearce and his associates would have us accept the reality of multiple perspectives and seek to find some rules within those divergent belief systems that can pull us together. For instance, the Soviet Union and the United States must communicate rules for getting along in order to keep the world intact, but they certainly function from different "meaningful pictures" of the world.[34]

Individual Meaning in Community

Viktor Frankl, well known for his investigation into the meaning of life, recognized the necessity of acknowledging the existence of multiple meanings. His general criterion for a "legitimate" meaning is that the vision of one individual not make it impossible for another's vision to be actualized. Of course, such a general rule cannot always be followed, but it is similar to the notion of individual rights within a democracy. Specifically, Frankl suggested three ways in which one can find meaning. First, one can give something to the world in terms of talents. Second, one can take something from the world, such as pleasure and enjoyment. And third, a person can choose to assume a particular stance or attitude, even in the midst of an unchangeable circumstance.[35] In each case, Frankl has suggested a way out of absurdity in the midst of multiple social realities.

Take the case of Ruth as an example of finding meaning through giving. Her husband died after the children left home, and she found herself with too much empty time. She was easily tempted to spend the day looking at old family photos, rearranging the children's bedrooms, or crying over her situation. One morning, while Ruth was doing her routine of filling time, she looked out into the icy Minnesota snow and saw a half-frozen duck. For some reason, this creature had not flown south. She went out, carefully picked up the almost dead animal, and took it to her heated garage where she fed it and loved it back to health. It was not long before she had seven "winter" ducks to care for. The following winter days found Ruth spending more and more time with the ducks and less time reflecting on old memories.

In the early spring, Ruth freed the ducks at the Mississippi River. But she had also freed herself, as she cared for the ducks that long winter. During that time, something happened to Ruth; she once again felt needed and significant. Each Minnesota winter now finds her searching for "winter" ducks that insist upon staying in the northland. And after school each day, one might find a number of neighborhood children feeding ducks and listening to stories in a warm garage. This Minnesota lady of the ducks has found meaning in life from giving to others.

Frankl contended that it is possible to contribute to human community by finding meaning through taking. Examine, for instance, the illustration of a young pastor named Chris. Chris was a good pastor, according to his church members. He provided thoughtful Sunday messages, conducted efficient meetings, and worked well with the youth. He also took visitation seriously. Some would even say that Chris was the model of a giving servant.

Chris' ministry proceeded well, but over a period of time, his joy of serving diminished. Chris worked just as hard, but he no longer felt a great sense of fulfillment from his work. Finally, Chris developed a severe and persistent headache. In the local hospital, they ran test after test to find the cause. As each test recorded negative results, his mental and physical anguish continued.

When the hospital released Chris, a friend requested that he visit an old gentleman chiropractor known as the "country doctor." With apprehension Chris approached the old man, only to be told to take off his shirt and lie down. As the "doctor" engaged in a number of neck and back manipulations, he inquired about Chris' long work days. He then suggested that Chris take advantage of the summer days and ride his bicycle to each daily visit for the next two weeks.

After the first week of bike riding to the "country doctor's," the headaches stopped. Chris inquired about what had relieved his pain. The doctor simply told him that he had "burned himself out" by not doing anything for himself. He admonished Chris for being so arrogant that he felt he always had to give, rather than to take. As Frankl would agree, sometimes we must take in order to continue to have something to give.

The final option Frankl spoke of is through the stand we take toward the unchangeable. We have all met someone who provided us with a model of how to suffer defeat, even death. These individuals are able to rise to life's challenges. Such examples provide us with courage. But if life seems absurd and without meaning, how does one cope with life by taking a stand against the absurd? An attempt to answer such a question is embodied in Maurice Friedman's discussion of one of Camus' characters in *The Plague*, Dr. Rieux. "'If there is a God,' says Camus' atheist healer Dr. Rieux in *The Plague*, 'I should think as he sits above in silence, he would want us to fight the order of death.' If 'the plague' teaches that there is more to admire than despise in men, it is because of the courage to address and respond, not *in spite of* death and the absurd, but precisely *to* and including them."[36] Friedman interpreted Dr. Rieux as able to find meaning by facing the unchangeable and the inevitable. Meaning came from the stance or attitude taken in the midst of what he could not control.

In a time of multiple meanings for some, meaninglessness for others, and utter confusion for more than a few, there are no easy answers for our communication in human community. Maybe today, the hero of limited resources is left with not giving in to simple answers that embrace idols of certainty—or allowing the absurd to grasp the whole of life. We are left walking a narrow ridge through extremes that call us to discover meaning within human community by taking, giving, and, at times, just standing in the face of the absurd and saying, "I do what I do, because I can do no other." Gandhi similarly suggested, "If I stood before the prospect of finding meaning in a minority of one voice, I humbly believe that I would have the courage to remain in such a hopeless minority. This is for me the only truthful position!"[37] Perhaps life is only absurd when we deny the presence of absurdity and when we are overwhelmed by it. Absurdity must be recognized while it is fought through communication with others that is rooted in giving, taking, and assuming responsibility for a stand or attitude. In the final analysis, it seems that absurdity may win only when we fail to communicate in a human community that is concerned about a vision of the narrow-ridge dual focus of self and other.

9

POWER AND RESPONSIBILITY

MARTIN Buber on power and responsibility in a nuclear age:

> It is now high time for men to tell politicians: "We do not want mankind
> to embark upon annihilating itself. We do not want you to proceed with
> gambling, the stake of which is the life of the human race, and in which
> both partners must lose.
>
> "We have given you the power you hold because we believed you to be
> persons who under any circumstances know what they do. We see we
> have been mistaken. The frenzy of the game has deprived you of the
> capacity to know the true nature of the game you play and whither it may
> lead. You are familiar with all the tricks and perform them methodically,
> but you are not aware that under your hands the game has changed into
> another one."[1]

The above quotation reflects Buber's concern that politicians recognize the impact of their decisions on the nuclear issue. Today, as in
the immediate aftermath of Hiroshima[2] and Nagasaki, the nuclear
issue is still significant. However, as important as the nuclear concern is, I want to stress Buber's more subtle point that many leaders
may not fully understand how "the game has changed." In this time of
limited resources and increasing polarized communication, do our
leaders realize how much "the game has changed"? For instance,

what is the responsibility of leaders within a university when the credentials of assistant professors seeking tenure must exceed those of many older tenured full professors in the same department? What should be the response of leadership in some professions in which such vast numbers seek employment with too few openings? What should be the role of leaders when a worker moves to a new geographical area, but because of the high cost of housing and interest rates is not able to purchase a home comparable with that of his or her co-workers?

What is going to be the response of leadership to the growing use of second-class workers? Universities are hiring fixed-term faculty that cannot be granted tenure and can be easily released. Some airlines are claiming that the way to keep down expenses is to hire part-time people without a full benefit package. Some students in my managerial communication class have said, "This is only temporary. Soon we will use more of the Japanese management style of lifetime employment and this fear will cease." While we may be able to learn from the Japanese system, it is not the total answer to the problems within human community. The success of the Japanese approach is due partly to its use of a two-class system of protected and "non-protected" workers.

> The much-vaunted lifetime employment and guaranteed promotion plans apply to only about 35 percent of employees in large, successful [Japanese] firms. Lifetime employment lasts until age 55, when a worker is retired with a lump-sum payment of five or six years' salary but no pension. Since the environment of Japanese firms is not immune to uncertainty, a number of methods are used to smooth out the effects of seasonal or cyclical swings. A large force of temporary workers, mostly women, are employed by each major firm. They are laid off during slack periods and receive neither benefits nor job security. Many other Japanese workers are employed in satellite firms that exist solely to provide goods and services to a single industrial giant on a contract basis. The workers in these firms also have little job security.[3]

As stated above, some universities are now employing such a "class system," and the federal government has suggested paying new postal workers less than those who already have jobs. While the above issues will not destroy a planet in the same sense as the nuclear threat of which Buber spoke, the response of our leadership to such issues will either enhance our human community or push us farther into a new "cheap labor" program that generates a second-class worker in organizations. Leaders need to examine such social time bombs as closely as their potential threat warrants. In times of communicative crisis and polarized communication, leadership must utilize power in ways which address our unique problems and enhance human community.

A major concern about leadership most readily identified with the notion of human community is the reluctance to use power. Such a leadership philosophy carries with it a genuine and sincere conviction that people should be treated with a dignity that recognizes responsibility for themselves; an attempt to aid others "too much" is seen as an act of paternalism. Undeniably, there can be positive aspects to this "hands-off" approach to human growth. But it is an extreme position that is grounded in an individualistic world view, rather than one of interdependence. A communicator working with such a laid-back leadership style handicaps himself or herself by backing away from the use of power. As Joanna Macy suggested, when we fail to grasp the interconnectedness of persons on a planet shrinking in resources and space, we are left with a "psychic numbing" that encourages our powerlessness[4] and perpetuates the outdated myth of individualism.

The antiquated questioning of power of the 1960s is still verbalized by some in this decade. It is unfortunate that the attitude embodied in the once infamous gestalt prayer of Fritz Perls is still meaningful to some leaders wishing to invite human community. Perls' well-known prayer or poem emphasizes a "do your own thing" attitude with a desire to limit the power of others' expectations. Interestingly, many who are familiar with Perls' gestalt prayer have forgotten the last line that reads, "If not, it can't be helped."[5] This final element of the verse gives the impression that one should not go out of the way to make contact with another individual.

The now classic response to Perl's "Prayer" originated with Walter Tubbs. This verse is much more akin to Buber's philosophy of the interhuman than Perls' message.

If I just do my thing and you do yours,
We stand in danger of losing each other
And ourselves.

I am not in this world to live up to your expectations;
But I am in this world to confirm you
As a unique human being.
And to be confirmed by you.

We are fully ourselves only in relation to each other;
The I detached from a Thou
Disintegrates.

I do not find you by chance;
I find you by an active life
Of reaching out.

Rather than passively letting things happen to me,
I can act intentionally to make them happen.

I must begin with myself, true;
But I must not end with myself:
The truth begins with two.[6]

At one time, I believed that the attitude represented by Perls was a necessary antithetical response in a societal dialectic, in that too much control of others required an opposing action. Individuals such as Tubbs and Philip Slater have critiqued the "hands-off" philosophy as a form of control. While refusing to exercise power, those in control are granted even more power in their continuing operations.

> Individualism . . . is a narcotic, and when its virtues are touted by those in power, it's a useful divide-and-conquer technique. For example, it gives the individual the "freedom" to stand alone as a powerless and inevitably naive consumer against massive organizations like ITT, the federal government, General Motors, and so on. Cooperation, organization, and coordination are necessary for human survival, and individualism is a romantic denial of this—a denial that leads to still larger and more impersonal organization. In the end, it's the huge bureaucracies that derive the benefits of individualism. Their life is made easier when they can say, "Go do your own thing; we'll mind the store."[7]

To do justice to those affirming the notion of taking responsibility only for oneself, it must be said that a "hands-off" approach was not meant as a selfish venture by most proponents. Such a philosophy was adopted for a much different reason—limiting abuses of power of one person over another. In retrospect, those who accepted this "powerless" stance made two mistakes. The first was to believe that power should always be avoided. And the second was to believe that life together can ever be lived without power.

Power by itself is neither good nor bad; rather, it is natural and inevitable—just as communication and conflict are unavoidable within a human community. A communicator working from a narrow-ridge concern for self and other recognizes power as natural and practical. Unlike some who have tried to compensate for too much control in our society by rejecting the use of power, Buber called for the embracing of extremes, while not being totally claimed by either option. Buber's orientation suggests taking some, but not total responsibility for another. A narrow-ridge response requires walking a tightrope between the extremes of martyrdom and individualism. Even a self-serving understanding of negotiating, as revealed in the following quotation, affirms a position on power and relationships that is behaviorally in concert with a narrow-ridge philosophy, although the motivation is questionable.

> You should always bear in mind that even if you never negotiate with the same opponent again, you may be negotiating with that opponent's close friend or business associate or acquaintance. If you annihilate your opponent, you can be sure that the chances are very good that your opponent will not speak highly of you if the opponent learns that you are negotiating with the opponent's friend, business associate, or acquaintance. In such an event, your road to negotiating success with any of these other individuals can only be more difficult. Contrast that to a situation in which your opponent has departed the negotiation feeling good about the outcome and even, perhaps, feeling like a winner. His report to his friend can only serve to help you . . . increase your negotiation power.[8]

Buber was concerned that the power to manipulate and use another increases with a decrease in the power to enter into relation.[9]

Buber wanted power to invite mutual relation out of a "living center"—a common purpose or agenda for the community. His concentration on power required doing what was needed to assist the growth of the community. Feelings are secondary, although important, in this living relation. Dialogically, for Buber, feelings for each other often grow out of relation together, but feelings are not enough to keep a community together.[10] In short, a common task carried out in the narrow-ridge spirit of concern for self and other must empower the group. Buber affirmed power associated with the carrying out of a central task or center as more fundamental than the feeling the members of a community have about each other. However, a task or center cannot be imposed on a community. A central focus must be invited, organically take root, and then guide a community. Buber did not believe each group or organization would become a community; it is the common center that empowers a group into community life.

In summary, the use of power can be quite compatible with a narrow-ridge orientation. However, if as inviters of human community we are to use power, we need to understand the various types and forms of it that are available to us. Some uses of power are congruent with Buber's narrow-ridge approach, while others are not. A good introduction to power possibilities is contained in Rollo May's now classic *Power and Innocence*. In a study of May's material, approaches that are or are not consistent with a narrow-ridge orientation become more apparent.

Power Combinations

The phrase "power combination" implies that power does not emerge in a vacuum. It also involves another person or another object, event, skill, organizational power, and so forth. Power, by its very nature, involves more than oneself. "Power is the ability to cause or prevent change. . . . Ancient Greek philosophers defined power as being—that is to say, there is no being without power. And since power is the ability to change, Heraclitus held that being is in continual flux. This definition has come down the mainstream and tributaries of philosophy through the ages to contemporary ontological thinkers like Paul Tillich, who describes power similarly as 'the power of being.'"[11] An ontological view of power equates the notion with being and cannot envision life without it. Power in the ontological sense is a social phenomenon between persons and events that is unavoidable and inevitable. The question, then, is no longer "Do you have power and how do others influence you with their power?" It is "Will you admit having power and attempt to understand its influence?" Learning to work with power as an ontological or fundamental activity of being shifts the focus from accumulation of power to management of power between persons.

If power is ontological, central to being, and unavoidable, we must contend with it. Or we simply abdicate our responsibility to those who are not only aware of the inevitability of power, but who may seek it for a questionable reason, such as psychological gratification. Rollo May referred to this as "exploitive power," in that violence or the threat of violence is used to keep another in place.[12] There may be times when such power must be used to protect persons, but at other times it is used to oppress the weaker foe just to satisfy a psychological desire for domination.

"Manipulative power" is another misuse of power. One may maneuver another person into assisting one's own goals without the other catching on.[13] Granted, manipulation may be needed when one has little power in a relationship. For centuries, slaves manipulated masters with conversations of double meanings. The slave had to please the master, while manipulating the master to treat him or her well.[14] The problem changes, however, when the person in power uses such a method. Brockriede referred to the person in power who seeks to manipulate as the seducer.[15] For instance, let us suppose Henry is a new young manager. He has been working in the company for three months when his immediate superior shares the following information with him privately during coffee break: "It is good to have you on staff, Henry. You are doing such fine work for us. I really believe you will move up quickly through our organization. Maybe I should not say anything, but I like you so much I must offer some important information off the record. I notice you and Tom have been having quite a few lunches together. Tom will be on his way out of our organization within a few weeks. I would not associate with him." However, what Henry has not been told is that an official decision has not yet been made to actually release Tom. Tom is in conflict with this immediate supervisor who is offering the off-the-record account and who wants to make a case that Tom does not relate well with his employees. At this point, the supervisor is trying to make Henry fit the pattern so that his chief rival (Tom) will be marginalized out of power. The supervisor's conversational style with Henry reflects the seduction of the manipulator that all of us have seen at one time or another.

Rollo May discussed the problem of "competitive power," when one person's success is another person's loss. He felt such a view of power could be both destructive and beneficial.[16] I, too, believe that there is a constructive competition and a destructive form of competition I refer to as "agreed-upon" deceit. Normally, what we call competition I would label agreed-upon deceit.

A number of years ago, I was a ninth-grade football coach. We had an excellent team that year, which prompted the sports writer for the school newspaper to interview me about the "competition" in our league the week before the city championship. I stated we had no constructive competition in our league, only agreed-upon deceit. If we really believed in constructive competition, I would not try to take advantage of the other team's weaknesses. Instead, if I perceived a weak place in the other team's defense, I would inform their coach when we were going to run in that direction. Such forewarning would then permit our strength to encounter theirs and both teams could improve. But, unfortunately, what we do is to take advantage of the weaker person, team, group, or organization without helping either improve. Agreed-upon deceit may help us win a game, but can simultaneously cause us to deteriorate as a team. If we cannot help the weaker opponent challenge us, then the lack of what I call "constructive competition" may reinforce poorly executed skills. In short, agreed-upon deceit can result in no improvement for either team. But if we can work with others on their weaknesses and let them make adjustments, then perhaps we can become stronger as we encounter a stronger opponent.

May also spoke of "nutrient power,"[17] with which one person assists another in ways which help growth. In its ideal form, this is the role of the teacher or the parent. There is still another form of power that fits the goal of the narrow ridge very closely: integrative power.[18] The use of integrative power involves working with another in order to get the task completed in a role akin to constructive competition, a role May called "the critic." The role of a critic walking the narrow ridge is to press his or her position, while still caring for the listener. It is a task that combines "Power and Love," the title of the following poem by Martin Buber.

1

Our hope is too new and too old—
I do not know what would remain to us
Were love not transfigured power
And power not straying love.

2

Do not protest: "Let love alone rule!"
Can you prove it true?
But resolve: Every morning
I shall concern myself anew about the boundary
Between the love-deed-Yes and the power-deed-No
And pressing forward honor reality.

3

We cannot avoid
Using power,
Cannot escape the compulsion
To afflict the world,
So let us, cautious in diction
And mighty in contradiction,
Love powerfully.[19]

This integration of power and love is fundamental to the constructive critic, who recognizes that ideas offered for discussion must be challenged in order for the strength of an idea to be tested. In my terms, integrative power relies on constructive competition, not agreed-upon deceit.

As John Stuart Mill, in his *Essay on Liberty*, says: "If opponents of all important truths do not exist, it is indispensable to imagine them and supply them with the strongest arguments which the most skillful devil's advocate can conjure up." . . . Our narcissism is forever crying out against the wounds of those who would criticize us or point out our weak spots. We forget that the critic can be doing us a considerable favor. Certainly, criticisms are often painful, and one has to embrace one's self in the face of them. [But criticism is necessary for growth.][20]

For those in leadership positions, whether official or unofficial, power is inevitable. All forms of power may at times be needed for human community to prosper. But it is the power role of the critic that seems so central to the blending of the narrow ridge and the ontological reality of power in a productive fashion.

Critic as Leader

A leader who does not want to use power limits his or her role as critic. When this view was most in vogue, nonjudgment was a major orientation in communication studies. Human communication studies attempted to differentiate between judgment of the person and judgment of behavior. In the practical enactment of this approach, however, some found it difficult to judge another's behavior without violating the person. Because of the difficulty of separating person and action, some assumed the stance of ethical relativism, which resulted in a tendency to criticize only those who were inclined to criticize others.

These decliners of judgmental leadership were not "protesters without a cause." They wanted to usher in a new human community by modeling a nonjudgmental communication style. While it was a noble effort, it was also doomed to fail because of the ontological nature of power and judgment. It is possible to withhold judgment, but impossible not to engage in it, unless one believes in absolute objectivity.

Judgment is an ontological or inevitable stance. Judgment is based on perspective, and a number of scholars contend that aperspectivity is not attainable. What is present here is a clash of world views: one purporting detachment and objectivity, and the other being the natural result of judgment. The ability to rise above the ongoing moment of life that is necessary for objectivity is also required for nonjudgment. To critique the "objectivity" position is simultaneously to critique the perspective of "nonjudgment."

An important work that reinforced the critique of the "illusion of objectivity" and implicitly that of nonjudgment was Floyd W. Matson's *Broken Image: Man, Science, and Society*. Matson documented the evolution of the notion of objectivity and showed how it no longer can be accepted in light of the "new" discoveries, that is, Einstein's theory of relativity and Heisenberg's principle of uncertainty. Heisenberg made the notion of objectivity virtually meaningless with his conclusion that it is a "fact that we cannot observe the course of nature without disturbing it."[21]

Deetz asserted that the very act of choosing a methodology is a subjective act. "The critique of the so-called 'objective' sciences is not aimed at their presumed objectivity but their inability/lack of desire to examine their own subjectivity carried in their methods and concepts and to be aware of the social/political consequences of their peculiar subjective stance."[22] Proponents of the work of Gadamer and European philosophy within the existential-phenomenological tradition affirm that the mere choice of what to study and how to investigate it is a subjective act.[23] Even if one believes in scientific objectivity, the question remains whether such standards can be applied to issues of value, rather than fact. The scope of this book has fallen within the value question, as we ask how to invite dialogue in community. As Miller and Nicholson suggested, *"there exists no universally accepted set of procedures for resolving moral disputes. Such circumstances are not found in scientific inquiry."*[24]

Existential-phenomenological literature describing the human's inability to escape influencing what is observed generally uses Martin Heidegger's notion of "being-in-the world." This phrase implies that we cannot stand above history and record something; our being there and our looking make a difference. The human, then, is not an ahistorical figure, but is enveloped by and in the midst of history in the making at every moment.

> [The human's historicity] is the . . . fundamental structure of his "being-in-the-world." This structure shows most lucidly that "world" is not the sum total of objectively given entities existing in and by themselves but rather the situational locus in which man finds himself embedded at any given time. . . . [A person's] action is thus not a free projecting of possibilities but is conditioned and therefore limited by tradition, that is, by the remote origins of the individual and historical human situation.[25]

Accepting the critique of objectivity when applied to the notion of nonjudgment has two major consequences. First, we need to admit that our perspective is limited and does influence our judgments. Second, we need to reaffirm the importance of dialectic in the pursuit of truth in community life. A communicator who accepts the impossibility of nonjudgment and works as a critic out of a narrow-ridge sensitivity acknowledges his or her perspective without seeing it as the absolute truth. Buber recognized the constant lurking of limits in our perspectives. If a person came to Buber for counseling, he did not try to act as if he were not an authority figure. He allowed himself to be viewed as a leader in a situation in which his counsel and judgment were sought out.[26] For Buber, every exchange had limits placed on it; he recognized that perspective was impossible to avoid. "A very important point in my thinking is the problem of limits. Meaning, I do something, I try something, I will something, and I give all my thoughts in existence into this doing. And then I come at a certain moment to a wall, to a boundary, to a limit that I *cannot* ignore. This is true, also, for what interests me more than anything: human effective dialogue. . . . [E]ven in dialogue, full dialogue, there is a limit set."[27]

Buber was willing to test his own limits. He was willing to allow his perspective to be examined and challenged. He was willing to persuade another, but only as he was simultaneously willing to be persuaded. A Buberian commitment to the narrow ridge exposes beliefs and attitudes. Each brings a unique position. In dialogue, each individual must be willing to let the other's stance challenge his or her own, to test ideas, while still affirming the personhood of the challenger. Perhaps one of the biggest misconceptions of Buber's work is that he did not seek to persuade or to fight for ideas.[28] Buber tried very hard not to limit the pursuit of truth. He wanted the critic to affirm the person, but he also invited an open and active exchange that permitted the challenging of ideas.

Thus, the leader in a critical role must be willing to change as well as to be changed. Leadership may require taking some unpopular stands that critique the work of others. And conversely, leaders must listen to the critiques of their own policies and actions openly enough that they might be changed as well. Buber's goal was "as far as possible, to change something in the *other*, but also let *me* be changed by *him*. . . . I felt I have not the right to want to change another if I am not open to be changed by him as far as it is legitimate."[29]

Leadership within Community

When one is open to others in Buber's narrow-ridge fashion, it may indeed be difficult to be a prophet in one's own country. When we encounter our leaders frequently, we begin to discount their power because of the inevitable visibility of their flaws. Thus, a leader who encourages human community may be walking on thin ice. By inviting a sense of community that allows others to get to know him or her, the leader may be placing himself or herself out of the role of leader. Others may no longer be able to offer respect when flaws become visible. Yet Buber saw this as a necessary risk for a leader to take.

Buber set high leadership standards, which is consistent with his emphasis on the education of the "great character." Not all have the ability to be called to leadership and still be open to persons. Because of Buber's high standards, he has been called an elitist. If by elitist it is meant that Buber did not see all as having the same gifts and talents, the criticism is accurate. If by elitist it is meant that the person of leadership should be able to uphold the values of the community, the label is correct. If by elitist critics meant that not all persons are willing to commit themselves to living a narrow-ridge concern for one another, they are correct again. However, if the term is understood to mean that someone is unresponsive to everyday issues and insensitive to the common person's plight, Buber was not elitist. Buber sought a "person of character" that can be found in all realms of life—a person who stands above the crowd, not to glorify himself or herself, but because concern for the community makes that person unique.

While in high school, I worked at a power plant in order to finance eventual college tuition payments. The man who maintained leadership in this setting for the greatest number of years was not only competent and a good worker, he was able to listen to his fellow workers and respond openly to their comments. Unlike many others, he could even be convinced to change his mind. But when he felt that he was correct, he fought for the right to state his case. Over the course of his forty years of employment at this power plant, he had been granted and denied responsibility many times by various administrations. However, this man's unique capacity of being open to both friendly and negative comments allowed him repeatedly to re-enter leadership positions. But whether in or out of favor with the management, this man remained the "great character" of the power plant workers.

Another person of "great character," Todd, was a former orderly at a local hospital. Todd took full advantage of his good benefit package and "retired" at the age of fifty-six. But Todd was far from inactive as he worked days and many nights on his beautiful large yard, garden, car, older house, and friends' and neighbors' projects. Todd always seemed to have time to bolster neighbors' spirits by encouraging their work projects and assisting when needed. Todd also spent much of his summer with his children and grandchildren, who came regularly to visit. He spent much time teaching and helping the youngsters with various crafts and skills. He also listened to others' ideas and encouraged people to risk undertaking a project, no matter what it was, and then made himself available when tough problems were encountered. This man believed in people using their time constructively, and he wanted to help the young people learn satisfaction from work.

Todd only had a high-school education, but he was the respected teacher of the family and neighborhood. When a person who knew him well was once asked why so many young people flocked around Todd, the answer was: "Todd believes in good honest work. He believes in young people. He believes in supporting, but not smothering. And the kids recognize that Todd is not just concerned about their projects, he is concerned about them." The "great character" need not hold an office in order to lead; sometimes being a neighborhood leader can contribute as much, if not more, to the quality of our human community.

Todd would never have had such a positive effect on young people, if he had forced himself upon them. He recognized that such relationships had to come slowly with time. Similarly, Buber did not tell a person he was out to build his or her character. If he had done so, a strong character in the group may have rebelled against imposed community and dropped out.[30] Another pitfall, according to Buber, is talking too much about "making a community." Thus, as a conflict consultant for churches, I frequently advise leaders to try and invite community, but not to constantly talk about it. One of the best potential contributors to community may be the person who rebels against the forcing of community.

Buber's "great character" must be willing to tolerate conflict and to work through it with the person. To turn one's back on a challenge is to stifle community. One university administrator practiced an authoritarian management style. He held as his eleventh commandment, "Thou Shalt Not Rock the Boat." While the man was a good administrator, he was not as good as he might have been. Perhaps if he could have entered into conflict with other quality thinkers instead of demanding loyalty, he could have been much more. But according to Buber's standards, this administrator did not respond as a great character. He was not willing to test status quo positions or affirm opponents, if such questioners and rule violators could be discouraged.

> The great character can be conceived neither as a system of maxims nor as a system of habits. It is peculiar to him to act from the whole of his substance. That is, it is peculiar to him to react in accordance with the uniqueness of every situation which challenges him as an active person. . . . All this does not mean that the great character is beyond the acceptance of norms. No responsible person remains a stranger to norms. But the command inherent in a genuine norm never becomes a maxim and the fulfillment of it never a habit.[31]

The administrator in the above example loved the manageability of rules and regulations. But this man was not the leader Buber would have sought. Buber's "great character" knows the rules, but has the courage to violate them when necessary and recognizes that others must sometimes violate the rules as well.

Buber also recognized that the "great character" is too often viewed as the "enemy of the people." The great character, like the person at the power plant, may lose an official position for stating what he or she believes. Those that follow the power structure frequently want no association with leaders who hold no official position. At one company, a well-liked woman was being reviewed to see if her contract would be renewed; a group of four managers were to make this decision. The four managers were contacted by four other lower-level managers who claimed that the person under review was not competent. Each one of the four lower managers was then given the chance to testify regarding this person's incompetence at an open public review meeting. Only one was willing to do so; the other three were afraid of negative repercussions initiated by the "boss" of this division for testifying against someone he personally liked.

When the sole person of character made her public statement, the other three acted as if they knew nothing of the accusations. They did not talk to or make any contact with the new "problem person" of the company. This person of "great character," willing to publicly proclaim her view of truth, was considered an "enemy of the people." She eventually left her job because of the "coldness" of others toward her. This person was willing to place the long-range good of a human community at a higher level than her own success. The words of Martin Buber point to the struggle of her situation. Today the great characters are still 'enemies of the people,' they who love their society, yet wish not only to preserve it but to raise it to a higher level. To-morrow they will be the architects of a new unity of mankind."[32]

Clearly, then, the demands of leadership for the "great character" are more than many of us can withstand. Not all are cut out for leadership in a dialogical community. Buber pointed to the following characteristics of a dialogical leader. First, a leader needs to come to terms with the ontological nature of power and judgment. Second, the leader must be willing to use power and judgment in persuading others in accordance with a vision. Third, such a leader recognizes that his or her own vision is limited and is therefore open to being persuaded to change perspective. And fourth, such a leader must embrace a long-range perspective that extends beyond immediate recognition by one's fellows and calls the community to a higher level, while simultaneously being open to having that vision tested by counter perspectives.

Buber's view of leadership and power provides us with a challenge. The leader must be open to persuade and to be persuaded. One must hold to the traditions of a community, but violate those beliefs, if necessary. Indeed, this is the key to Buber's concept of the narrow ridge. One can not embrace an absolute without being willing to hold it open for discussion and debate. Perhaps Buber's view of leadership is congruent with the work of individuals like Richard Weaver, who rejected relativism and called for ethics to emerge from a belief system, a set of enduring social values.[33] That enduring set of values is at the heart of any community and cannot be ignored. But neither should those values become so carved in stone that violation is not possible. For Buber's "great character," taking the risk of violating the norm is not only necessary, but is the very standard by which the person of "great character" must be measured.

The life of Dietrich Bonhoeffer provides a portrait of the type of leader Buber would affirm. Bonhoeffer loved community and is sometimes referred to as a theologian of community. Bonhoeffer wrote perhaps one of the purest books on pacifism ever written, *Cost of Discipleship*.[34] But he later participated in an assassination attempt on Adolph Hitler. Bonhoeffer knew the standards of pacifism, but he still violated them.[35] Just as a military officer may not be able to follow every order, the "great character" may have to judge behavior, stand against it, and at times even violate norms held to be sacred and true. In short, the leadership style described by Buber was not meant for all. Indeed, he would have agreed with Truman's famous statement, "If you can't stand the heat, stay out of the kitchen."[36] The "great character" not only can stand the heat, but recognizes it as necessary in the testing of ideas and of our leaders.

10

THE COMMUNITY OF DIALOGUE

MARTIN Buber on dialogue in community:

> Man has always had his experiences as I, his experiences with others, and with himself; but it is as We, ever again as We, that he has constructed and developed a world out of his experiences. . . . Man has always thought his thoughts as I, and as I he has transplanted his ideas into the firmament of the spirit, but as We he has ever raised them into being itself, in just that mode of existence that I call "the between" or "betweenness." . . . It is to this that the seventh Platonic epistle points when it hints at the existence of a teaching which attains to effective reality not otherwise than in manifold togetherness and living with one another, as a light is kindled from leaping fire. Leaping fire is indeed the right image for the dynamic between persons in We.[1]

The implications of Martin Buber's dialogue for communication and human community can be summarized in the central theme of Buber's work—some form of community needs to be nourished in groups and organizations for life to be ultimately worth living. *I* is the beginning of dialogue in community, but it is not sufficient. The *We* of communicative exchange must emerge for Buber's version of human community to be invited. This *We* embraces the *I* and the *Thou*, the me and the you, the person and the event with each being accessible to the other.

The interdependent thrust of Buber's philosophical anthropology makes the notion of the narrow ridge central to communication and community for two reasons. First, Buber's narrow ridge speaks to the community concern of affirming self and other, tradition and change, which has been emphasized throughout this book. Second, the notion of the narrow ridge embraces the importance of contradictions; life is frequently not an either/or, but a simultaneous yes and no. For instance, I recently went to my son's PTA meeting, where I witnessed an animated discussion on whether or not we should give our children contradictory messages. My son is in kindergarten and, like his classmates in this suburban school, has brought home literature on not trusting strangers, that is, not talking to unknown people, not accepting rides from individuals he does not know, and running from any adult that might try to inappropriately touch him. Some of the parents at the PTA meeting, including myself, were worried about how they could teach the necessary suspicion and still have their children develop good attitudes about people in general.

If Martin Buber were asked to provide an answer to this complex problem, I believe he would suggest that we teach both suspicion and good will toward others. Children need to be "streetwise" and they need to love people. Both messages must be communicated. One without the other leaves the child naive or cynical. Martin Buber pointed to the complexity of living the contradictions inherent in a narrow-ridge philosophy, as he borrowed from the Eastern philosophy of Tao.

> . . . the teaching of Tao, the Way, which is itself unconditional unity, yet bears, encompasses, and rhythmically regulates the alternation of the opposites and opposing processes, their correspondences and contradictions, their battles and their couplings. . . . [A]ll . . . are only appearances and acts of the two primal essences yin and yang. . . . [Buber went on to quote a story from Lao Tze.] "If the whole world were insane except for you," he says to the complaining father of a mentally ill son, "then it would be you who would be the insane one."[2]

The narrow-ridge embracing of contradictions and opposites implies a picture of a dialogic community that is neither for the dictator, nor for one who wants easy answers. Buber did not offer us a technique or formula,[3] but rather pointed the way to dialogue in community. Bearing in mind Buber's acceptance of contradiction and complexity, let us examine his conception of the essential *We* of community.

Essential We

Martin Buber's notion of the essential *We* affirmed both the individual and the community.

> What corresponds to the essential *Thou* on the level of self-being, in relation to a host of men, I call the essential *We*.
>
> The person who is the object of my mere solitude is not a *Thou* but a *He* or a *She*. The nameless, faceless crowd in which I am entangled is not a *We* but the "one." But as there is a *Thou* so there is a *We*. . . .
>
> By *We* I mean a community of several independent persons, who have reached a self and self-responsibility, the community resting on the basis of this self and self-responsibility, and being made possible by them. The special character of the *We* is shown in the essential relation existing, or arising temporarily, between its members; that is, in the holding sway within the *We* of an ontic directness which is the decisive presupposition of the *I–Thou* relation. The *We* includes the *Thou* potentially. Only men who are capable of truly saying *Thou* to one another can truly say *We* with one another.[4]

Buber went on to describe some groups in which the essential *We* was present. He spoke of the person that can labor with others and slowly awaken among them a sense of trust, belonging, and purpose.[5] Buber described a style of communication that seeks change in perception, not by forcing people to comply, but by offering new insights that can be accepted after the establishment of trust. This form of *We* in groups does not emerge over night. Perhaps this is why some religious leaders are counseled to use the first two years at a "new" location just to get to know the people, before implementing any changes.

Paulo Freire, in *Pedagogy of the Oppressed*, used a method that is similar to Buber's call for a slow and deliberate inviting of the essential *We*. The forcing of community is consistent with what Freire called the "banking concept." Information is stuffed into a person's head and he or she is then expected to remember it on command. Freire claimed that many communities suffer from a "let-me-tell-you" sickness. He did not reject the notion of authority, but stated that authority had to be delegated by the people, not just imposed on them. An authority figure can only invite a feeling of *We* when he or she gains trust and is given the go-ahead to lead.[6]

Buber also spoke of how the sacrifices of some people can invite the *We* of community. Buber believed sacrifice is, at times, needed for the health of a cause or community. Of course, any time we open the door to such a statement there may be rebellion against what seems to be a martyr position. Buber clearly did not advocate sacrifice for the sake of martyrdom. For Buber, sacrifice was a response to the call of the moment that could not be answered in a less demanding fashion. Buber might have agreed with Christopher Lasch, who lamented the contemporary tendency to omit sacrifice and commitment to a higher loyalty in the common definition of love.[7]

Both Buber and Lasch pointed to a love that is not limited to happiness. Feeling good is indeed significant, but it cannot be the fundamental ground of community. Commitment to values higher than one's own narcissism seems crucial to the invitation of human community. Glenn Tinder made this point in *Community: Reflection on a Tragic Ideal*. He offered the notion of civility as an alternative to our perception of happiness in community. Tinder directed us toward tolerance of plurality and diversity.[8] Civility and tolerance require one's own needs, at times, to go unfulfilled. Assistance of another in the community is an act of love that is not solely centered on one's own self, but seeks to aid the wider community.

In order to see this type of commitment in more vivid terms, let us investigate the following example. Three young scholars were applying for a faculty position in Peace Studies at a major university. The first candidate, Sue, very much wanted the position, but as she heard more about the job she felt that one of the other candidates would assist the program more. The second candidate, Tom, had majored in Peace Studies, but did not really feel a commitment to the subject matter. He worked hard for the position in order to support his family with a good income. The final possible faculty member, Hank, had much relevant experience in Peace Studies, as well as recent academic training.

The screening committee narrowed the list to these three persons and then implemented a very unorthodox procedure. They asked the three final applicants to decide among themselves which one they thought would be the "best" person for the position. The candidates tried to agree on criteria for making the decision. Both Sue and Hank felt that the candidate should be the one who could "best" bring information and commitment to Peace Studies for the students at the university. Tom, on the other hand, felt the job should be awarded on the basis of financial need on the part of the applicant. After all, were not all three qualified enough to make it to the final cut? Finally, Tom called for a vote. The results were one vote for Tom and two for Hank. The department examined the vote and selected Sue for the position. Sue was academically not as qualified as Hank, but she seemed to be a good judge of the ability of others, as well as herself, and she appeared determined to work for the best interests of the students. She was willing to sacrifice for the betterment of the larger group. This characteristic got her the job. The departmental hiring committee saw her ability to look beyond herself as central to the development and nurturing of human community. The department members at the university believed that the credentials of the three candidates were fairly well matched and the additional characteristic Sue brought was a role model of a scholar so committed to the pursuit of truth that she would vote against herself in order to promote the "best" for a community.

Although the selection procedure described above was quite unusual, I am intrigued by the courage to make a decision on more than just academic qualifications. Our human community, it seems, can benefit from leaders who actively take the risk to lead our youth, not just protect their own individual futures. Perhaps a student of Sue's will one day state something similar to what I shared about one of my former professors, Paul Keller. When I was asked to provide a comparison of Paul's work to that of Martin Buber, I concluded my remarks with the following: "Our world desperately needs more great characters like Paul Keller to carry us into the next century and hopefully beyond."[9] Great characters are willing to sacrifice, work, and struggle for a human community that includes them, but does not revolve around them.

In Search of Principles

Buber believed in nurturing the bondedness of people in community through voluntary association and trust and a vision capable of accepting the need to sacrifice for a larger community. Buber called for communication that stretched the person, group, or organization to locate options not readily apparent. He practiced this approach in his reconciliation work between the Jews and Arabs. Buber favored a union between Jews and Arabs that permitted autonomy and a concern for the other side's constructive destiny.

> The basis on which a federative union can be established is, by necessity, so that for each of the two partners the full national autonomy is preserved; neither one should be allowed to injure in any point the national existence of the other.
>
> In order that so immense a work, and unprecedented work in fact, may succeed, it is indeed necessary that spiritual representatives of the two people enter into a true dialogue with one another, a dialogue based on shared sincerity and mutual recognition alike. . . . These spiritual representatives must be independent in the full sense of this word; they must be individuals whom no consideration of any kind hinders from serving the right cause without reservation. If here and now a dialogue between such persons will come about, its significance will spread far beyond the boundaries of the Near East; it may show whether in the late hour of history the spirit of humankind can influence our destiny.[10]

Buber's call for representatives that can serve the "right" cause without reservation reflects a need for principle to bind the essential *We*, regardless of what others may think. Similarly, Gandhi called people out of their prideful stances into a willingness to struggle for goals higher than their own individual concerns. Gandhi went into conflict situations with the goal of discovering truth, not simply fighting for a predetermined outcome. The principle that Gandhi adhered to was the need to allow the resolution of a conflict to emerge in conversations between opponents. He did not seek a priori resolutions to conflict that would have called into question the requirement of openly listening to the opposition.[11]

It is interesting to note that Buber and Gandhi did correspond with one another. They eventually parted ways on the question of whether nonviolence could be used by the Jewish people against the Nazis. Buber did not believe that this was possible. He did not envision nonviolence as a technique appropriate for all situations. Buber contended that the situation in Germany, unlike India's struggle against the British, did not permit a nonviolent strategy. The two men also disagreed on the Jews settling in Palestine with Arabs already occupying the land. [12]

Although Buber did not fully agree with Gandhi, he did attempt to take Gandhi's concerns seriously and not predetermine his response without genuinely attending to Gandhi's challenge.

> I have been very slow in writing this letter to you, Mahatma. I made repeated pauses—sometimes days elapsing between short paragraphs— in order to test my knowledge and my way of thinking. Day and night I took myself to task, searching whether I had not in any one point over- stepped the measure of self-preservation allotted and even prescribed by God to a human community, and whether I had not fallen into the grievous error of collective egotism. Friends and my own conscience have helped to keep me straight whenever danger threatened. [13]

The importance of the above exchange, for our purposes, is not who was "right," but that Buber responded out of a search for principle or truth, not simply a justification of his own position. Gandhi's use of "principle" and "truth" parallels Buber's discussion of the notion of the "between." [14] Buber referred to the "between" as an "ontological reality." He visualized the realm of the "between" as potentially available to all people, but not always visible. The "between can be invited, but not forced.

To be able to conceptualize Buber's notion of the "between" as an "ontological reality," we must give up the notion that we alone can possess or own a communicative exchange. Answers emerge in the relationship, not from one party or the other. For instance, if two people are struggling for the best way to stop a labor strike and one person convinces the other of a particular position after much argu- ment, no one person is the victor. Without the opponent, the selected idea could not have been tested and eventually confirmed. The answer was given birth in the dialogue between the contestants.

Buber did not view the "between" or what he also referred to as the "interhuman" as a psychological phenomenon. He did not want to stress a possessive view of information or "truth." Clearly, not all psychologies center truth around the individual—many have an interactive theme. Thus, it was not psychology in general that Buber rejected. It was a tendency to center information around and/or in the person.

It is basically erroneous to try to understand the interhuman phenomena as psychological. When two men converse together, the psychological is certainly an important part of the situation, as each listens and each prepares to speak. Yet this is only the hidden accompaniment to the conversation itself, the phonetic event fraught with meaning, whose meaning is to be found neither in one of the two partners nor in both together, but in their dialogue itself, in the "between" which they live together.[15]

Gandhi provided a concrete example of the "between" in decision making.[16] But as one invites a principle or "truth" to emerge "between" persons, it is often difficult to know whether one is choosing an option that actually emerged "between" persons or simply responding to one's internal perception or a priori truth held before encountering the other. Discussion of Buber's notion of the "interhuman" or the "between" and of "the courage to address and the courage to respond" were major topics for Maurice Friedman in his partially autobiographical work on dialogue, *Touchstones of Reality*. Friedman spoke of the limits of the psyche as a touchstone of reality and stressed the danger of mistaking truth for the psyche, or what goes on inside oneself.[17]

The dialogic community that Buber and Friedman called us to is not a place where people have no will or personal uniqueness, but it is a home where the isolated person is not sufficient. We need to be called out into contact, into dialogue, into meeting with others and events. Buber lamented that the modern person is frequently unwilling to be called into responsibility—to have a "truth" emerge "between" him or her and another being. There is little dialogue or possibility of finding "truth" when one's mind is made up before the interaction.[18] In concert with his interactional and nonpossessive view of truth, Buber emphasized that dialogical leadership discovers "truth" not inside one's individual being or in an absolute command, but "between" partners in dialogue.

> Whatever the way, man enters into the dialogue again and again; imperfect entry, but one that is not refused. . . . All that happens is here experienced as dialogue; what befalls man is taken as a sign; what man tries to do and what miscarries is taken as an attempt and a failure to answer, as a stammering attempt to respond as well as one can. . . . [T]hey

make real that which has been laid upon them from outside of themselves, make it real with the free will of their own being, in the autonomy of their person. [19]

In bringing together Buber's and Gandhi's material, one must answer how the notion of the "between" can assist in the struggle for principle in everyday living. How can we be sure that we are following the emergent answer "between" us and not just our own individual concern? And what allows us to know what is and what is not the "best" action at a particular point in time? Buber's answer is that we must open ourselves to dialogue with those that seek to challenge and discipline us. Such openness is a safeguard against acts of individual pride cloaked as a struggle for principle "between" persons.

To place a quality finding or solution above our own success permits the life and vitality of the essential *We* of community to be nurtured, as we affirm the right of our opponents to challenge our positions. Buber called for the proletariat and the bourgeoisie to attempt to comprehend the other side's position and to listen with openness. [20] In everyday communicative life within a community, this affirming of opponents means the encouraging of courage. It is no small challenge to be able to withstand criticism from another whose position is at odds with one's own.

While speaking at a college on some of the implications of Martin Buber's work, I was asked the following question: "What could help communication majors live the life of dialogue of which Buber spoke?" While there are many possible answers to this question, one of the most significant to me is the toughening of one's skin. I sometimes feel that communication majors do not have enough courage to listen openly to what they do not like to hear. We frequently teach our communication students how to be caring and empathic communicators without giving them the tools to deal with a rude or brusque returning style. Although Buber wanted people in community to be sensitive about how they spoke to others, it is fruitless to dwell on how impersonally others may speak in return. Dialogue is invited not only by openness, but by the courageous person who persists when others would have fled! [21]

Even as one openly encounters another individual, dialogical courage may require making decisions without the approval or sanction of others. David Riesman called a person with this courage "inner-directed." While Riesman's "inner" terminology does not sufficiently emphasize the notion of dialogue between tradition and personal uniqueness that is the hallmark of Buber's writing, Riesman's work is of relevance here. In his 1950 edition of *The Lonely Crowd,* he discusses the difference between living in *abundance* and living in *scarcity.* Riesman's arguments are on target, but his yesterday is once again our contemporary moment—his abundance is now our scarcity.

> The hard enduringness and enterprise of the inner-directed types are somewhat less necessary under these conditions [Again, what Reisman called "new" conditions in 1950 would be those of abundance. The thesis of this book is that today's "new" conditions are those of perceived scarcity.] Increasingly, *other people* are the problem, not the material environment. . . . Furthermore, the "scarcity psychology" of many inner-directed people, which was socially adaptive during the period of heavy capital accumulation that accompanied transitional growth of population, needs to give way to an "abundance psychology" capable of "wasteful" luxury consumption of leisure and of the surplus product.[22]

The person who can function the best in a scarcity environment is the "inner-directed" person, according to Riesman. Since 1950, several generations have been brought up in abundance rather than scarcity. The implication is that we today ("other-directed" people) are as ill prepared to deal with our current environment as Riesman's "inner-directed" person was prepared to cope with abundance three decades ago. We have now reversed course. If we substitute the word scarcity for abundance, then Riesman is still on target. We are still ill-prepared to deal with the contemporary moment.

The "inner-directed" vocabulary, however, is not sufficient because it can too easily result in the "do-your-own-thing" movement or the hard-core "self-made" person taking care of his or her own. The "other-directed" person is too easily convinced to conform and follow. Neither of these is ideal for a dialogical community. But it seems that we do need the courage of the "inner-directed" person to assist the communities in which we live, rather than just take from them. Maurice Friedman spoke of the courage necessary for the person concerned about human community and possessing a value system at odds with what might be in vogue at the moment.

When I came to teach at Sarah Lawrence College in 1951, I was dismayed
by the utter lack of social concern on the part of the students even when
their own boyfriends were risking their lives in the Korean War. By 1958
this situation had decisively changed with the Civil Rights Movement, the
Northern Student Movement, SNCC, and the beginnings of the "freedom rides" in the South. . . . *But the joy of finding unknown comrades
walking beside one must also include the courage to walk alone again if it
should prove necessary.*[23]

Individuals inviting dialogue may have to once again walk alone.
The notion of community is not the primary concern of many today.
The current question seems to be how one can gain a "competitive
edge" or how one's status can be augmented. *Newsweek* devoted
feature coverage to the 1980s competitive set, the yuppies, young,
urban professionals. These individuals, in stereotyped form, are
considered the young status seekers, aggressive trend setters, and
affluent spenders. According to Rosabeth Moss Kanter, professor of
management at Yale, yuppies are known "not so much by their
willingness to work hard for the corporation, but their devotion to
accumulating power and getting rich."[24] However, this upwardly
mobile group must also be aware of the increasing competition for
limited resources. As interesting as the yuppies may be to the media,
the question is whether such a group will respond to the needs of an
increasingly interdependent society and world. If so, this group will
need to go beyond thinking centered on "me," "my idea," "our
kind," or "our group."

On the Edge of the Abyss

As one of my thoughtful colleagues suggested, we are at the edge of
the abyss with the chance to learn and adapt. If we fail, we may go the
way of the great dinosaurs of the past. Webster's definition of abyss
states the following: "1. the bottomless gulf, pit, or chaos of the old
cosmogonies; 2.a. an immeasurably deep gulf or great space, b.
intellectual or spiritual profundity; also vast moral depravity."[25] In
terms of human community, it seems that many of us are looking
down into that great abyss without asking how we can narrow or close
it. Instead, we ask how we can keep that bottomless pit from en-

gulfing "me" and "my hopes" for a better and brighter future. Once again, Christopher Lasch's theme is pertinent—we are leaving the social values of the past and replacing them with the self-concerned desire just to survive.[26]

Arthur Dyck, in his book *On Human Care*, provocatively quoted Russian dissident and exile Aleksandr Solzhenitsyn. Solzhenitsyn maintained that Western democracies can avert decline from within by distinguishing "clearly between good and evil."[27] Dyck further stated that our culture needs to continue to pursue such a goal, not by justifying what we want to do, but by a willingness to permit our ideas to be critiqued at any moment, in hopes of making the correct decision. Dyck's point is that our actions should evolve from thoughtful positions, not just comfortable and unexamined ideologies.[28]

One of the major social critics of this century, H. Richard Niebuhr, has called us to be responsible people by accepting a teleological or future-oriented vision that may admittedly change with the circumstances, but that is needed to move us forward.[29] Such a vision is similar to my emphasis on a philosophical system that can guide our actions. The problem today, however, is that we seem reluctant or unable to look beyond our own survival. "The poor have always had to live for the present, but now a desperate concern for personal survival, sometimes disguised as hedonism, engulfs the middle class as well."[30]

A recent summary article on interpersonal communication has stated that dialogue is increasingly viewed as less important than more pragmatic approaches to communication.[31] The emphasis on social exchange theory (at least some interpretations of this approach) in the communication discipline presently seems to be more popular than dialogue. This current perspective is recorded in the following statement:

> The assumption that a motivating force in interpersonal communication is self-interest is consistent with the Social Exchange Theories. . . .
>
> While this author is not going to defend the argument that people involved in interpersonal relationships are necessarily engaged in mutual exploitation, we will examine a set of theories that argue that the guiding force of interpersonal relationships is the advancement of both parties' self-interests.[32]

Such pragmatism of self-interest strikes at the heart of the community Martin Buber envisioned that embraced the dialogical tension of self, other, and community principles. The question is: What can stir people to embrace the struggle for community and not just survival?

The marketing person that Erich Fromm found so detrimental to human community is being offered once again as a communicative model. The "marketing" communicator is making use of an age-old method—bartering. Exchange value, rather than helpfulness or service to the whole community, becomes the criterion for decision-making. Instead of selling material goods, the marketing communicator is trained to sell himself or herself. Fromm stated that we have moved from the productive individual who stated, "I am what I do," to the marketing orientation of "I am as you desire me." This marketing communicator has placed appearance on a more fundamental stage than actual performance.[33] It is interesting to note how applicable Fromm's "marketing orientation" (1947), like Riesman's work (1950), is today.

We are on the edge of an abyss that threatens to engulf, not to embrace the narrow ridge. When asked to speak to a group of ministers about peace education, I admitted that in daily communication there is something that frightens me almost as much as nuclear war—the interpersonal violence we are experiencing in a time of perceived limited resources. Fromm witnessed similar problems decades ago. It seems that the communicative health of living in community is still in question.

Why Community?

If enthusiasm for communication strategies seems to be at odds with dialogue and the essential *We* of community, a fundamental question must be asked. Should one devote time to what seems an unpopular and risky venture? This question can only be answered by each person in his or her own unique situation, but it is clear that if one answers affirmatively, the struggle against the mood of our culture will not be an easy one.

Ernest Bormann's discussion of fantasy themes in groups and organizations sheds light on this topic. Bormann theorized that people tend to live in accordance with the narrations of myths and stories that surround their daily living.[34] We can change the context in which we interpret our own lives by changing the myths and stories that guide us. Such change is not easy, but these processes are slowly occurring. Our fantasy themes are now including women and minorities in executive positions, business, and major political offices. As the narration changes to make such events more within the vision of young people, we begin to live a new narration. Narration in community does not only mirror events; it opens the possibilities for events to actually take place.

The use of narration in this work embraces a socially constructed view of reality.[35] Because of this narrative ability, Walter Fisher called the human by a new metaphor: *homonarrans*.[36] In the midst of crisis or a change from abundance to perceived limited resources, there is a clash of narrations. Fisher stated that the clashing of narratives engenders the hope for a consolidating narrative.

> From the perspective of the narrative paradigm, the dynamic of this situation is that rival stories are being told. Any story, any form of rhetorical communication, not only says something about the world, it also implies an audience, persons who conceive of themselves in very specific ways. If a story denies a person's self-conception, it does not matter what it says about the world. In the instance of protest, the rival factions' stories deny each other in respect to self-conceptions and the world. The only way to bridge this gap, if it can be bridged through discourse, is by telling stories that do not negate the self-conceptions people hold of themselves.[37]

In light of Fisher's suggestion to find a narrative that bridges multiple self-perceptions, it is clear that narrative about community cannot rest on just one philosophical system or moral ground. For some, a narrative claiming to benefit "me" or "my kind" by being concerned about both self and other will gather attention. In some settings, a narrative about a dialogic community cannot be voiced in a rhetoric of moral passion; rather, a pragmatic plea for the adoption of a long-term perspective is more persuasive. Perhaps in such instances, a "fantasy theme" or narration embracing a "new" pragmatism, a pragmatism in the school of William James, who called people to an individualism sympathetic to community, may be needed.[38] Perhaps this "new" pragmatism will embrace Kafka's person of faith, who when asked, "Why carry on?" simply replied, "I cannot do otherwise."[39] The abyss is frightening enough that our narration about human community can be grounded in pragmatic language. We need not speak of human community only in terms of moral and ethical issues. We face the struggle for quality human association and, by the predictions of many, for life itself.

It is interesting that William James and B. F. Skinner both taught at Harvard, but wrote about "community" in much different ways.[40] James might be called the champion of individual will, while Skinner, in *Walden Two*, imposed a utopian community. The writings of James seem to offer more hope for human community from a dialogical perspective than the work of Skinner. Skinner's perspective reflects a more desperate tone, a belief that the human being alone without coercion, without reward or punishment, cannot find a way to unfold the possibilities of community.

What the pragmatic James might call for today would not be a dictated totalitarian sense of community or an insensitive individualism. Perhaps he would call us much closer to Buber's understanding of community—where the community is invited, not forced. It seems that we are left with the ethical or moral choice of imposing community in hopes of saving the world or inviting community with the full realization that if we fail, a second chance may not be available. Even though inviting community through narration may not assure its development, forcing community will destroy the opportunity for dialogue to guide the group or organization. Dialogically, maybe a pragmatic narrative voicing concern for others in order to assure our own survival is a better alternative than forced community that destroys the bonds of communicative freedom between persons in groups and in organizational life.

Martin Buber reached this same conclusion after the Communist experiments of Lenin and Marx. Lenin did not permit the necessary voluntary association to permit community to happen. Marx was at least ambiguous on the notion of voluntary association in producer and consumer collectives. Lenin made them mandatory. When this group association was made mandatory, the original contribution of community building was destroyed.[41] Community cannot be forced by decree. Lenin also moved to a very centralized view of the state government as collective. Both of these moves by Lenin were at odds with Buber's approach to community.[42] Buber believed that community had to happen initially in small groups and organizations. It cannot be imposed on a whole group or country. Community cannot be forced, nor expected to emerge without a common purpose for which people can gather.

> Community should not be made into a principle; it, too, should always satisfy a situation rather than an abstraction. The realization of community, like the realization of any idea, cannot occur once and for all time; always it must be the moment's answer to the moment's question, and nothing more. . . . The real essence of community is to be found in the fact—manifest or otherwise—that it has a centre. The real beginning of a community is when its members have a common relation to the centre overriding all other relations: the circle is described by the radii, not by the points along its circumference. . . .[A] community need not be "founded." Wherever historical destiny had brought a group of men together in a common fold, there was room for the growth of a genuine community.[43]

If we are left with voluntary commitment to community and recognition of the importance of a center out of which community can emerge, then narration or communication must carry the essence of our center. For a community to survive, it must have a story. That story must be one that individuals can relate to, feel a part of, and affirm. It is a communicative vision of where we are going and why that keeps a community vibrant and healthy. Time is needed for people to tell their stories and to retell them. If we become too efficient in time use, we may close the door to a sense of community within our group and our organization.

There is no one center that can claim the attention of every group, but a dialogic center does need to include a sensitivity to both self and other. A corporation that assumes a center of profit without a social concern is not a place for the narrow ridge or a dialogic community. A family in which the parents always center on the wishes of the children is not the home of the narrow ridge either. The narrow ridge requires a balancing of concern for self and other in proportionate amounts for what is needed by the situation, with recognition that at times some need more assistance than others. In short, our collective center may not emerge from a common religious or philosophical base; it may come from a base-line concern that we want to see our accomplishments passed on to the next generation.

Our groups and organizations need dialogue, perhaps even more in a time in which community is suspect and competition is translated as taking advantage of another's weakness. While the task is great, dialogically we can at least invite participation in a narrow-ridge narration that envisions groups, organizations, and a world for all, not just "my" kind. Dialogically, our task may not be to implement what Buber pointed us toward, but rather to make sure that such a story or vision is kept alive, in order to keep the conversation going with those who might envision a much different picture of tomorrow! If we can keep the conversation going within groups and organizations and permit narratives and visions of a "better" world to be offered for critique and review, future generations may inherit a world in which the struggle for community is still worth the risk.

NOTES
BIBLIOGRAPHY
INDEX

NOTES

Introduction

1. See for example, Charles T. Brown and Paul W. Keller, *Monologue to Dialogue: An Exploration of Interpersonal Communication* (Englewood Cliffs, NJ: Prentice Hall, 1973); Frank E. X. Dance, "Communication and Ecumenism," *Journal of Communication* 19 (1969): 14–21; Richard L. Johannesen, "The Emerging Concept of Communication as Dialogue," *Quarterly Journal of Speech* 57 (1971): 373–81; Floyd Matson and Ashley Montagu, eds., *The Human Dialogue: Perspectives on Communication* (New York: The Free Press, 1967); John Poulakos, "The Components of Dialogue," *Western Journal of Speech Communication* 38 (1974): 199–212; John Stewart, *Bridges Not Walls: A Book About Interpersonal Communication* (Reading, MA: Addison-Wesley, 1973); and Stewart, "Foundations of Dialogic Communication," *Quarterly Journal of Speech* 64 (1978): 183–201; Ronald C. Arnett, "Toward a Phenomenological Dialogue," *Western Journal of Speech Communication* 45 (1981): 201–12; Rob Anderson, "Phenomenological Dialogue: Humanistic Psychology and Pseudo Walls: A Response and Extension," *Western Journal of Speech Communication* 46 (Fall 1982): 344–57; Ronald C. Arnett, "Rogers and Buber: Similarities, Yet Fundamental Differences," *Western Journal of Speech Communication* 46 (Fall 1982): 358–72; and Ronald C. Arnett and Gordon Nakagawa, "The Assumptive Roots of Empathic Listening: A Critique," *Communication Education* 32 (Fall 1983): 368–78.

2. The perspective of dialogue used here is that of Buber and Maurice Friedman, a primary American interpreter of Buber's work. The reader can consult the bibliography to find additional supporting material used in the interpretation of Buber's work.

177

3. Martin Buber, *Paths in Utopia* (Boston: Beacon Press, 1958), pp. 80–95.

4. Buber, *Paths in Utopia*, pp. 7–8.

5. Edward M. Kennedy, "A Tribute to Senator Robert F. Kennedy," *Representative American Speeches: 1967–1968*, ed. Lester Thonssen (New York: H. W. Wilson, 1968), p. 178.

6. Christopher Lasch, *The Culture of Narcissism: American Life in an Age of Diminishing Expectations* (New York: W. W. Norton, 1979), p. 100.

7. For a discussion on the notion of image as a guiding point for human perceptions, see Maurice Friedman, *The Hidden Human Image* (New York: Dell Publishing, 1974).

8. Karlyn Keene, "American Values: Change and Stability—A Conversation with Daniel Yankelovich," *Public Opinion* (December/January 1984): 3.

9. Abraham Maslow, *Motivation and Personality*, 2nd ed. (New York: Harper & Row, 1970); and William Schutz, *The Interpersonal Underworld* (Palo Alto, CA: Science and Behavior Books, 1966).

10. Lasch, p. 19.

11. The term "social Darwinism" was given its original impetus by sociologist Herbert Spencer, who tied the social and biological findings together. An introductory critique of this approach is found in Ashley Montagu, *On Being Human* (New York: Hawthorn Books, 1966), pp. 19–26.

12. Carl R. Rogers, *A Way of Being* (Boston: Houghton Mifflin, 1980), pp. 301–6.

13. "U.S. Catholic Bishops' Pastoral Letter on Catholic Social Teaching and the U.S. Economy," *Catholic Herald*, November 22, 1984, 1A–35A.

14. Ellen Goodman, "Haves, Have-Nots Now Coldly Judged as Winners, Losers," *Los Angeles Times*, November 13, 1984, part 2.

15. Keene, pp. 2–3.

16. Unfortunately, after a number of years of retelling this story, I can no longer locate its original source.

17. A number of people have examined the need for advocacy in science. One of the more intriguing studies consisted of interviews with forty respected scientists. See Ian Mitroff, "The Myth of Objectivity or Why Science Needs a New Psychology of Science," *Management Science* 18 (1972): B613–B618.

18. See for example, B. Aubrey Fisher, *Perspectives on Human Communication* (New York: Macmillan, 1978), p. 7.

19. Martin Buber, *Between Man and Man* (New York: Macmillan, 1972), pp. 19–20.

20. Maurice Friedman, *The Confirmation of Otherness: In Family, Community, and Society* (New York: Pilgrim Press, 1983), pp. 249–60; and *Hidden Human Image*, pp. 358–71.

21. Ephraim Fischoff, "Introduction," *Paths to Utopia*, p. xi.

22. Hans-Georg Gadamer, *Truth and Method* (New York: Seabury Press, 1975), pp. 357–58.

1. The Communicative Crisis

1. Martin Buber, "Hope for This Hour," in *The Human Dialogue: Perspectives on Communication*, ed. Floyd W. Matson and Ashley Montagu (New York: The Free Press, 1967), p. 307.

2. Maurice Friedman, *The Hidden Human Image* (New York: Dell Publishing, 1974), pp. 358–74.

3. Martin Buber, *The Knowledge of Man: A Philosophy of the Interhuman* (New York: Harper & Row, 1965), pp. 72–88.

4. Ronald C. Arnett, *Dwell in Peace: Applying Nonviolence to Everyday Relationships* (Elgin, IL: Brethren Press, 1980).

5. Rollo May, *Power and Innocence: A Search for the Sources of Violence* (New York: Dell Publishing, 1976), p. 220.

6. Paul Watzlawick, Janet Beavin, and Don Jackson, *Pragmatics of Human Communication: A Study of Interactional Patterns, Pathologies, and Paradoxes* (New York: W. W. Norton, 1967), pp. 68–69.

7. Gregory Bateson, *Steps to an Ecology of Mind* (New York: Ballantine Books, 1974), pp. 61–71.

8. Gerald I. Nierenberg, "The Art of Negotiating," in *Peacemaking: A Guide to Conflict Resolution for Individuals, Groups and Nations*, ed. Barbara Stanford (New York: Bantam Books, 1974), p. 41.

9. See May's *Power and Innocence*, which is based on this theme. See also Martin Buber, *A Believing Humanism: Gleanings* (New York: Simon and Schuster, 1969), p. 45; Martin Luther King, Jr., "Let Us Be Dissatisfied! *Gandhi Marg* 12, no. 3 (July 1968): 222; and Theodore Roszak, "Gandhi and Churchill: A Dialogue on Power," in *Peacemaking*, p. 404.

10. In my previous work, the dual possibilities of power as either destructive or constructive are detailed in chapter format. See Arnett, *Dwell in Peace*, pp. 77–78.

11. Buber, *The Knowledge of Man*, p. 77.

12. Charles R. Berger and William Douglas, "Thought and Talk: Excuse Me, But Have I Been Talking to Myself?" *Human Communication Theory: Comparative Essays*, ed. Frank E. X. Dance (New York: Harper & Row, 1982), pp. 53–55.

13. Martin Buber, *Between Man and Man* (New York: Macmillan, 1972), p. 105.

14. Anatol Rapoport, "Strategy and Conscience," in *The Human Dialogue*, pp. 92–93.

15. The theme of contemporary society failing to ask questions concerning the possible unethical ramifications of technologically feasible actions is a major point in James W. Douglass, *The Non-Violent Cross: A Theology of Revolution and Peace* (New York: Macmillan, 1973); and Eric Fromm, *The Revolution of Hope: Toward a Humanized Technology* (New York: Bantam Books, 1971).

16. Rapoport, pp. 94–95.

17. Lois Ramiro Beltran, "Research Ideologies in Conflict," *Journal of Communication* 25 (1975): 187–93.

18. See, for example, Hans-Georg Gadamer, *Truth and Method*, ed. and trans. Garrett Barden and John Cumming (New York: Seabury Press, 1975), pp. 356–58; Ludwig Landgrebe, *Major Problems in Contemporary European Philosophy*, trans. Kurt F. Reinhardt (New York: Frederick Ungar, 1977), pp. 117–18; and Richard Palmer, *Hermeneutics: Interpretation Theory in Schleiermacher, Dilthey, Heidegger, and Gadamer* (Evanston, IL: Northwestern Univ. Press, 1969), pp. 144–48.

19. Werner Heisenberg, *Physics and Philosophy* (New York: Harper & Row, 1958); Floyd W. Matson, *The Broken Image* (Garden City, NY: Anchor Books, 1964); Michael Polanyi, *Personal Knowledge: Towards a Post-Critical Philosophy* (New York: Harper Torchbooks, 1964); and Polanyi, *The Tacit Dimension* (New York: Doubleday, 1967).

20. See, for example, two special issues of the *Western Journal of Speech Communication*, Winter 1977 and Winter 1978; Ronald C. Arnett, "Communication as Dialogical Interpretation," *Speech Association of Minnesota Journal* 7 (1980): 14–20; Barry Brummett, "Some Implications of 'Process' of 'Intersubjectivity': Postmodern Rhetoric," *Philosophy and Rhetoric* 9 (1976): 21–51; and Kenneth R. Williams, "Reflections on a Human Science of Communication," *The Journal of Communication* 23 (1973): 239–50.

21. Martin Buber spoke of the illusion of objectivity in a variety of his works. It is most poignantly described in his discourse on education in *Between Man and Man*, pp. 83–117.

22. Rapoport, p. 95.

23. Rapoport, p. 95.

24. Strategic thinking is a form of monologue in Buber's terms. The productive characteristics of this form of human interaction will be discussed later in the text. This chapter has detailed the negative features of monologue; however, upon occasion, such interaction may be demanded by the situation.

25. Philip Slater, *Earthwalk* (New York: Anchor Press, 1974), p. 113.

26. Christopher Lasch, *The Culture of Narcissism: American Life in an Age of Diminishing Expectations* (New York: W. W. Norton, 1979), p. 91.

27. See, for example, the many best sellers that suggest looking out for oneself and provide a quick "how-to" win or profit package for the reader. The titles may change, but the "me-ism" strategy continues to be reflected.

28. Lasch, p. 100.

29. Buber, *Between Man and Man*, p. 16.

30. Buber, "Hope for this Hour," *Human Dialogue*, pp. 220–21.

2. The Narrow Ridge

1. Martin Buber, *The Way of Response* (New York: Schocken Books, 1966), p. 55.

2. Erik Erikson, *Gandhi's Truth: On the Origin of Militant Nonviolence*

(New York: W. W. Norton, 1969); and Gene Sharp, *Gandhi as a Political Strategist, with Essays on Ethics and Politics* (Boston: Porter Sargent Publishers, 1979).

3. Buber, *The Way of Response*, p. 110.

4. Milton Rokeach, *The Open and Closed Mind* (New York: Basic Books, 1960), p. 60.

5. Rokeach, p. 392.

6. Roger Fisher, *International Conflict for Beginners* (New York: Harper & Row, 1970), pp. 29–31.

7. Lewis Coser, *The Functions of Social Conflict* (New York: The Free Press, 1956), pp. 87–88.

8. Roger Fisher was interviewed by Dan Rather on the CBS News' Special Report, "Shiite Moslem Hijackers of TWA Flight 847," June 18, 1985.

9. Meg Greenfield, "After the Ayatollah," *Newsweek*, December 17, 1979, 116.

10. Mark Hickson III, "Saul Alinsky: American Marxian Strategist?" in *Marxian Perspectives on Human Communication*, ed. Mark Hickson III and Fred Jandt (Rochester, NY: PSI Publishers, 1976), p. 28.

11. Ian I. Mitroff, *Creating a Dialectical Social Science: Concepts, Methods, and Models* (London: D. Reidel Publishing, 1981).

12. Dag Hammerskjold, *Markings* (New York: Alfred A. Knopf, 1977), p. 151.

13. Joyce Hocker Frost and William W. Wilmot, *Interpersonal Conflict* (Dubuque, IA: W. C. Brown, 1978), p. 28.

14. Gregory Bateson, *Steps to an Ecology of Mind* (New York: Ballantine Books, 1974), p. 70.

15. William Lederer and Don Jackson, *Mirages of Marriage* (New York: W. W. Norton, 1968), pp. 161–73.

16. Maurice Friedman, *Martin Buber: The Life of Dialogue* (Chicago: Univ. of Chicago Press, 1976), p. 3.

17. Aubrey Hodes, *Martin Buber, An Intimate Portrait* (New York: Viking Press, 1971), p. 57.

18. Martin Buber, *I and Thou* (New York: Charles Scribner's Sons, 1958), p. 18.

19. Buber, *I and Thou*, pp. 22–23.

20. For another interesting perspective on I–Thou in community, the work of Dietrich Bonhoeffer is of interest. See, for example, Dietrich Bonhoeffer, *The Communion of Saints* (New York: Harper & Row, 1963), pp. 22–37.

21. Such a distinction is implied in all the works of Viktor Frankl. See, for example, *The Will to Meaning* (New York: Plume Books, 1969); and *The Unheard Cry for Meaning* (New York: Simon and Schuster, 1978).

22. The following "Fiddler" discussion is adapted from a speech given by Paul Keller to Manchester College Alumni, North Manchester, Indiana, May 19, 1979.

23. Richard Johannesen, *Ethics in Human Communication*, 2nd ed. (Prospect Heights, IL: Waveland Press, 1983), p. 49.

24. Martin Buber, *Pointing the Way: Collected Essays* (New York: Harper & Row, 1957), p. 57.

25. Buber, *Pointing the Way*, p. 323.

26. Hodes, p. 111.

27. Hodes, pp. 112–15.

28. Maurice Friedman, *The Confirmation of Otherness in Family, Community, and Society* (New York: The Pilgrim Press, 1983), pp. 123–24, cited an interview with Boszormenyi-Nagi recorded in Richard D. Stanton, "Dialogue in Psychotherapy: Martin Buber, Maurice Friedman, and Therapists of Dialogue," (Ph.D. diss., Union Graduate School/West, 1978), p. 181.

29. Friedman, *The Confirmation of Otherness*, p. 124.

30. For an examination of the practical use of contradictions, see Ian Mitroff, Richard O. Mason, and Vincent P. Barabba, "Policy As Argument—A Logic For Ill-Structured Decision Problems," *Management Science* 28, no. 12 (1982): 1391–1403.

31. Buber, *I and Thou*, p. 81.

32. Martin Buber, *Israel and the World: Essays in a Time of Crisis* (New York: Schocken Books, 1948), p. 17.

3. Existential Mistrust: The Failure to Listen

1. Martin Buber, *The Knowledge of Man: A Philosophy of the Interhuman* (New York: Harper & Row, 1965), pp. 87–88.

2. See, for example, Howard Kirschenbaum, *On Becoming Carl Rogers* (New York: Dell Publishing, 1979). Kirschenbaum's biography of Rogers reveals the validity of this statement. Rogers' emphasis has been attitude, not technique, but many poor imitators of Rogers have emphasized technique, including Dr. Charles Truax (a developer of the empathic listening scales), whom Rogers confronted on more than one occasion.

3. Calvin Hall and Gardner Lindzey, *Theories of Personality* (New York: John Wiley and Sons, 1970), pp. 278–81.

4. Martin Buber, "Hope for This Hour," in *The Human Dialogue: Perspectives on Communication*, ed. Floyd W. Matson and Ashley Montagu (New York: The Free Press, 1967), p. 308.

5. Viktor Frankl, *The Unheard Cry for Meaning: Psychotherapy and Existentialism* (New York: Simon and Schuster, 1978), p. 14.

6. Frankl, *The Unheard Cry for Meaning*, p. 57.

7. Josef Bleicher, *Contemporary Hermeneutics: Hermeneutics as Method, Philosophy, and Critique* (London: Routledge & Kegan Paul, 1980), p. 1.

8. Martin Buber was a former student of Wilhelm Dilthey. Buber considered Dilthey the founder of the history of philosophical anthropology. See for example, *Between Man and Man* (New York: Macmillan, 1972), p. 126.

9. Ronald C. Arnett, "Rogers and Buber: Similarities, Yet Fundamental Differences," *Western Journal of Speech Communication* 46 (Fall 1982): 371–72.

10. Bleicher, p. 3.

11. Paulo Freire, *Pedagogy of the Oppressed* (New York: Seabury Press, 1974), p. 31.

12. Ronald C. Arnett and Gordon Nakagawa, "The Assumptive Roots of Empathic Listening: A Critique," *Communication Education* 32 (1983): 368–78.

13. Carl R. Rogers has expressed concern about how some of his concepts, such as empathy, have been misused. See Rogers' biography *On Becoming Carl Rogers*, pp. 278–90.

14. Abraham Maslow, *The Farther Reaches of Human Nature* (New York: The Viking Press, 1973), pp. 67–69.

15. Maurice Friedman did a similar critique in *The Hidden Human Image* (New York: Dell Publishing, 1974), pp. 274–85.

16. Aubrey Fisher made this point in *Perspectives on Human Communication* (New York: Macmillan, 1978), pp. 95–96.

17. Dean Barnlund, "Toward a Meaning-Centered Philosophy of Communication," *Journal of Communication* 12 (1962): 197–211.

18. William Pemberton, "The Transactionist Assumption," in *Bridges Not Walls*, ed. John Stewart (Reading, MA: Addison-Wesley Publishing, 1973), pp. 30–32.

19. Ronald C. Arnett, "Nonviolent Peacemaking: A Look at Assumptions," *Journal of Peace and Change* (Winter, 1979–1980): 7–10.

20. Friedman, *Hidden Human Image*, p. 280.

21. Friedman, *Hidden Human Image*, p. 283.

22. Sidney Jourard, *The Transparent Self* (New York: Van Nostrand Reinhold, 1971), p. 6.

23. Martin Buber, *A Believing Humanism: Gleanings* (New York: Simon and Schuster, 1969), p. 152.

24. Ronald C. Arnett, *Dwell in Peace: Applying Nonviolence to Everyday Relationships* (Elgin, IL: Brethren Press, 1980), p. 136.

25. For further accounts, see for example, "The Bizarre Tragedy in Guyana," *US News and World Report*, December 4, 1978, 25–29; Dole Paul Johnson, "Dilemmas of Charismatic Leadership: The Case of the People's Temple," *Sociological Analysis* 40 (1979): 315–23; and "Nightmare in Jonestown," *Time*, December 4, 1978, 16–21.

26. Buber, *A Believing Humanism*, pp. 148–49.

27. Charles T. Brown and Paul W. Keller, *Monologue to Dialogue: An Exploration of Interpersonal Communication* (Englewood Cliffs, NJ: Prentice-Hall, 1973), p. 20.

28. Carl R. Rogers, *The Freedom to Learn* (Columbus, OH: Charles E. Merrill, 1969), pp. 255–56.

29. David Riesman, *The Lonely Crowd* (New Haven, CT: Yale Univ. Press, 1950), pp. 19–22.

30. Martin Buber, *The Knowledge of Man*, ed. Maurice Friedman (New York: Harper & Row, 1965), p. 76.

31. Buber, *A Believing Humanism*, p. 151.

4. Monologue: Centering on Self

1. Martin Buber, *Between Man and Man* (New York: Macmillan, 1972), p. 168.

2. Buber, *Between Man and Man*, pp. 19–21.

3. Martin Buber, *I and Thou* (New York: Charles Scribner's Sons, 1958), pp. 24–25.

4. Maurice Friedman, *Martin Buber: The Life of Dialogue* (Chicago: Univ. of Chicago Press, 1976), pp. 123–24.

5. Sigmund Freud, *Civilization and Its Discontents* (New York: W. W. Norton, 1962), p. 92.

6. Maurice Friedman, *The Hidden Human Image* (New York: Dell Publishing, 1974), p. 38.

7. Howard Kirschenbaum, *On Becoming Carl Rogers* (New York: Dell Publishing, 1979), p. 138.

8. Kirschenbaum, pp. 202–3.

9. Carl R. Rogers, "The Interpersonal Relationship: The Core of Guidance," in *Bridges Not Walls: A Book about Interpersonal Communication*, ed. John Stewart, 2nd ed. (Reading, MA: Addison-Wesley Publishing, 1977), p. 247.

10. Carl R. Rogers, *A Way of Being* (Boston: Houghton Mifflin, 1980), p. 45.

11. Morton Deutsch, "Conflicts: Productive and Constructive," *Journal of Social Issues* 25 (1969): 10.

12. Brent D. Ruben, "Communication and Conflict: A System-Theoretic Perspective," *Quarterly Journal of Speech* 64 (1978): 20.

13. Abraham H. Maslow, *Motivation and Personality*, 2nd ed. (New York: Harper & Row, 1970), p. 150.

14. Maurice Friedman, "Aiming at the Self: The Paradox of Encounter and the Human Potential Movement," *Journal of Humanistic Psychology* 16 (1976): 6.

15. Kirschenbaum, p. 369.

16. Abraham H. Maslow, *The Farther Reaches of Human Nature* (New York: The Viking Press, 1973), p. 15.

17. Alan Watts, *Psychotherapy East and West* (New York: Ballantine Books, 1972).

18. One can be a proponent of humanism without accepting every assumption of humanistic psychology. The two terms have some common ground, but should not be seen as identical.

19. Maurice Friedman, ed., "Dialogue Between Martin Buber and Carl R. Rogers," in *The Knowledge of Man* by Martin Buber (New York: Harper & Row, 1965), pp. 166–84.

20. Maurice Friedman, "Introductory Essay," *The Knowledge of Man*, pp. 29–33; Maurice Friedman, *Touchstones of Reality: Existential Trust and the Community of Peace* (New York: E. P. Dutton, 1974), p. 247; and Ronald C. Arnett, "Rogers and Buber: Similarities, Yet Fundamental Differences," *Western Journal of Speech Communication* 45 (Summer 1981): 358–72.

21. Richard Johannesen, in a letter to me, posed an important question: Does Rogers' emphasis on following an innate, inner impulse minimize the role of conscious choice? With much caution, I would suggest that yes, following innate inner impulses may limit conscious choice. Such a proposition begins to reflect a deterministic posture, which seems at significant odds with Rogers' orientation.

However, this problem is too complicated to fully explicate here. What is of concern is the understanding of language. Perhaps Rogers would assert that "truth" is "findable" a priori to speech, yet fully wrapped up in experience. In short, choice making need not always be conscious, but as Polanyi would describe, sometimes tacit. The above linguistic position and its counter, held by Gadamer, are stated in Hans-Georg Gadamer, *Truth and Method,* (New York: Continuum Press, 1975), pp. 366–96. My personal position is in agreement with Gadamer, but both positions have philosophical support from different quarters.

22. Julia Wood made this point about the social nature of the human in *Human Communication: A Symbolic Interactionist Perspective* (New York: Holt, Rinehart, and Winston, 1982).

23. Maurice Friedman, *The Confirmation of Otherness in Family, Community, and Society* (New York: The Pilgrim Press, 1983), pp. 150–51.

24. Martin Buber, *Good and Evil* (New York: Charles Scribner's Sons, 1953), pp. 99–106.

25. Buber, *Good and Evil,* pp. 99–101.

26. Buber, *The Knowledge of Man,* pp. 92–93.

27. Hanna Colm, "Healing as Participation: Tillich's Therapeutic Theology," in *The Human Dialogue: Perspectives on Human Communication,* ed. Floyd W. Matson and Ashley Montagu (New York: The Free Press, 1967), p. 275.

28. Kirschenbaum, p. 148.

29. Friedman, *The Confirmation of Otherness,* pp. 150–51.

30. Buber, *The Knowledge of Man,* pp. 169–73.

31. An excellent discussion of the difference between Rogers' and Buber's positions regarding mutuality and role is present in Maurice Friedman, "Healing Through Meeting and the Problematic of Mutuality," *Journal of Humanistic Psychology* 25 (Winter 1985): 13–17.

32. Carl R. Rogers, *Client-Centered Therapy: Its Current Practice, Implications, and Theory* (Boston: Houghton Mifflin, 1965), p. 497.

33. Calvin Hall and Gardner Lindzey, *Theories of Personality* (New York: John Wiley and Sons, 1970), p. 529.

34. Leo Tolstoy, *The Death of Ivan Ilych and Other Stories* (New York: The New American Library, 1960), p. 152.

35. Roderick P. Hart and Don Burks, "Rhetorical Sensitivity and Social Interaction," *Speech Monographs* 39 (1972): 75–91; Roderick P. Hart, Robert E. Carlson, and William F. Eadie, "Attitudes Toward Communication and the Assessment of Rhetorical Sensitivity," *Communication Monographs* 47 (1980): 2–22; and Donald Darnell and Wayne Brockriede, *Persons Communicating* (Englewood Cliffs, NJ: Prentice-Hall, 1976), pp. 176–78.

36. "A Conversation with Gregory Bateson," *Communication: Ethical and Moral Issues*, ed. Lee Thayer (New York: Gordon and Breach Science Publishers, 1973), p. 248.

37. Buber, *Between Man and Man*, pp. 19–21.

38. Friedman, *The Confirmation of Otherness*, p. 150.

39. Maurice Friedman made a similar point, differentiating a dialogical position from that of Rogers' organismic impulses in *The Healing Dialogue in Psychotherapy* (New York: Aronson, 1985), p. 55.

5. Organizational Involvement: A Place of Hiding

1. Martin Buber, *Paths in Utopia* (Boston: Beacon Press, 1958), pp. 135–36.

2. See, for example, Christopher Lasch, *The Culture of Narcissism: American Life in an Age of Diminishing Expectations* (New York: W. W. Norton, 1979). Also, a series of four papers was presented on this subject at the 1980 Speech Communication Association Convention in New York.

3. Some analysts of labor and management disputes have described the climate of the 1980s as one of "give backs" in terms of union workers and "take backs" in terms of nonunion workers. As Lasch in his work on narcissism stated, the situation is not one of growth, but survival.

4. Herman Mau and Helmut Krausnick, *German History: An Assessment by German Historians* (London: Oswald Wolff Publishers, 1959), pp. 16–20.

5. Philip Slater, *The Pursuit of Loneliness: American Culture at the Breaking Point*, 2nd ed. (Boston: Beacon Press, 1976), p. 8.

6. Paul Watzlawick, John Weakland, and Richard Fisch, *Change: Principles of Problem Formation and Problem Resolution* (New York: W. W. Norton, 1974), pp. 31–39.

7. Muzafer Sherif, *In Common Judgment* (Boston: Houghton Mifflin, 1966), p. 157; and Muzafer Sherif and Carolyn W. Sherif, *Social Psychology* (New York: Harper & Row, 1969), pp. 142–45.

8. Martin Buber, *Between Man and Man* (New York: Macmillan, 1965), p. 64.

9. Herbert Marcuse, *Negotiations: Essays in Critical Theory* (Boston: Beacon Press, 1968), p. 268.

10. Buber, *Between Man and Man* pp. 40–82. This essay, "The Question to the Single One," is an elaboration of Buber's 1933 address referred to in the text.

11. Buber, *Between Man and Man*, p. 55.

12. Buber, *Between Man and Man*, p. 82.

13. Slater, p. 164.

14. Martin Luther King, Jr., "Vietnam and the Struggle for Human Rights," in *War and the Christian Conscience: From Augustine to Martin Luther King, Jr.*, ed. Albert Marrin (Chicago: Henry Regnery, 1971), p. 304.

15. Buber, *Between Man and Man*, p. 83.

16. Joseph Bensman and Robert Lilienfeld, *Between Public and Private: Lost Boundaries of the Self* (London: Free Press, 1979), p. 88.

17. Erich Fromm, *The Revolution of Hope: Toward a Humanized Technology* (New York: Harper & Row, 1968); David Riesman, *The Lonely Crowd* (New Haven: Yale Univ. Press, 1963); William Whyte, *The Organization Man* (Garden City, NY: Doubleday, 1957).

18. Richard L. Johannesen provided a summary of the "group-think" phenomenon in *Ethics of Human Communication*, 2nd ed. (Prospect Heights, IL: Waveland Press, 1982), pp. 97–98.

19. Whyte, pp. 171–72.

20. Gene Sharp, *Gandhi as a Political Strategist* (Boston: Porter Sargent, 1979), p. 11.

21. Dietrich Bonhoeffer, *Life Together* (New York: Harper & Row, 1954), p. 35.

22. Viktor Frankl, *Man's Search for Meaning: An Introduction to Logotherapy* (New York: Pocket Books, 1974), p. 89.

23. Martin Buber, *The Knowledge of Man* (New York: Harper & Row, 1965), pp. 126–27.

24. Buber, *The Knowledge of Man*, p. 126.

25. Buber, *The Knowledge of Man*, pp. 121–48.

26. Buber, *Between Man and Man*, pp. 108–17.

27. Richard L. Lael, *The Yamashita Precedent: War Crimes and Command Responsibility* (Wilmington, DE: Scholarly Resources Inc., 1982), pp. 123–28.

28. Erwin Knoll and Judith Nies McFadden, *War Crimes and the American Conscience* (New York: Holt, Rinehart, and Winston, 1970), p. 46.

29. What is called for here is an *I–Thou* attitude in decision-making that looks beyond immediate benefit to oneself and asks the value of these actions to you and I together in community. Martin Buber, *I and Thou* (New York: Charles Scribner and Sons, 1958), pp. 14–15.

30. Howard Kirschenbaum, *On Becoming Carl Rogers* (New York: Delta, 1979), pp. 90–95.

31. Kirschenbaum, pp. 138–39.

32. Maurice Friedman, *Hidden Human Image* (New York: Dell Publishing, 1974), p. 368.

6. The Search for the Ethical Community

1. Martin Buber, *A Believing Humanism: Gleanings* (New York: Simon and Schuster, 1969), pp. 96–97.

2. Richard L. Johannesen, *Ethics in Human Communication*, 2nd ed. (Prospect Heights, IL: Waveland Press, 1981), pp. 20–65.

3. John J. Makay and William R. Brown, *The Rhetorical Dialogue* (Dubuque, IA: William C. Brown, 1972), p. 27; cited in Johannesen, pp. 55–56.

4. See for example, Henry W. Johnstone, Jr., "Toward an Ethics for Rhetoric," *Communication* 6 (1981): 305–14; and Johannesen, *Ethics in Human Communication*, 2nd ed., pp. 61–62.

5. Wayne Brockriede, "Arguers as Lovers," *Philosophy and Rhetoric* 5 (Winter 1972): 1–11.

6. David W. Augsburger, *The Love-Fight* (Harrisonburg, VA: Choice Books, 1973).

7. Paul W. Keller, "Interpersonal Dissent and the Ethics of Dialogue," *Communication* 6 (1981): 300–301.

8. Buber, *Between Man and Man*, pp. 34–39.

9. I found it interesting that a similar warning is in William H. Whyte, Jr., *The Organization Man* (New York: Doubleday & Co., 1956), pp. 121–42. Whyte discussed, in that mid-fifties book, the danger of relationship sensitivity taking over content and productivity. I am making a similar point three decades later. When relationships become narcissistic and forgetful of a goal beyond affirming one another, something is missed within the community— the principles that initially brought that group of people together.

10. Dietrich Bonhoeffer, *Life Together* (New York: Harper & Row, 1954), pp. 26–30.

11. Richard Walton, *Interpersonal Peacemaking: Confrontations and Third Party Consultations* (Reading, MA: Addison-Wesley, 1969), p. 5.

12. Rudy Henry Wiebe, *Peace Shall Destroy Many* (Toronto: McClelland and Stewart, 1972), p. 5.

13. Wiebe, p. 84.

14. Thomas R. Nilsen, *Ethics of Speech Communication*, 2nd ed. (Indianapolis: Bobbs-Merrill, 1974), p. 63.

15. Nilsen, *Ethics of Speech Communication*, p. 95.

16. Thomas I. Emerson, *The System of Freedom of Expression* (New York: Random House, 1970), pp. 98–101.

17. Dennis R. Smith and L. Keith Williamson, *Interpersonal Communication: Roles, Rules, Strategies, and Games* (Dubuque, IA: William C. Brown, 1977), p. 263.

18. Irving Janis, *Victims of Groupthink* (Boston: Houghton Mifflin, 1972), p. 13.

19. Based on the work of James Sargent and Gerald Miller, "Some Differences in Certain Behaviors of Autocratic and Democratic Leaders," *Journal of Communication* 21 (September 1971): 245.

20. Maurice Friedman, *The Hidden Human Image* (New York: Dell Publishing, 1974), p. 359.

21. Eric Hoffer, *Ordeal of Change* (New York: Harper & Row Publishers, 1963), p. 11.

22. Em Griffin, *Getting Together: A Guide to Good Groups* (Downers Grove, IL: InterVarsity Press, 1982), p. 187.

23. Randy Y. Hirokawa, "Improving Intra-Organizational Communication: A Lesson From Japanese Management," *Communication Quarterly* 30 (1981): 39.

24. Paul W. Watzlawick, Janet Helmick Beavin, and Don D. Jackson, *Pragmatics of Human Communication: A Study of Interactional Patterns, Pathologies, and Paradoxes* (New York: W. W. Norton, 1967), p. 86.

25. John Stewart, "Interpersonal Communication—A Meeting Between Persons," in *Bridges Not Walls: A Book About Interpersonal Communication*, ed. John Stewart (Reading, MA: Addison-Wesley, 1982), p. 18.

26. Albert Camus, *Resistance, Rebellion, and Death* (New York: Random House, 1960), pp. 102–3.

27. Martin Buber, *Israel and the World: Essays in a Time of Crisis* (New York: Schocken Books, 1948), p. 42.

28. Peter M. Blau and Marshall W. Meyer, *Bureaucracy in Modern Society*, 2nd ed. (New York: Random House, 1971), pp. 156–57.

29. Emerson, p. 9.

30. Emerson, p. 20.

31. Maurice Friedman, *Martin Buber: The Life of Dialogue* (Chicago: Univ. of Chicago Press, 1976), p. 218.

32. Buber, *A Believing Humanism*, p. 211.

33. Graydon Snyder, Dean and Professor of New Testament Theology, Bethany Theological Seminary, Oak Brook, IL.

34. Sam Keen, *Voices and Visions* (New York: Harper & Row, 1974), p. 24.

7. Freedom: The Unity of Contraries

1. Martin Buber, *The Way of Response* (New York: Schocken Books, 1966), p. 111.

2. "Degrees Gathering Dust for Frustrated Grads," *US News and World Report*, January 24, 1983, 81–82.

3. See, for example, the following recent studies: Richard Kamber, "Marketing the Humanities," *Liberal Education* 68 (Fall 1982): 233–47; Raymond F. Zammuto, "Are the Liberal Arts an Endangered Species?" *Journal of Higher Education* (March/April 1984): 184–211; and Warren Bryan Martin, "Education For Character, Career, and Society," *Change* 15 (January/February 1983): 35–42.

4. Buber, p. 166.

5. Joan V. Bondurant, *Conquest of Violence: The Gandhian Philosophy of Conflict* (Berkeley: Univ. of California Press, 1971), p. viii.

6. Susan B. Shimanoff, *Communication Rules: Theory and Research* (Beverly Hills, CA: Sage Publishers, 1980), pp. 209–11.

7. Michael Parenti, *Power and the Powerless* (New York: St. Martin's Press, 1978), p. 66.

8. Martin Buber, *Between Man and Man* (New York: Macmillan, 1965), pp. 92–93.

9. Herman Hesse, *Siddhartha* (New York: New Directions, 1951), p. 83.

10. Viktor Frankl, *Man's Search for Meaning: An Introduction to Logotherapy* (New York: Pocket Books, 1974), pp. 212–13.

11. Gordon Allport, "Preface" to Frankl, *Man's Search for Meaning*, p. xi.

12. Maurice Friedman, "Introduction" to Martin Buber, *Between Man and Man*, p. xviii.

13. Marx W. Wartofsky, *Feurerbach* (Cambridge: Cambridge Univ. Press, 1982), p. 3.

14. Maurice Friedman, *Martin Buber: The Life of Dialogue*, 3rd ed. (Chicago: The Univ. of Chicago Press, 1976), pp. 135–44.

15. The phrase "trained incapacity" was brought to my attention by a former graduate-school professor, Kenneth Williams.

16. Steven Strasser, *Phenomenology and the Human Sciences* (Atlantic Highlands, NJ: Humanities Press, in association with Duquesne Univ., 1980), pp. 237–40.

17. Richard Palmer, *Hermeneutics: Interpretation Theory in Schleiermacher, Dilthey, Heidegger, and Gadamer* (Evanston, IL: Northwestern Univ. Press, 1969), pp. 118–21.

18. John Stewart, "Interpretive Listening: An Alternative to Empathy," *Communication Education* 32 (1983): 387.

19. William Barrett, *The Illusion of Technique: A Search for Meaning in a Technological Civilization* (Garden City, NY: Anchor Books, 1978), p. 85.

20. Donald P. Cushman, Barry Valentinsen, and David Dietrich, "A Rules Theory of Interpersonal Relationships," in *Human Communication Theory*, ed. Frank E. X. Dance (New York: Harper & Row, 1982), p. 95.

21. Rollo May, *Love and Will* (New York: Dell Publishing, 1969), p. 215.

22. Leslie H. Farber, *The Ways of the Will: Essays Toward a Psychology and Psychotherapy of Will* (New York: Basic Books, 1965), pp. vii–ix.

23. Farber, p. 15.

24. Maurice Friedman, *Touchstones of Reality: Existential Trust and the Community of Peace* (New York: E. P. Dutton, 1974), pp. 318–31.

25. Barrett, p. 289.

26. Martin Buber provided his most extensive description of the notion of direction in *Good and Evil* (New York: Charles Scribner's Sons, 1953).

27. Buber, *Between Man and Man*, p. 92.

28. Carl R. Rogers, *Freedom to Learn* (Columbus, OH: Charles E. Merrill, 1969), pp. 266–67.

29. Maurice Friedman, *The Hidden Human Image: A Heartening Answer to the Dehumanization of Our Age* (New York: Dell Publishing, 1974), p. 283.

30. Sidney Jourard, *The Transparent Self* (New York: Van Nostrand, 1964), p. 5.

31. Buber, *The Way of Response*, p. 119.

32. Friedman, *The Hidden Human Image*, p. 5.

33. The transactional nature of will and call is portrayed by Maurice Friedman in chapter 7, "The Tension between Personal Calling and Social Role," in *Confirmation of Otherness in Family, Community, and Society* (New York: The Pilgrim Press, 1983), pp. 51–62.

34. J. L. Mehta, *The Philosophy of Martin Heidegger* (New York: Harper & Row, 1971), p. 91.

35. Hans-Georg Gadamer, *Truth and Method* (New York: Continuum Publishing, 1975), p. 238.

36. Thomas Merton, *No Man Is an Island* (New York: Doubleday, 1967), p. 16.

37. Maurice Friedman, *Martin Buber: The Life of Dialogue* (Chicago: Univ. of Illinois Press, 1976), pp. 57–61.

38. Edith Hamilton, *Mythology: Timeless Tales of Gods and Heroes* (New York: The New American Library, 1964), p. 78.

39. Edward M. Kennedy, "A Tribute to Senator Robert F. Kennedy," *Representative American Speeches: 1967–1968*, ed. Lester Thonssen (New York: H. W. Wilson, 1968), p. 178.

40. Stanley Hauerwas, *A Community of Character: Toward A Constructive Christian Social Ethic* (Notre Dame, IN: Univ. of Notre Dame Press, 1981), p. 18.

41. See, for example, Martin Buber, *On the Bible: Eighteen Studies* (New York: Schocken Books, 1968).

42. Adir Cohen, "The Question of Values and Value Education in the Philosophy of Martin Buber," *Teachers College Record* 80 (1979): 763–66.

43. Graydon Snyder, Professor of New Testament Theology, Bethany Theological Seminary, Oak Brook, IL.

8. Meaning in Community: Is This All There Is?

1. Martin Buber, *On Judaism* (New York: Schocken Books, 1967), p. 212.

2. Maurice Friedman has used Buber's orientation to develop what might be termed an optimistic struggle with the absurd. See Maurice Friedman, *The Hidden Human Image* (New York: Dell Publishing, 1974), pp. 146–64.

3. John F. Kennedy, "Inaugural Address," in *Famous Speeches in American History*, ed. Glenn R. Capp (Indianapolis: Bobbs-Merrill, 1963), p. 239.

4. Robert M. Riepenhoff, "Teen Suicide a Real Concern," Brookfield Survey Finds," *The Milwaukee Journal*, June 27, 1985, 1, 12.

5. Gerald M. Goldhaber, *Organizational Communication* (Dubuque, IA: W. C. Brown, 1983), p. 72.

6. Philip Slater, *The Pursuit of Loneliness: American Culture at the Breaking Point* (Boston: Beacon Press, 1976), p. 197.

7. Joseph Bensman and Robert Lilienfeld, *Between Public and Private: Lost Boundaries of the Self* (New York: The Free Press, 1979), pp. 28–90.

8. Samuel M. Ehrenhalt, "The Nature of Education," *Current* (November 1983): 17.

9. "The Annual Survey—Wanted: New College Grads," *Changing Times* (Fall 1984): 38.

10. Russell W. Rumberger, "The Growing Imbalance Between Education and Work," *Phi Delta Kappa* (January 1984): 342.

11. "Degrees Gathering Dust For Frustrated Grads," *U.S. News and World Report*, January 24, 1983, 81; and Anne McDougall Young, "Research Trends in Higher Education and Labor Force Activity," *Monthly Labor Review* (Fall 1983): 39–41.

12. Robert Jay Lifton and Eric Olson, "The Nuclear Age," *Death: Current*

Perspectives, ed. Edwin S. Schneidman, 2nd ed. (Palo Alto, CA: Mayfield Publishing, 1980), p. 63.

13. Robert Doolittle, *Orientations to Communication and Conflict* (Palo Alto, CA: Science Research Associates, 1976), pp. 9–10.

14. One of the most "popular" pieces to reflect this view during the 1960s was Paul Goodman's *Growing Up Absurd: Problems of Youth in the Organized Society* (New York: Vintage Books, 1960).

15. Christopher Lasch used the world of professional sports as a real-life caricature to point out the phenomenon of narcissism in the guise of loyalty to the group. *The Culture of Narcissism: American Life in an Age of Diminishing Expectations* (New York: W. W. Norton, 1979), pp. 203–11.

16. Albert Camus, *Resistance, Rebellion, and Death* (New York: Vintage Books, 1977), pp. 10–11.

17. Friedman, *The Hidden Human Image*, p. 150.

18. Bensman and Lilienfeld, p. 4.

19. Matthew Rothschild, "Central Employment Agency," *Progressive* (Fall 1984): 18–20.

20. Bensman and Lilienfeld, p. 137.

21. Christopher Jencks, "Rethinking the Benefits of Higher Education," *Journal of Thought* (June 1982): 265.

22. Alan Watts spoke of this form of action as liberation from one's cultural *maya* in *Psychotherapy East and West* (New York: Ballantine Books, 1972), p. 21.

23. Although Buber would not totally agree with Carl Rogers' individual solutions to the problem of accepting absurdity in order to conform, he would concur that the problem of introjecting the values of others is significant in our culture, as people seek to belong. See for example, Carl Rogers, *Client-Centered Therapy* (Boston: Houghton Mifflin, 1965), p. 149.

24. Sam Keen, *Voices and Visions* (New York: Harper & Row, 1974), p. 109.

25. Buber pointed to this issue when he discussed the notion of responsibility. See, for example, Martin Buber, *Between Man and Man* (New York: Macmillan, 1965), pp. 16–17.

26. Barry Brummett provided a rhetorical community view of meaning and truth in "A Defense of Ethical Relativism as Rhetorically Grounded," *Western Journal of Speech* 45 (1981): 286–98.

27. Martin Buber, *The Knowledge of Man: A Philosophy of the Interhuman* (New York: Harper & Row, 1965), pp. 82–85.

28. Isaac Bashevis Singer, "Yentl, the Yeshiva Boy," *The Collected Works of Isaac Bashevis Singer* (New York: Farrar, Straus, and Giroux, 1982), pp. 149–69.

29. Jacques Ellul, *Propaganda* (New York: Knopf, 1965), p. 257.

30. Vernon E. Cronen, W. Barnett Pearce, and Linda M. Harris, "The Coordinated Management of Meaning: A Theory of Communication," in *Human Communication Theory*, ed. Frank E. X. Dance (New York: Harper & Row, 1982), p. 63.

31. Cronen, Pearce, and Harris, p. 68.

32. Cronen, Pearce, and Harris, pp. 82–83.

33. Cronen, Pearce, and Harris, p. 79.

34. The work of Barnett Pearce and associates seems to be built on good common-sense models of conflict resolution that emphasize the notion of common ground and superordinate goals bringing those of divergent belief systems together. See, for example, M. Sherif et al., *Intergroup Conflict and Cooperation: The Robber's Cave Experiment* (Norman: Univ. of Oklahoma, 1961); and Herbert W. Simmons, *Persuasion: Understanding, Practice and Analysis* (Reading, MA: Addison Wesley, 1976), pp. 151–68.

35. Viktor Frankl, *The Will to Meaning: Foundations of Logotherapy* (New York: New American Library, 1965), p. 70.

36. Friedman, *Hidden Human Image*, p. 160.

37. Aubrey Hodes, *Martin Buber: An Intimate Portrait* (New York: Viking Press, 1971), p. 165.

9. Power and Responsibility

1. Martin Buber, *A Believing Humanism* (New York: Simon and Schuster, 1967), p. 203.

2. For an excellent account of the six years of devastation after the dropping of the bomb, see *Children of Hiroshima* (London: Taylor and Francis, 1981).

3. Ann Harriman, "The Rise and Fall of the Third Wave," *National Forum* (Summer 1984): 29.

4. Joanna Macy, "Buddhist Approaches to Social Action," *Journal of Humanistic Psychology* 24 (Summer 1984): 128.

5. Frederick S. Perls, *In and Out the Garbage Pail* (New York: Bantam Books, 1972), p. i.

6. Walter Tubbs, "Beyond Perls," *Journal of Humanistic Psychology* 16 (Spring 1976): 5.

7. Philip Slater, *The Pursuit of Loneliness: American Culture at the Breaking Point* (Boston: Beacon Press, 1976), p. 138.

8. John Ilich, *Power Negotiating: Strategies for Winning in Life and Business* (Reading, MA: Addison Wesley, 1980), p. 168.

9. Martin Buber, *I and Thou* (New York: Charles Scribner's Sons, 1958), p. 39.

10. Buber, *I and Thou*, p. 45.

11. Rollo May, *Power and Innocence: A Search for the Sources of Violence* (New York: Dell Publishers, 1972), pp. 99–100.

12. May, pp. 105–6.

13. May, pp. 106–7.

14. Thomas Kochman, "Toward an Ethnography of Black American Speech Behavior," in *Rappin' and Stylin' Out: Communication in Urban Black America*, ed. Thomas Kochman (Chicago: Univ. of Chicago Press, 1972), pp. 246–58. Kochman described shucking and signifying as ways of manipulation for one's survival with a more powerful foe.

15. Wayne Brockriede, "Arguers as Lovers," *Philosophy and Rhetoric* 5 (Winter 1972): 1–11.

16. May, pp. 108–9.

17. May, p. 109.

18. May, pp. 109–13.

19. Martin Buber, *A Believing Humanism*, p. 45.

20. May, pp. 109–10.

21. Floyd W. Matson, *The Broken Image: Man, Science, and Society* (New York: Anchor Books, 1964), p. 126.

22. Stanley Deetz, "Introduction," in *Phenomenology in Rhetoric and Communication*, ed. Stanley Deetz (Washington, DC: Center for Advanced Research in Phenomenology and University Press of America, 1981), p. 2.

23. See for example, Hans-Georg Gadamer, *Truth and Method* (New York: Continuum, 1975), pp. 146–214.

24. Gerald R. Miller and Henry E. Nicholson, *Communication Inquiry: A Perspective on a Process* (Reading, MA: Addison-Wesley, 1976), p. 229.

25. Kurt F. Reinhardt, trans., *Major Problems in Contemporary European Philosophy*, by Ludwig Landgrebe (New York: Frederick Ungar, 1966), pp. 117–18.

26. Martin Buber, *The Knowledge of Man: A Philosophy of the Interhuman* (New York: Harper & Row, 1965), pp. 171–75.

27. Buber, *The Knowledge of Man*, p. 175.

28. Buber's work has upon occasion been placed in the "expressionist" camp of communication that tends to celebrate feelings without any persuasive goal. Buber was willing to be persuasive, as he was simultaneously open to the other's view.

29. Buber, *The Knowledge of Man*, pp. 167–68.

30. Martin Buber, *Between Man and Man* (New York: Macmillan, 1972), p. 105.

31. Buber, *Between Man and Man*, pp. 113–14.

32. Buber, *Between Man and Man*, p. 116.

33. Cited in Wayne C. Minnick, "A New Look at the Ethics of Persuasion," *The Southern Speech Communication Journal* 45 (1980): 362.

34. Dietrich Bonhoeffer, *The Cost of Discipleship* (New York: Macmillan, 1975).

35. William Jay Peck, "The Role of the 'Enemy' in Bonhoeffer's Life and Thought," in *A Bonhoeffer Legacy: Essays in Understanding*, ed. A. J. Klassen (Grand Rapids, MI: William B. Eerdman's Publishing, 1981), p. 347.

36. Merle Miller, *Plain Speaking: An Oral Biography of Harry S. Truman* (New York: G. P. Putnam's and Sons, 1973), p. 19.

10. The Community of Dialogue

1. Maurice Friedman, *The Confirmation of Otherness in Family, Community, and Society* (New York: Pilgrim Press, 1983), p. 31, which was taken from Martin Buber, *The Knowledge of Man: A Philosophy of the Interhuman* (New York: Harper Torchbooks, 1966), p. 107.

2. Buber, pp. 92–93.

3. Martin Buber, *Between Man and Man* (New York: Macmillan, 1965), p 16.

4. Buber, *Between Man and Man*, pp. 175–76.

5. Buber, *Between Man and Man*, p. 176.

6. Paulo Freire, *Pedagogy of the Oppressed* (New York: Seabury Press, 1974).

7. Christopher Lasch, *The Culture of Narcissism: American Life in a Time of Diminishing Expectations* (New York: W. W. Norton, 1979), pp. 42–43.

8. Glenn Tinder, *Community: Reflections on a Tragic Ideal* (Baton Rouge: Louisiana State Univ. Press, 1980), pp. 187–99.

9. Ronald C. Arnett, "A Teacher and Friend: A Dedication for Dr. Paul W. Keller," *Bulletin of the Peace Studies Institute* (Spring 1983): 2.

10. Martin Buber, *A Land of Two Peoples: Martin Buber on Jews and Arabs*, ed. Paul R. Mendes-Flohr (New York: Oxford Press, 1983), p. 305.

11. Mark Juergensmeyer, *Fighting with Gandhi: A Step-By-Step Strategy For Resolving Everyday Conflicts* (New York: Harper & Row, 1984), p. 15.

12. See the exchange between Gandhi and Buber in *A Land of Two Peoples*, pp 106–26.

13. Buber, *A Land of Two Peoples*, p. 125.

14. V. V. Ramana Murti, "Buber's Dialogue and Gandhi's Satyagraha," *Journal of the History of Ideas* 24, no. 4 (1968): 605–13.

15. Buber, *Knowledge of Man*, p. 75.

16. For a further discussion of the relationship between Gandhi's approach to truth and Buber's notion of the "between," see Ronald C. Arnett, *Dwell in Peace: Applying Nonviolence to Everyday Relationships* (Elgin, IL: Brethren Press, 1980), pp. 131–36; and Murti, "Buber's Dialogue and Gandhi's Satyagraha," pp. 605–13.

17. Maurice Friedman, *Touchstones of Reality: Existential Trust and the Community of Peace* (New York: E. P. Dutton, 1972), pp. 247–58.

18. Martin Buber, *On the Bible: Eighteen Studies* (New York: Schocken Books, 1982), p. 11.

19. Buber, *On the Bible*, p. 149.

20. Buber, *Between Man and Man*, pp. 33–39.

21. Charles T. Brown and Paul W. Keller, *Monologue to Dialogue* (Englewood Cliffs, NJ: Prentice-Hall, 1973), p. 199.

22. David Riesman, *The Lonely Crowd* (New Haven, CT: Yale Univ. Press, 1963), p. 18.

23. Friedman, *Confirmation of Otherness*, p. 287.

24. "The Year of the Yuppie," *Newsweek*, December 31, 1984, 17.

25. *Webster's Seventh New Collegiate Dictionary* (Springfield, MA: G. & C. Merriam, 1976), p. 4.

26. Lasch, p. 32.

27. Arthur J. Dyck, *On Human Care* (Nashville, TN: Abingdon, 1980), p. 169.

28. Dyck, pp. 171–72.

29. H. Richard Niebuhr, *The Responsible Self* (New York: Harper & Row, 1968), pp. 60–61.

30. Lasch, p. 64.

31. Joe Ayres, "Four Approaches to Interpersonal Communication: Review, Observation, Prognosis," *Western Journal of Speech Communication* 48 (Fall 1984): 408–40.

32. Michael E. Roloff, *Interpersonal Communication: A Social Exchange Approach* (Beverly Hills, CA: Sage Publications, 1981), pp. 11–14.

33. Erich Fromm, *Man for Himself: An Inquiry into the Psychology of Ethics* (Greenwich, CT: Fawcett Publications, 1947), pp. 75–89.

34. Ernest G. Bormann, "Symbolic Convergence: Organizational Communication and Culture," in *Communication and Organizations: An Interpretive Approach*, ed. Linda L. Putnam and Michael E. Pacanowsky (Beverly Hills, CA: Sage, 1983), pp. 99–122.

35. Robert Scott, "Narrative Theory and Communication Research," *Quarterly Journal of Speech* 70 (1984): 197–98.

36. Walter R. Fisher, "Narration as a Human Communication Paradigm: The Case of Public Moral Argument," *Communication Monographs* 51 (March 1984): 6.

37. Fisher, p. 16.

38. William Barrett, *The Illusion of Technique: A Search for Meaning in a Technological Civilization* (Garden City, NY: Anchor Books, 1978), pp. 336–38.

39. Barrett, p. 306.

40. Barrett, pp. 344–45.

41. Martin Buber, *Paths in Utopia* (Boston: Beacon Press, 1958), pp. 122–24.

42. Buber, *Paths in Utopia*, p. 13.

43. Buber, *Paths in Utopia*, pp. 134–35.

BIBLIOGRAPHY

Anderson, Rob. "Phenomenological Dialogue: Humanistic Psychology and Pseudo Walls: A Response and Extension." *Western Journal of Speech Communication* 46 (Fall 1982): 344–57.

"The Annual Survey—Wanted: New College Grads." *Changing Times* (Fall 1984): 39–51.

Arnett, Ronald C. "Communication as Dialogical Interpretation." *Speech Association of Minnesota Journal* 7 (1980): 14–20.

——. *Dwell in Peace: Applying Nonviolence to Everyday Relationships.* Elgin, IL: Brethren Press, 1980.

——. "Nonviolent Peacemaking: A Look at Assumptions." *Journal of Peace and Change* (Winter 1979–1980): 7–10.

——. "Rogers and Buber: Similarities, Yet Fundamental Differences." *Western Journal of Speech Communication* 46 (Fall 1982):358–72.

——. "A Teacher and Friend: A Dedication for Dr. Paul W. Keller." *Bulletin of the Peace Studies Institute* (Spring 1983): Cover–3.

——. "Toward a Phenomenological Dialogue." *Western Journal of Speech Communication* 45 (1981): 201–12.

Arnett, Ronald C., and Gordon Nakagawa. "The Assumptive Roots of Empathic Listening: A Critique." *Communication Education* 32 (Fall 1983): 368–78.

Augsburger, David W. *The Love-Fight.* Harrisonburg, VA: Choice Books, 1973.

Ayres, Joe. "Four Approaches to Interpersonal Communication: Review, Observation, Prognosis." *Western Journal of Speech Communication* 48 (Fall 1984): 408–40.

Barnlund, Dean. "Toward a Meaning-Centered Philosophy of Communication." *Journal of Communication* 12 (1962): 197–211.

Barrett, William. *The Illusion of Technique: A Search for Meaning in a Technological Civilization.* Garden City, NY: Anchor Books, 1978.

Bateson, Gregory. *Steps to an Ecology of Mind.* New York: Ballantine Books, 1974.

Beltran, Lois Ramiro. "Research Ideologies in Conflict." *Journal of Communication* 25 (1975): 187–93.

Bensman, Joseph, and Robert Lilienfeld. *Between Public and Private: Lost Boundaries of the Self.* London: Free Press, 1979.

"The Bizarre Tragedy in Guyana." *US News and World Report*, December 4, 1978, 25–29.

Blau, Peter M., and Marshall W. Meyer. *Bureaucracy in Modern Society*, 2nd ed. New York: Random House, 1971.

Bleicher, Josef. *Contemporary Hermeneutics: Hermeneutics as Method, Philosophy, and Critique.* London: Routledge & Kegan Paul, 1980.

Bondurant, Joan V. *Conquest of Violence: The Gandhian Philosophy of Conflict.* Berkeley: Univ. of California Press, 1971.

Bonhoeffer, Dietrich. *The Communion of Saints.* New York: Harper & Row, 1963.

———. *The Cost of Discipleship.* New York: Macmillan, 1975.

———. *Life Together.* New York: Harper & Row, 1954.

Brockriede, Wayne, "Arguers as Lovers." *Philosophy and Rhetoric* 5 (Winter 1972): 1–11.

Brown, Charles T., and Paul W. Keller. *Monologue to Dialogue: An Exploration of Interpersonal Communication.* Englewood Cliffs, NJ: Prentice-Hall, 1973.

Brummett, Barry. "A Defense of Ethical Relativism as Rhetorically Grounded." *Western Journal of Speech* 45 (1981): 286–98.

———. "Some Implications of 'Process' of 'Intersubjectivity': Postmodern Rhetoric." *Philosophy and Rhetoric* 9 (1976): 21–51.

Buber, Martin. *A Believing Humanism: Gleanings.* New York: Simon and Schuster, 1969.

———. *Between Man and Man.* New York: Macmillan, 1972.

———. *Good and Evil.* New York: Charles Scribner's Sons, 1953.

———. *I and Thou.* New York: Charles Scribner's Sons, 1958.

———. *Israel and the World: Essays in a Time of Crisis.* New York: Schocken Books, 1948.

———. *The Knowledge of Man: A Philosophy of the Interhuman.* New York: Harper & Row, 1965.

———. *A Land of Two Peoples: Martin Buber on Jews and Arabs*. Edited by Paul R. Mendes-Flohr. New York: Oxford Press, 1983.

———. *On Judaism*. New York: Schocken Books, 1967.

———. *On the Bible: Eighteen Studies*. New York: Schocken Books, 1982.

———. *Paths in Utopia*. Boston: Beacon Press, 1958.

———. *Pointing the Way: Collected Essays*. New York: Harper & Row, 1957.

———. *The Way of Response*. New York: Schocken Books, 1966.

Camus, Albert. *Resistance, Rebellion, and Death*. New York: Random House, 1960.

Capp, Glenn R., ed. *Famous Speeches in American History*. Indianapolis: Bobbs-Merrill, 1963.

Cohen, Adir. "The Question of Values and Value Education in the Philosophy of Martin Buber." *Teachers College Record* 80 (1979): 743–70.

Coser, Lewis. *The Function of Social Conflict*. New York: The Free Press, 1956.

Dance, Frank E. X., ed. *Human Communication Theory: Comparative Essays*. New York: Harper & Row, 1982.

Dance, Frank E. X. "Communication and Ecumenism." *Journal of Communication* 19 (1969): 14–21.

Darnell, Donald, and Wayne Brockriede. *Persons Communicating*. Englewood Cliffs, NJ: Prentice-Hall, 1976.

Deetz, Stanley, ed. *Phenomenology in Rhetoric and Communication*. Washington, DC: Center for Advanced Research in Phenomenology and University Press of America, 1981.

"Degrees Gathering Dust for Frustrated Grads," *US News and World Report*, January 24, 1983, 81–82.

Deutsch, Morton. "Conflicts: Productive and Constructive." *Journal of Social Issues* 25 (1969): 7–40.

Doolittle, Robert. *Orientations to Communication and Conflict*. Palo Alto, CA: Science Research Associates, 1976.

Douglass, James W. *The Non-Violent Cross: A Theology of Revolution and Peace*. New York: Macmillan, 1973.

Dyck, Arthur J. *On Human Care*. Nashville, TN: Abingdon, 1980.

Ehrenhalt, Samuel M. "The Nature of Education." *Current* (November 1983): 15–24.

Ellul, Jacques. *Propaganda*. New York: Knopf, 1965.

Emerson, Thomas I. *The System of Freedom of Expression*. New York: Random House, 1970.

Erickson, Erik. *Gandhi's Truth: On the Origin of Militant Nonviolence*. New York: W. W. Norton, 1969.

Farber, H. Leslie. *The Ways of the Will: Essays toward a Psychology and Psychotherapy of Will*. New York: Basic Books, 1966.

Fisher, B. Aubrey. *Perspectives on Human Communication*. New York: Macmillan, 1978.

Fisher, Roger. *International Conflict for Beginners*. New York: Harper & Row, 1970.

Fisher, Walter R., "Narration as a Human Communication Paradigm: The Case of Public Moral Argument." *Communication Monographs* 51 (March 1984): 1–22.

Frankl, Viktor. *Man's Search for Meaning: An Introduction to Logotherapy*. New York: Pocket Books, 1974.

———. *The Unheard Cry for Meaning: Psychotherapy and Existentialism*. New York: Simon and Schuster, 1978.

———. *The Will to Meaning*. New York: Plume Books, 1969.

Freire, Paulo. *Pedagogy of the Oppressed*. New York: Seabury Press, 1974.

Freud, Sigmund. *Civilization and Its Discontents*. New York: W. W. Norton, 1962.

Friedman, Maurice. "Aiming at the Self: The Paradox of Encounter and the Human Potential Movement." *Journal of Humanistic Psychology* 16 (1976): 5–35.

———. *The Confirmation of Otherness in Family, Community, and Society*. New York: Pilgrim Press, 1983.

———. *The Healing Dialogue in Psychotherapy*. New York: Aronson, 1985.

———. "Healing Through Meeting and the Problematic of Mutuality." *Journal of Humanistic Psychology* 25 (1985): 7–40.

———. *The Hidden Human Image*. New York: Dell Publishing, 1974.

———. *Martin Buber: The Life of Dialogue*. Chicago: Univ. of Chicago Press, 1976.

———. *Touchstones of Reality: Existential Trust and the Community of Peace*. New York: E. P. Dutton, 1972.

Fromm, Erich. *Man for Himself: An Inquiry into the Psychology of Ethics*. Greenwich, CT: Fawcett Publications, 1947.

———. *The Revolution of Hope: Toward a Humanized Technology*. New York: Bantam Books, 1971.

Frost, Joyce Hocker, and William W. Wilmot. *Interpersonal Conflict*. Dubuque, IA: W. C. Brown, 1978.

Gadamer, Hans-Georg. *Truth and Method*. New York: Seabury Press, 1975.

Goldhaber, Gerald M. *Organizational Communication.* Dubuque, IA: W. C. Brown, 1983.

Goodman, Ellen. "Haves, Have-Nots Now Coldly Judged as Winners, Losers." *Los Angeles Times,* November 13, 1984, part 2, 5.

Goodman, Paul. *Growing Up Absurd: Problems of Youth in the Organized Society.* New York: Vintage Books, 1960.

Greenfield, Meg. "After the Ayatollah." *Newsweek,* December 17, 1979, 116.

Griffin, Em. *Getting Together: A Guide to Good Groups.* Downers Grove, IL: InterVarsity Press, 1982.

Hall, Calvin, and Gardner Lindzey. *Theories of Personality.* New York: John Wiley and Sons, 1970.

Hamilton, Edith. *Mythology: Timeless Tales of Gods and Heroes.* New York: The New American Library, 1964.

Hammarskjold, Dag. *Markings.* New York: Alfred A. Knopf, 1977.

Harriman, Ann. "The Rise and Fall of the Third Wave," *National Forum* (Summer 1984): 28–30.

Hart, Roderick P., and Don Burks, "Rhetorical Sensitivity and Social Interaction." *Speech Monograph* 39 (1972): 75–91.

Hart, Roderick P., Robert E. Carlson, and William F. Eadie. "Attitudes toward Communication and the Assessment of Rhetorical Sensitivity." *Communication Monographs* 47 (1980): 2–22.

Hauerwas, Stanley. *A Community of Character: Toward a Constructive Christian Social Ethic.* Notre Dame, IN: Univ. of Notre Dame Press, 1981.

Heisenberg, Werner. *Physics and Philosophy.* New York: Harper & Row, 1958.

Hesse, Herman. *Siddhartha.* New York: New Directions, 1951.

Hickson, Mark, III, and Fred Jandt, eds. *Marxian Perspectives on Human Communication.* Rochester, NY: PSI Publishers, 1976.

Hirokawa, Randy Y. "Improving Intra-Organizational Communication: A Lesson From Japanese Management." *Communication Quarterly* 30 (1981): 35–40.

Hodes, Aubrey. *Martin Buber, An Intimate Portrait.* New York: Viking Press, 1971.

Hoffer, Eric. *Ordeal of Change.* New York: Harper & Row, 1963.

Ilich, John. *Power Negotiating: Strategies for Winning in Life and Business.* Reading, MA: Addison-Wesley, 1980.

Janis, Irving. *Victims of Groupthink.* Boston: Houghton Mifflin, 1972.

Jencks, Christopher. "Rethinking the Benefits of Higher Education." *Journal of Thought* (June 1982): 257–66.

Johannesen, Richard L. "The Emerging Concept of Communication as Dialogue." *Quarterly Journal of Speech* 57 (1971): 373–82.

———. *Ethics in Human Communication*. 1981; Prospect Heights, IL: Waveland Press, 1983.

Johnson, Dole Paul. "Dilemmas of Charismatic Leadership: The Case of the People's Temple." *Sociological Analysis* 40 (1979): 315–23.

Johnstone, Henry W. "Toward an Ethics for Rhetoric." *Communication* 6 (1981).

Jourard, Sidney. *The Transparent Self*. New York: Van Nostrand Reinhold, 1971.

Juergensmeyer, Mark. *Fighting with Gandhi: A Step-By-Step Strategy for Resolving Everyday Conflicts*. New York: Harper & Row, 1984.

Kamber, Richard. "Marketing the Humanities." *Liberal Education* 68 (Fall 1982): 233–47.

Keen, Sam. *Voices and Visions*. New York: Harper & Row, 1974.

Keene, Karlyn. "American Values: Change and Stability—A Conversation with Daniel Yankelovich," *Public Opinion* (December/January 1984): 2–33.

Keller, Paul. "But on the Other Hand . . . ." A Speech given to Manchester College Alumni, Manchester College, North Manchester, Indiana, May 19, 1979.

———. "Interpersonal Dissent and the Ethics of Dialogue." *Communication* 6 (1981): 287–303.

King, Martin Luther, Jr. "Let Us Be Dissatisfied!" *Gandhi Marg* 12, no. 3 (July 1968): 218–29.

Kirschenbaum, Howard. *On Becoming Carl Rogers*. New York: Dell Publishing, 1979.

Klassen, A. J., ed. *A Bonhoeffer Legacy: Essays in Understanding*. Grand Rapids, MI: William B. Eerdman's Publishing, 1981.

Knoll, Erwin, and Judith Nies McFadden. *War Crimes and the American Conscience*. New York: Holt, Rinehart, and Winston, 1970.

Kochman, Thomas, ed. *Rappin' and Stylin' Out: Communication in Urban Black America*. Chicago: Univ. of Chicago Press, 1972.

Landgrebe, Ludwig. *Major Problems in Contemporary European Philosophy*. Translated by Kurt F. Reinhardt. New York: Frederick Ungar, 1977.

Lael, Richard L. *The Yamashita Precedent: War Crimes and Command Responsibility*. Wilmington, DE: Scholarly Resources Inc., 1982.

Lasch, Christopher. *The Culture of Narcissism: American Life in an Age of Diminishing Expectations.* New York: W. W. Norton, 1979.

Lederer, William, and Don Jackson. *Mirages of Marriage.* New York: W. W. Norton, 1968.

Macy, Joanna. "Buddhist Approaches to Social Action." *Journal of Humanistic Psychology* 24 (1983): 117–29.

Makay, John J., and William R. Brown. *The Rhetorical Dialogue.* Dubuque, IA: William C. Brown, 1972.

Marcuse, Herbert. *Negotiations: Essays in Critical Theory.* Boston: Beacon Press, 1968.

Marrin, Albert, ed. *War and the Christian Conscience: From Augustine to Martin Luther King Jr.* Chicago: Henry Regnery, 1971.

Martin, Warren Bryan. "Education for Character, Career, and Society." *Change* 15 (January/February 1983): 35–42.

Maslow, Abraham. *The Farther Reaches of Human Nature.* New York: Viking Press, 1973.

———. *Motivation and Personality.* 2nd ed. New York: Harper & Row, 1970.

Matson, Floyd W. *The Broken Image: Man, Science, and Society.* Garden City, NY: Anchor Books, 1964.

Matson, Floyd, and Ashley Montagu, eds. *The Human Dialogue: Perspectives on Communication.* New York: The Free Press, 1967.

Mau, Herman, and Helmut Krausnick. *German History: An Assessment by German Historians.* London: Oswald Wolff Publishers, 1959.

May, Rollo. *Love and Will.* New York: Dell Publishing, 1969.

———. *Power and Innocence: A Search for the Sources of Violence.* New York: Dell Publishing, 1976.

Mehta, J. L. *The Philosophy of Martin Heidegger.* New York: Harper & Row, 1971.

Merton, Thomas. *No Man Is an Island.* New York: Doubleday, 1967.

Miller, Gerald, and Henry E. Nicholson. *Communication Inquiry: A Perspective on a Process.* Reading, MA: Addison-Wesley, 1976.

Miller, Merle. *Plain Speaking: An Oral Biography of Harry S. Truman.* New York: G. P. Putnam's and Sons, 1973.

Minnick, Wayne C. "A New Look at the Ethics of Persuasion." *The Southern Speech Communication Journal* 45 (1980): 352–62.

Mittroff, Ian. *Creating a Dialectical Social Science: Concepts, Methods, and Models.* London: D. Reidel Publishing, 1981.

———. "The Myth of Objectivity or Why Science Needs a New Psychology of Science." *Management Science* 18 (1972): B613–B618.

Mittroff, Ian, Richard O. Mason, and Vincent P. Barabba. "Policy As Argument—A Logic For Ill-Structured Decision Problems." *Management Science* 28 (1982): 1391–1404.

Montagu, Ashley. *On Being Human*. New York: Hawthorn Books, 1966.

Murti, V. V. Ramana. "Buber's Dialogue and Gandhi's Satyagraha." *Journal of the History of Ideas* 24, no. 4 (1968): 605–13.

Niebuhr, H. Richard. *The Responsible Self*. New York: Harper & Row, 1968.

"Nightmare in Jonestown," *Time* December 4, 1978, 16–21.

Nilsen, Thomas R. *Ethics of Speech Communication*. 2nd ed. Indianapolis: Bobbs-Merrill, 1974.

Palmer, Richard. *Hermeneutics: Interpretation Theory in Schleiermacher, Dilthey, Heidegger, and Gadamer*. Evanston, IL: Northwestern Univ. Press, 1969.

Parenti, Michael. *Power and the Powerless*. New York: St. Martin's Press, 1978.

Perls, Frederick S. *In and Out the Garbage Pail*. New York: Bantam Books, 1972.

Polanyi, Michael. *Personal Knowledge: Towards a Post-Critical Philosophy*. New York: Harper Torchbooks, 1964.

———. *The Tacit Dimension*. New York: Doubleday, 1967.

Poulakos, John. "The Components of Dialogue." *Western Journal of Speech Communication* 38 (1974): 199–212.

Putnam, Linda L., and Michael E. Pacanowsky, eds. *Communication and Organizations: An Interpretive Approach*. Beverly Hills, CA: Sage Publications, 1983.

Riepenhoff, Robert M. "Teen Suicide a Real Concern, Brookfield Survey Finds," *The Milwaukee Journal* June 27, 1985, 1, 12.

Riesman, David. *The Lonely Crowd*. New Haven, CT: Yale Univ. Press, 1963.

Rogers, Carl R. *Client-Centered Therapy: Its Current Practice, Implications, and Theory*. Boston: Houghton Mifflin, 1965.

———. *The Freedom to Learn*. Columbus, OH: Charles E. Merrill, 1969.

———. *A Way of Being*. Boston: Houghton Mifflin, 1980.

Rokeach, Milton. *The Open and Closed Mind*. New York: Basic Books, 1960.

Roloff, Michael E. *Interpersonal Communication: A Social Exchange Approach*. Beverly Hill, CA: Sage Publications, 1981.

Rothschild, Matthew. "Central Employment Agency." *Progressive* (Fall 1984): 18–21.

Ruben, Brent D. "Communication and Conflict: A System-Theoretic Perspective." *Quarterly Journal of Speech* 64 (1978): 202–10.

Rumberger, Russell W. "The Growing Imbalance between Education and Work." *Phi Delta Kappa* (January 1984): 342–46.

Sargent, James, and Gerald Miller. "Some Differences in Certain Behaviors of Autocratic and Democratic Leaders." *Journal of Communication* 21 (September 1971): 233–52.

Schneidman, Edwin S., ed. *Death: Current Perspectives*. 2nd ed. Palo Alto, CA: Mayfield Publishing, 1980.

Schutz, William. *The Interpersonal Underworld*. Palo Alto, CA: Science and Behavior Books, 1966.

Scott, Robert. "Narrative Theory and Communication Research." *Quarterly Journal of Speech* 70 (1984): 197–221.

Sharp, Gene. *Gandhi as a Political Strategist, With Essays on Ethics and Politics*. Boston: Porter Sargent Publishers, 1979.

Sherif, Muzafer. *In Common Judgment*. Boston: Houghton Mifflin, 1966.

Sherif, Muzafer et al. *Intergroup Conflict and Cooperation: The Robber's Cave Experiment*. Norman: Univ. of Oklahoma, 1961.

Sherif, Muzafer, and Carolyn W. Sherif. *Social Psychology*. New York: Harper & Row, 1969.

Shimanoff, Susan B. *Communication Rules: Theory and Research*. Beverly Hills, CA: Sage Publishers, 1980.

Simmons, Herbert W. *Persuasion: Understanding, Practice and Analysis*. Reading, MA: Addison-Wesley, 1976.

Singer, Isaac Bashevis. *The Collected Works of Isaac Bashevis Singer*. New York: Farrar, Straus, and Giroux, 1982.

Slater, Philip. *Earthwalk*. New York: Anchor Press, 1974.

———. *The Pursuit of Loneliness: American Culture at the Breaking Point*. 2nd ed. Boston: Beacon Press, 1976.

Smith, Dennis R., and L. Keith Williamson. *Interpersonal Communication: Roles, Rules, Strategies, and Games*. Dubuque, IA: William C. Brown, 1977.

Stanford, Barbara, ed. *Peacemaking: A Guide to Conflict Resolution for Individuals, Groups and Nations*. New York: Bantam Books, 1974.

Strasser, Steven. *Phenomenology and the Human Sciences*. Atlantic Highlands, NJ: Humanities Press in association with Duquesne University, 1980.

Stewart, John, ed. *Bridges Not Walls: A Book About Interpersonal Communication*. Reading, MA: Addison-Wesley, 1973.

Stewart, John. "Foundations of Dialogic Communication." *Quarterly Journal of Speech* 64 (1978): 183–201.

———. "Interpretive Listening: An Alternative to Empathy." *Communication Education* 32, no. 4 (1983): 379–92.

Thayer, Lee, ed. *Communication: Ethical and Moral Issues.* New York: Gordon and Breach Science Publishers, 1973.

Thonssen, Lester, ed. *Representative American Speeches: 1967–1968.* New York: H. W. Wilson, 1968.

Tinder, Glenn. *Community: Reflections on a Tragic Ideal.* Baton Rouge: Louisiana State Univ. Press, 1980.

Tolstoy, Leo. *The Death of Ivan Ilych and Other Stories.* New York: The New American Library, 1960.

Tubbs, Walter. "Beyond Perls." *Journal of Humanistic Psychology* 12, no. 2 (Fall 1972): 5.

Walton, Richard. *Interpersonal Peacemaking: Confrontations and Third Party Consultations.* Reading, MA: Addison-Wesley, 1969.

Wartofsky, Marx W. *Feuerbach.* Cambridge, MA: Cambridge Univ. Press, 1982.

Watts, Alan. *Psychotherapy East and West.* New York: Ballantine Books, 1972.

Watzlawick, Paul, Janet Beavin, and Don Jackson. *Pragmatics of Human Communication: A Study of Interactional Patterns, Pathologies, and Paradoxes.* New York: W. W. Norton, 1967.

Watzlawick, Paul, John Weakland, and Richard Fisch. *Change: Principles of Problem Formation and Problem Resolution.* New York: W. W. Norton, 1974.

Webster's Seventh New Collegiate Dictionary. Springfield, MA: G. & C. Merriam, 1976.

Western Journal of Speech Communication, Winter 1977 and Winter 1978.

Wiebe, Rudy Henry. *Peace Shall Destroy Many.* Toronto: McClelland and Stewart, 1972.

Whyte, William. *The Organization Man.* Garden City, NY: Doubleday, 1957.

Williams, Kenneth R. "Reflections on a Human Science of Communication." *The Journal of Communication* 23 (1973): 239–50.

Wood, Julia. *Human Communication: A Symbolic Interactionist Perspective.* New York: Holt, Rinehart, and Winston, 1982.

"The Year of the Yuppie," *Newsweek,* December 31, 1984, 14–24.

Yoichi, Fokushima, ed. *Children of Hiroshima.* London: Taylor and Francis, 1981.

Young, Anne McDougall. "Research Trends in Higher Education and Labor Force Activity." *Monthly Labor Review* (Fall 1983): 39–41.

Zammuto, Raymond F. "Are the Liberal Arts an Endangered Species?" *Journal of Higher Education* (March/April 1984): 184–211.

INDEX

Ronald C. Arnett, Chairperson and Associate Professor of Interpersonal Communication at Marquette University, received his Ph.D. from Ohio University. He has served as editor, associate editor, and editorial board member for scholarly journals. The author of many articles, he received the Outstanding Article of the Year Award for 1979 from the Religious Communication Association. His first Book, *Dwell in Peace: Applying Nonviolence to Everyday Relationships*, was published in 1980 by Brethren Press and is currently in its third printing.